Rocky Mountain Railroad Odyssey

NILS ERIKSEN

Eriks Journey through North America

CHAPTER 1

Opening

Edmonton, this year, December 28.

My sister Amelia led a rather solitary life. She seemed oblivious to it, absorbed as she was in her work as a biologist. She hadn't truly grasped the extent of her isolation, a common occurrence when one's perspective on the situation differs from that of an outsider. Amelia's solitude had its roots in a deeply unhappy engagement that had soured. Since then, she had become cautious about forming new connections. However, she wasn't the sole individual leading a life of seclusion. He, too, was wholly engrossed in his work, striving as a journalist to sustain a struggling magazine. And this, too, had its reasons.

So, Erik's and Amelia's circumstances bore similarities despite their geographical separation. Yes, they were roughly the same age. Yet, their youth diverged: Amelia had grown up in a sheltered environment within a friendly settlement in the western part of our Canadian town. On the other hand, Erik had been a rebel during his youth, driven by his own motivations. But let him recount that story himself within these pages.

However, these are mere surface details. The crux of their relationship lies in how harmoniously they mesh. This becomes apparent at first sight. Their conversations even flow as though they've been intertwined forever. Sometimes, observing them, I find myself amazed. What intrigues me is that despite the vast distance, they've managed to bridge the gap. Amelia's life has been marked by far more trials than mine. My own path has been much smoother. But we'll delve into that later.

Amelia resides in Edmonton, Canada. This city, my hometown, rests along the North Saskatchewan River. This river winds its way to Hudson Bay in northern Canada, connecting to the North Atlantic through the Labrador Sea. One could suggest that a message placed in a bottle in the river amidst the Canadian Rockies could traverse Edmonton and ultimately find its place in the Atlantic Ocean. Meanwhile, Erik inhabits Hamburg, situated on the banks of the Elbe River. The Elbe flows into the North Sea, also linked to the North Atlantic. A message in a bottle might find its way into the river, encountering the message from Canada on its journey across the Atlantic. But what would be the odds of such an occurrence? And what were the chances that my sister would fall in love with a man from Hamburg while in Canada?

I encounter Erik once again in Edmonton. He walks along the snow-covered sidewalk in the "Strathcona" neighborhood, where I also find myself strolling. The air is frigid, causing my breath to freeze. Snow has drifted in from the Rocky Mountains, and the cold holds the city in its grip. When people venture outside, they move with haste—from their cars or the bus to stores, cafés, restaurants, or directly to their warm apartments. Winters in Canada are cold, and in Alberta, even more so.

Erik told me that he felt as though he had entered a different realm when he first arrived here. Strathcona struck him as a relaxed, lively neighborhood near the University of Alberta in Edmonton. Life thrived on the streets, and his spirits remained high. Today seemed distant, like it belonged to a different world.

His friend Frank from Germany had just called him. Frank inquired whether Erik would embark on the journey again if he knew how it would conclude. I had already posed the same question to Erik.

"The question of all questions," Erik responds, clutching his cell phone tighter as he navigates the icy path. "Why are you asking me the ultimate question now?"

"Because I'm concerned."

"But there's only one answer: Absolutely, I would."

"You've seen and experienced so much. However, you've also lost a lot, especially since you no longer have a job in Germany."

"The job isn't what matters to me. It pales in comparison to this. I see what I've gained. I've encountered two individuals who truly mean something to me. All of this, so far from home. One of those people is the love of my life."

Erik pauses and takes a deep breath. The conversation and the snowy street corner in Edmonton catch him off guard. Yet, it doesn't matter.

"I can't quantify the journey. It unfolded as it had to. What significance is there now in labeling it as good or bad? One thing is certain: there was never another option."

"Then I suppose everything occurred as it should have."

"That's how it is. But I'll be there. I'll call you again."

Erik ends the call. He decides there's a better time to continue reflecting on the past months. He must compose himself and, at the very least, project strength. If not him, then who? "We're all trying to do this. The responsibility isn't yours alone," I assure him. "We're all striving to support my sister."

Erik slips his cold hands into the pockets of his thick coat. I accompany him for a short distance down 82nd Avenue. At the intersection of 112th Street, we bid each other farewell with a firm handshake. "Best wishes," I convey. "And give my regards to Amelia. I plan to visit her tonight. Perhaps we can convene then."

"I wish you the best as well. Erik turns onto the street and says, "Maybe we will cross paths later."

A "Starbucks" café lines the path. In the past, he would have contemplated stopping for an "Americano." "Oh well," Erik mutters to himself and enters the café. The air carries a pleasant aroma of coffee and spices. It offers a sense of comfort akin to the lingering Christmas decorations. He queues up at the counter. He orders an "Americano" and a latte with cinnamon dusting the milk foam.

"Would you like these in larger mugs?" the waitress inquires. "It'll help keep them warm a bit longer out there."

"That would be much appreciated." He pays and retrieves the two cups from the counter.

With hopes that they'll remain warm, he resumes his stroll. He advances along 112th Street before making a left turn. Before him stands the University of Alberta Hospital. It's one of the largest hospitals in Western Canada and evokes a sense of reassurance. Over the past two weeks, Erik has been coming here regularly. With the latte in its cinnamon-adorned cup, he has made this journey.

He navigates his way to the entrance as if on autopilot. It's astonishing how swiftly one can adapt to such routines, he muses. Day after day, and sometimes even at night, he finds himself here. The circumstances are unfortunate: He isn't spending Christmas with his beloved in one of Strathcona's charming homes with brick facades, nor in one of the picturesque single-family houses in the city's suburbs, not even in the nearby Rocky Mountains or beyond them, on the Pacific Coast's scenic shores. Instead, he celebrates Christmas with the love of his life here, at the University of Alberta Hospital, shortly after the holiday.

CHAPTER 2

The California Zephyr

Chicago, in August, one year earlier

This story starts in the summer a year and a half ago. I want to tell it in the present tense. That's how Erik told me about what happened when we sat together in Amelia's apartment in Edmonton. At that time, in August, Erik had come to Chicago with his friend Frank. His first encounter with trains in the U.S. was rather involuntary. "We can't get away from here," he says in a small, cramped hotel room. The decrepit air conditioner rattles loudly, and notepads lie on the bed before them. Erik and Frank write out the prices of the connections among themselves. They are planning to continue their journey.

Visiting the Windy City was at the top of their travel plans, and Chicago impressed them both. The city, with its sights, fascinated him almost as much as New York, which he and Frank already knew. From "Michigan Avenue" to "Millennium Park" on the lakefront and "Cloud Gate", Erik and Frank traveled through the city on foot and by the Loop. The trip was marked by spontaneity. "Actually, we didn't have any real planning, and we didn't have a plan," Erik admits. A travel agency specializing in flights in Hamburg had arranged an open jaw flight to North America for them. The return flight was scheduled to depart from San Francisco a few weeks later.

Erik had already discovered that traveling in the United States is comfortable and easy, especially if you travel by car, from motel to motel. Erik would never have thought of getting on a Greyhound bus. He also only knew about existing railroads - but he needed to figure out where and how they ran.

Of course, both could travel at short notice. But they would have to pay a hefty price for it. When they get stuck in their room, they go down the stairs to the lobby of the simple hotel and talk to the receptionist.

"We want to go from Chicago to the West Coast. But we can't make it. Because we don't get that booked," Frank says.

"What's so hard about booking a flight?" she asks with a laugh. "Surely two guys from Europe should be able to manage that."

"The problem is the price. No matter where we try, we can't find anything under $1,000 per person."

"Aha, so this is where it gets stuck. Then let me try it the old-fashioned way," says the receptionist. After noting the travel dates, she picks up the phone and calls a friend at a travel agency. She nods at the receiver, smiles at Erik and Frank, babbles - and then shakes her head.

"Sorry, guys, but you already looked right. If you want to fly, there's nothing under $1000 per person, from ORD to SFO."

Erik didn't realize it would be so expensive.

"I can tell you what Cindy says she would do in your situation." Cindy owns the travel agency. "She would take the train."

"Really? And is it expensive?"

"No, if you drive Coach, it's not expensive. It's not that bad;

at least that's what Cindy says." She advises them to go to "Union Station" and ask.

At an "Amtrak" counter in the station, Frank and Erik find an employee who reminds them of their receptionist: she seems friendly but resolute. She understands the plan and hacks away at her keyboard for a while. Then her face brightens: she has found two seats on one train and another. "Unfortunately, it's always more crowded in the Rockies than before," she sighs. "You have to take a break there."

Erik looks at her questioningly. She: "The train goes west once a day. And, wait a minute, it gets tight after Reno, too. But you could take the bus there."

"Not the bus, anything but that," Frank says. "You're right, not the bus," Erik counters.

"Can we make another longer stopover in Reno?" inquires Erik. "Hold on. Yes, you can stay there for two or three days." Now, it's getting to be too much for Frank. "What are we going to do for three days in Nevada? I want to go to San Francisco, to the coast, and party." This "partying" was one of Frank's life mottos. At the beginning of the trip, Erik thought it was funny. But as time went on, he found that a large part of his ventures consisted only of "partying," drinking, and meeting women.

But here and now, he turns that into an idea: "I'll tell you something: Reno is a fantastic place to party. It's not far from there to Lake Tahoe. I hear you can meet the greatest women there."

"Have you made any progress yet?" the counter attendant asks curiously. Erik winks at her, and it works: "Reno is a fantastic place to party, isn't it?"

"Oh yes," she replies, "that's where all the people who want to party go; the trains are full of happy people who want to party." Her voice has a certain irony, but it escapes Frank - fortunately. Otherwise, they would be on the bus after all.

So, for the two of them, it will be the "California Zephyr". The price is reasonable, at least compared to the plane.

Complete with luggage and tickets, Frank and Erik return to Union Station the following day. Erik thinks you can't tell what's inside this big station from the outside. He doesn't see any tracks anywhere. After the station was built in the 1920s, real estate speculators bought "the air above the tracks," and created new office buildings on top of it.

Today, however, this leads to the platforms being in a dark cave, Erik notes. But through the confusing corridors, they eventually find the train and also the correct carriage.

A train service attendant orders the passengers into the car. When Erik hesitates, he hisses, "Hurry, go, go." His tone brooks no argument. The man is an authority figure through and through, tolerating no games. Upstairs in the car, the coach service attendant introduces himself. Erik feels puzzled. This one has the goal of making people feel comfortable on board. But perhaps, Frank admits, the attendant was just having a bad day. At 2 pm, it sounds like "All Aboard" on the platform. The train departs on time.

Complete with luggage and tickets, Frank and Erik return to Union Station the following day. Erik thinks you can't tell what's inside this big station from the outside. He doesn't see any tracks anywhere. After the station was built in the 1920s, real estate speculators bought "the air above the tracks," as it was called, and created new office buildings on top of it.

Today, however, this leads to the platforms being in a dark cave, Erik notes, which could be better lit. That's why Union Station doesn't make a friendly impression on him when they step out onto the platforms. But through the confusing corridors, they eventually find the train and also the correct carriage.

A surprise awaits here: A conductor stands before the entrance, dressed in the "Amtrak" railroad company uniform. He orders the passengers into the car. To do this, he asks to see the tickets. Frank's turn and the conductor grumbles at him: "Upstairs!" When Erik hesitates, he hisses, "Hurry, go, go." His tone brooks no argument. The man is an authority figure through and through, tolerating no games. "Do conductors in the U.S. have more power than those in Europe? Are they perhaps something like "train bosses" to ensure they follow the rules and don't step out of line?" asks Erik Frank, but he can only shrug his shoulders. "Maybe that's the case."

When Erik worries about the rude "greeting" and looks for the seat on the upper deck of the coach, he, fortunately, experiences the exact opposite from the man below: Another "conductor" introduces himself by the name of "Henry" and welcomes the two "coach" passengers. Erik feels puzzled. Henry has the goal of making people feel comfortable on board. In front of the train, his companion seems primarily concerned with restraining the passengers and not letting them get out of line.

But perhaps, Frank admits, the "Conductor" was just having a bad day. At any rate, he likes the seats. The distance to the next row is considerable - they had yet to experience so much space on a train in Europe. At 2 pm, it sounds like "All Aboard" on the platform. Then, the doors are closed, and the train departs on time.

RAILS TO THE WEST

Erik stretches his legs out on the footrests and watches the "Superliner" car rumble out of the station. West of Chicago, these double-decker Superliners are found on almost all long-distance trains. After a few minutes, Frank complains about the slow pace. "Can't do any better, I guess, with the tracks," Erik says. "But it's on a schedule, so it has to get to Denver when it's supposed to."

"You guys are optimistic," says a younger fellow passenger, leaning across the aisle from the seat opposite. He speaks German, albeit with an accent.

Frank is pleased that the man addresses him in German. "Are we optimistic? Why?"

"Actually, the trains are never on time. Especially when you're traveling such a long distance. Where are you headed? To Denver? You'll be lucky if we get away with a few hours' delay."

A few hours' delay seems like a lot to Erik, but he doesn't find it overly alarming. As if on cue, the train then accelerates. The houses behind the window pass by more quickly. There is a lot of green, and streets alternate with gardens and railroad crossings.

In Naperville, Illinois, the "California Zephyr" stops after a good half hour, then an hour later in Princeton. After the factories and industrial areas of Chicago had passed, and even the suburbs seemed more sparsely populated, the train reached the flat land of Illinois. Outside the window, fields alternate with meadows and small groves of trees. The cloudy sky, the dead straight horizon, in front of it, as if on a backdrop, lie the fields. But it repeats itself as the hours pass. Another farm, a village, a railroad crossing - the "California Zephyr" leaves everything by its side. It gets more exciting when the train slows to pass a small town. Then Erik sees houses again, supermarkets, restaurants with giant billboards, and cars in front of traffic lights - small-town life in Illinois, after all.

The train now seems to him like a capsule that is shot through space. It feels different from in an airplane because there you are removed from "everything earthly," seeing the ground many thousands of meters below you or looking into a sea of clouds. No, Erik is thankful that he gets at least a feeling for the landscapes and places they pass on this train.

At the same time, there are other advantages: Erik can stretch out on his seat, listen to music on his smartphone, look outside, and ponder. He can pick up a book, read, or talk to the other passengers.

As if to prove there is a reality, the "Zephyr" slows down shortly after 5 pm. Some passengers stand up, probably because they know what's coming: the long bridge over the Mississippi - a highlight. Indeed, Erik thinks, the sound of the wheels changes, and you can feel the steel he rides on. There it is, in full width: the "Old Man River," the Mississippi, which divides the United States into two halves: the somewhat older, more developed America in the east and the "Pioneer Land," western America.

The train traverses the bridge, which spans over 0.4 miles in length. The steel struts fly past behind the window, and the water is brown-blue - if such a hue even exists, Erik thinks. Yes, there is. It's blue like a river, with a dash of brown, like the Mississippi adds. The "Burlington Rail Bridge" connects Chicago to Denver across the river. Beyond the bridge, the "Zephyr" slows down and rolls into the Burlington station on a big curve. Erik finds the light sandstone building with a circular waiting room behind the glass facade attractive. Another small town, said to have just over 24000 residents, looks exciting from the train window. There also appears to be a respectable little "downtown" north of the station. "I'm on the verge of ending this secluded-ness and getting off," he says, but Frank can stop him, "We still have the night on the train and tomorrow's day in Denver. We don't know if there are any seats on that train tomorrow." That's true, Erik thinks and sighs, "If you're traveling by train, it's best not to be spontaneous."

❄

After Burlington, the "California Zephyr" revs up again, as Frank and Erik notice. It completes the next 300 miles in five hours and crosses an entire state, Iowa, in the process. Just before 11 pm, the "Zephyr" arrives in its first major city after Chicago, Omaha, Nebraska. Neither knows anything about this place, which is supposed to have half a million inhabitants.

At least the train will take a break here, so the two of them can take a walk across the platform. Erik feels how good it feels to stretch his legs. Omaha has a strange train station, which could already indicate, that something "isn't right." There are three station buildings at once: the first is a vast, monumental 1930s structure, but it's on the other side of the tracks, cut off from the tracks. The platforms look run down. It isn't in use anymore. Today, the Art Deco building houses the "Durham Museum." It is named after the couple who managed to renovate the building, which was threatened with demolition after the decline of passenger service. The second one is not so monumental, a bit more classical. Frank and Erik are standing right in front of it: a fence separates the building from the platform, lit up as bright as day. This building is also not in use. After many years of vacancy, it has become the headquarters of a television station.

The actual station building is a concrete cuboid from the 1980s that sits directly in front of the train. It is single-story and of an impressive ugliness, as Erik finds: The concrete walls are enclosed by a dark flat brown roof. Erik asks the coach attendant, the friendlier of the two. "This is a "standard Amtrak" station," he explains, replacing the other two stations that closed in the early 1970s. At least the train goes to "downtown" Omaha, he says; the railroad doesn't even come downtown in many places. Amtrak wanted to redesign the stations in the

1970s and 1980s with such concrete blocks. They were supposed to give the railroad a modern image and, at the same time, save costs so that it wouldn't have to maintain the large station buildings. In some cities, these were simply to be demolished.

Frank and Erik are not unhappy when the call of "All Aboard" is heard, and they hurriedly board before the big train continues its journey west. "That's one side of train travel," Erik says, "you're cut off from reality, but that can be quite a positive thing. Look at the dark office buildings of downtown Omaha and the industrial areas. We're lucky to be sitting here in our cozy "coach" car." Again, Erik is pleased with how far back the seats recline, and there are blankets and pillows available from the service attendant. The lighting is pleasant, and the air hisses into the coach through invisible nozzles. This rumbling and gentle hissing should become for him the melody of a night on the train rolling through the vastness of North America.

Frank and Erik have known each other for ages, since college, to be exact. Both studied economics. After graduating, Frank went to work for an aviation company in sales - he had a marketing focus. Dealing with customers is part of his everyday life, with special key accounts like those in the aviation industry. Erik became a journalist, working for a renowned magazine in the dockland-district of Hamburg. It's a travel magazine that shines not only for its lavish reportage but also for its illustrations. However, one should say "shone" because the good times were over.

Erik took advantage of the opportunity that arose after his studies and a time at a daily newspaper: He was able to start working at a magazine. That was a lot of fun for him. Instead of the dry studies, he had to deal with people and stories. They weren't as superficial as in the daily newspaper but more in-depth, multi-layered, and critical. His favorite thing to do was to write reports. Erik loved to think about topics and research. He literally composed his texts. To accomplish this, he filed and polished them until they were outstanding. At least, that's what his friends and colleagues told him. But Erik's work had to be suitable not only in terms of lyrics but also in terms of content. That's why he preferred to devote himself to critical topics. These ranged from the working lives of Asian seamen on ferries in the Baltic Sea to the development of tourism in Greenland and the consequences for the Inuit. Whenever there were travel topics to back up with critical approaches, Erik raised his hand at the magazine's editorial conferences. The first years were a happy time: He could "pay his dues" and put something aside and live in an old apartment on the edge of the harbor in Hamburg's Portuguese Quarter.

After a few years, he became friends with a colleague: Andrea and Erik got along well and had similar tastes in choosing topics and writing. They had gone to Budapest together on reportage, and things sparked between them. They spent "roaring" nights in their hotel rooms on the Danube. Later, in Hamburg, they became a couple. But anyone who worked as closely together in an editorial department as the two of them did, and with the pressure, that prevailed in their jobs, were also going to have a difficult time in their private lives: Although they got along well, they were not supposed to live together. Erik noticed that Andrea refused to move in with him. He had often offered her to, especially since his apartment was near her work. But it all seemed to have become too close for her. Finally, one day, after they had been together for a good year and a half, they broke up. She had approached the breakup very matter-of-factly and almost coolly. Erik was troubled by this. When it came to love and relationships, he took everything very hard. It had never been about affairs for him, as they were not so rare in her editorial department. For him, it was about great love. He is an earnest guy in that respect. Andrea, on the other hand, was an efficient person. She also took the initiative to break up with him. She had no problem dismissing Erik as an affair of her past. He, on the other hand, did. They also tried to reduce their professional contact. Erik thought that was a shame, but he couldn't help it.

Because times weren't getting any better for the travel magazine, they both worked for. He was in his late thirties and sometimes wondered if he had chosen the wrong profession.

"Say, how's your magazine doing now?" Frank asks him as they lean back in their seats on the train.

"You know, times are rough in the industry. Circulations are dropping rapidly. Why do people no longer want to buy printed travel magazines? Of course, our quality was higher a few years ago - but we had a bigger budget then, too."

"And you can't counter it online?"

"The online offerings of our publishing house are growing. Much money is being invested in this, including in the forums where users can discuss God and the world. But even though the articles are now no longer free, it's not enough. The magazine can barely be financed with the little money these online subscriptions bring in." Although staff cuts slowly began at the publishing house, Erik still climbed the career ladder, driven by the ambition to make it.

He didn't realize then how much it pissed Andrea off that he was moving up to a senior position. At the same time, he was moving further and further away from the job as a reporter that he had started out with. It wasn't long before he was no longer doing his own research, writing his own magazine articles, but editing other writers' copy, mostly freelancers. Erik planned long stretches of magazine pages. To achieve this, he hardly ever had any outside appointments, but only spent time in the magazine's editorial office in their modern Hamburg building. He didn't realize how little he enjoyed the job. At the same time, the work was becoming increasingly "condensed. All this could still do little to him, he thought.

"But you have a new publishing director. He'll fix it, won't he?"

"I don't trust him with anything. He has a big mouth, and behind it is an astonishing emptiness. He could manage a small city magazine.

Erik didn't say how circulation was developing at his publication. They were themselves close to a city magazine. The shareholders had tasked the publishing director to make the editorial department more profitable. Things had become very uncomfortable. The editor-in-chief, a journalist with heart and soul, could not do much to counter him. The head of the publishing house had made it clear to everyone that "normal dedication" and "normal working hours" were no longer enough for the employees. If they wanted to keep their job long-term, they had to work harder and stay longer.

"But I also realize how much this job has taken me away from the job I once loved," Erik says.

"What do you call that publishing thing?"

"He's just the 'cookie monster.'"

"Why is that?"

"He doesn't bother with trifles. He eliminates everything that stands in his way and expends considerable energy on it. The employees who try, he eats like cookies. He'll do anything to get more cookies." Quickly, the workdays had grown to ten to eleven hours a day. Erik would go to the magazine in the morning and come out in the evening exhausted. "You wouldn't believe how much I needed this vacation," he says. "And you know what? I think you're having more fun with your sales job."

"No, it can't be. My job is rubbish."

"But at least you get to socialize. I sit in a neon-lit office all day and get to edit long articles and sort news. It's not great."

"There might be something to that, listening to you. Ten years ago, you were a creative person, and today, you're an administrator with a big computer screen to look at all day. You should change jobs sometime, badly.

"I'm changing industries at the same time. There can't be any future in what I'm doing."

"Maybe we should both change jobs, industries, and countries," Frank says. "The best thing would be to change continents right away." Erik could not have known how right he would be - nor that things would go further downhill for him.

The other passengers are silent or have fallen asleep. In some rows, you can see a reading light. Erik can't sleep in such seats, but it is different here. Many people in the rows of seats before him are wrapped in blankets. It looks cozy. Outside, Erik can't see much beyond the train window in the vastness of the Midwest. But there is a signal just flashed by, glowing in the darkness. Then there's the rumble, a slight hiss, and the dim light. Erik can even fall asleep as the big train rushes through the night, dreaming of dimmed light and gentle hissing.

DENVER STOPOVER

The following day, Erik finds the first glimpse of the Rocky Mountains looming on the horizon impressive. He can make them out long before Denver, Colorado. Around him, the land is flat in a mix of green fields and brown earth. The train travels a dead, straight track toward the mountain backdrop on the horizon. Closer and closer comes the chain of peaks rising from the landscape.

"What a relief to get out!" he says.

"I'd rather drive right through to the West Coast," finds Frank, rubbing sleep from his eyes.

"No, I also have to leave this tin can and see something of the country for once. We'd be racing through otherwise. We're not tourists who want to cross such a big country in a few days."

Fortunately, not all stations in the Midwest are as run-down as the Amtrak concrete cube in Omaha. Denver Union Station is the opposite of the dreary cube. The grand old station has been renovated and expanded, partly to serve as the hub of a new rapid transit system. They arrive in Denver at 7:30 am. After 1038 miles or 1,670 kilometers, from Chicago Union Station, it's over here, at least until tomorrow.

The train has to be maneuvered slowly into the terminus, for which it turns, and the last car is pushed onto the extended platform. Outside, there is a hustle and bustle. The two leave the train, and look for a café to have breakfast. The station concourse is bustling in the morning, with train passengers rushing through and commuters coming "downtown" from the suburban trains.

Frank and Erik sit down at a café on the station's forecourt. The buildings downtown look attractive to Erik: The older structures are made of brick and have something "western" about them, with their four or five stories. The square is busy, the café full. There is a warm morning sun shining from the sky.

At the table next to them, a man sits with a newspaper and a coffee. Erik estimates him to be in his mid-forties. He is wearing more casual clothes with his polo shirt and blue pants. Still, he looks like a businessman. He takes off his dark sunglasses and begins to leaf through a newspaper. It is the "New York Times," Erik notices. Curious, he looks over and asks where they are from. They tell him they flew here from Germany and are stopping in Denver.

"As you two travel across America, what's your next stop?"

Paul asks. "We're going to make one more stop in Reno before heading to San Francisco," Frank replies.

"In Reno? That's a perfect match. I have a package that needs to go," the man says. "No big deal. But it's for a business friend, and I don't like sending it in the mail. It would be much better if you could take it with you."

Erik is skeptical. "If it's important, wouldn't it be better to use a courier service?"

"Oh, these courier services take forever. And they're not safe either. No, if you get on the train, you could just take it with you, and then in Reno, my friend will pick it up. When are you going on?"

Erik would have yet to tell him, but Frank is quicker. "First thing in the morning, we'll be on our way."

"You know what, guys? You could use a few dollars for your travel fund. How about you get, well, let's say, $500 if you take the package with you?"

Erik raises his hands, but Frank is faster again. "That sounds like a good deal. If it's nothing illegal."

"No, never do illegal things. This is a statue I want to give to my friend. Don't worry. I'll give you $200 now, and you'll get the rest when you deliver the package. It's not a risk."

He pulls out his wallet and holds up four $50 bills. He hands them to Frank, who grins broadly. "I'll come to your plat-form tomorrow morning and give you the package. There's zero risk involved. If you get cold feet, you'll already have $200. But why should you?"

He folds the newspaper, puts on his sunglasses, and marches off. He leaves his coffee behind. "Frank, I don't have a good feel-ing," Erik says.

"It may sound a little strange. But think about it: $500 for a piece of luggage we take from Denver to Reno. Why not? Our travel fund could use it."

"That's not the only thing. I'm pretty sure I saw the man on the platform earlier."

"Well, he does say he likes to ride the train."

"Maybe. But he was talking to a passenger on our train. The one who asked you about the delay in German, right behind Chicago."

Frank shrugs. "So what if they do. Then maybe they know each other? I'm still in favor of taking the package tomorrow."

Although Erik doesn't feel good, he lets himself be persuaded. Because they could really use the money.

Finding a hotel in downtown Denver on a tight budget for two travelers from Europe is not exactly trivial. Branches of big hotel chains can be located on every street corner. Still, the rooms are costly downtown - neither Frank nor Erik had expected that. Finally, just south of the train station, they find a "premium hostel," a hostel lodging that markets itself as something better.

After checking in, they move into a vast and clean room on the third floor, which overlooks the street and the roofs of many other houses. The rooms in the hostel are individually decorated because they all have a theme. This one is probably meant to remind people of "urban skiers": mounted on the wall is a snowboard floating in front of a picture of skyscrapers. "That's quite original," Frank says. "Maybe it's a skateboard without wheels that the hostel operator screwed on there. But it looks funny."

Later, Frank and Erik learn that the really cheap hotels are motels located at the access ramps of the highway, but not in the middle of downtown. For train travelers, Motel 6, Super 8 or Holiday Inn would not be an alternative. But to go there with a city bus, they didn't feel like it. So, you pay a hefty "premium" surcharge if you want to stay in Denver right in the center. The hostel has a very modern lobby, with benches along the brick walls dividing the rooms. The bar serves "Beer on Tap." Frank and Erik sit down at the bar first. In the western part, Larimer Street is a hotspot for Denver nightlife. But it's a little early for that now.

Erik notices a couple who have sat in the next seating area: she has blond hair, will be around thirty years old, and looks very attractive. He is a downright quaint guy with a beard and a fuzzy head. He may be approximately forty. The two are dressed alternatively in old jeans and brightly patterned shirts that could well have come from a thrift store. Above all, they seem upbeat and have such a friendly way of talking to each other. Everything about these two seems harmonious, Erik thinks. Then, the man reaches out his hand and introduces himself.

"I'm Drake, and this is Eline. We're from Aspen. And you?" Frank and Erik also introduce themselves. They report they are travelers from Germany, crossing the U.S. by train. "Oh, wow," Eline slips out. "That's impressive. Wait. How are you doing on your big trip?" she asks in German. "Was that an American accent I heard or a Dutch one?" asks Frank.

"A little of both, I guess," Eline says. "I'm from the Netherlands." She continues in English as Drake looks at her questioningly.

"So you're here visiting, too?" asks Erik.

"Yeah, you could say that. It's a long visit because we both emigrated, Drake, as much as I did.

"You're not from Germany, are you?" says Erik to Drake.

"No, I'm from New York City, and Eline is from a village in the north of the Netherlands with a windmill," he says. "With only one windmill, that's how small the village is," she adds.

"But we've lived in Aspen, in the middle of the Rocky Mountains, for many years. We visit Denver for a few days to taste the big city air. You know: going out, theater, shopping, things like that. The hostel fits us relatively well. Even though parking is expensive, more expensive than at one of the motels on the interstate."

"We're on Amtrak, so we don't need a parking spot," Erik says. "But how are you two getting to Aspen?"

"It was like John Denver," Drake says. "Like Rocky Mountain High, which is the official anthem of this state."

"Drake was a staunch New Yorker," Eline tells me, "from the top of his head to the bottom of his feet. He worked at an investment bank."

"Yes, and from early in the morning until late at night. I raked in quite a bit of money, I can admit that. But otherwise, I didn't have much. A small apartment, no girlfriend, no family. I just lived for work and occasional party nights where I could spend the money."

Erik reports how well he can understand this. Although his job doesn't make him as much money as an investment banker in New York, he knows the working hours very well. And Frank also knows what Drake is talking about.

"But then Eline came into my life," Drake says, beaming happily at his wife.

"I was sort of stranded in New York. I had previously studied in the Netherlands and graduated. But then I didn't know what to do. So I flew to my sister, who was already living in New Amsterdam," she said, slightly tongue-in-cheek. "New Amsterdam" is the old Dutch name for New York. "Then Drake met me, and it was like we were just looking for each other. Me, the graduate from the Netherlands, visiting the wider world, and you ..."

"...the snooty investment banker looking for a fling with a Dutch girl."

"What were you looking for?"

"No, honey, I wasn't looking for adventure."

"I know you do," she says, stroking his face.

"We fell head over heels in love. It happened quickly, and it was very stormy. We didn't want to break up once we found each other. But we also slowly realized that it wasn't meant to continue in New York," Eline tells the story of the two. "Some people are crazy about living in New York. I admire those. For me, as a country girl, this city was too big, too hectic, and therefore too exhausting in the long run. Life in New Amsterdam is also quite expensive. Of course, if you have an investment banker for a boyfriend, it works," she laughs.

"But that didn't do much for me in the long run," Drake adds. "It's not like my days as a banker got shorter just because I met a great Dutch girl I'm completely in love with. It took me a while to realize this job wasn't for me. We need to build something new together; that was our thinking."

"That's why we did something great," Eline takes over again. "We crisscrossed the U.S. and figured out where to settle down. We were together, and we set off for a new life."

"Yes, I had also quit my job for that. I had a decent amount to put away, so we had funds to go with. I was willing to spring that for a good cause, a life with Eline in a place we liked."

"So we went west by wagon. The way you guys came by train, it wasn't until Denver that we really got fascinated. We got all the way to the Rockies and stopped in Aspen. That's where we stayed. Because Drake had discovered a 'business opportunity.'"

Erik listens spellbound as the two tell how they rented an empty café in Aspen and ran it. The place was open to skiers in the winter and hikers in the summer. "The first few years weren't easy until we were known and made money. The key difference is that when you do it for yourself, you accomplish a lot more than when it's for someone else."

"It was mainly for us," says Eline, "because we also married in Aspen. It was romantic, with a party, flowers, music and some friends that we flew in especially. They came from New York, but two friends of mine from the Netherlands made it there."

"Because we stayed in Aspen, and that's pretty far from anyone else we knew."

"And you can live on that?" inquires Frank.

Eline and Drake look at each other with grins. "Yes, we can live relatively well on it; it went better than we thought. We've given coffee consumption in the Rockies a good boost, anyway."

The two also invite Erik and Frank to come to Aspen and visit them there in their café. But whether it was really a serious invitation? Why not? The only thing is that Aspen is unfortunately not on their route at all. But the contact should not break off.

"Those two people," he later tells Frank, "they found happiness."

"Yes, and they've managed to build something together that they can live off of."

"With this, they show us only love counts!"

What the two didn't tell him he could later read on the web, after a simple search for "Eline" and "Drake": they don't have one café in Aspen open to skiers and hikers. They built an entire cafe chain in many towns and cities in Colorado and neighboring states. Obviously, Drake couldn't stay away from "business," and Eline had discovered her knack for running a chain of coffee shops. The two "Black Bear Coffee" owners seem to have made a fortune with their stores. They remained owners. They had the right idea just before "Starbucks" began to cover the far corners of the United States with coffee houses. Erik discovered while researching on the web that Eline and Drake have contributed to society with their proceeds.

Their alternative clothing made them look like mountain lovers, perhaps an alt-hippie couple living on "the skinny" and staying in a hostel close to Larimer Street in Denver.

Erik can't help but feel a little jealous. Drake had set himself up as a businessman on Wall Street, met the love of his life, and moved to the mountains with her. He leaves everything behind to build a new life, which he succeeds in doing. How he would love to follow such a path as well. At the same time, Erik thinks they both have remained likable; you couldn't tell who they were.

THROUGH THE ROCKY MOUNTAINS

The train picks up speed. Downtown Denver is behind them since they boarded the next "California Zephyr." A coach service attendant has assigned them two seats. Again, they sit in the upper deck of one of the "Superliner" coaches. The man with the package was indeed waiting for them on the platform: he was wearing the same polo shirt and sunglasses again, Erik noticed. The "parcel" was a dark leather suitcase, thick but not too big. It has a combination lock on the top. "But don't look inside," the man said, still laughing, and pressed the suitcase into their hands. Then, he quickly disappeared again into the hustle and bustle. Frank didn't seem to mind any of this, Erik thought. He slid the suitcase onto the shelf above their seats, grinned, and remarked, "Soon, we'll be $500 richer for a little courier service."

Now, the big train curves out of the city and "sets course" for the mountains they had seen on the horizon the day before. The seats seem just as comfortable to Erik as they were on the first leg of the trip, and even the train's windows have been washed. This is a nice touch by "Amtrak," Erik thinks. Before the spectacular ride through the mountains, the windows are cleaned. This custom goes back to the predecessor railroad company. There was once a train washing facility in Denver through which the former "San Francisco Zephyr," the predecessor that ran until 1970, was passed before ascending into the mountains. After Denver, the train climbs the hills in long switchbacks. The train spirals up meter by meter, so to speak. Actually, it's a tedious ride.

But when you're sitting back as a passenger, you don't mind, except for the ever-changing views of the valley, which also includes the city of Denver and its suburbs. Shortly before they enter the Front Range, as the mountain range is called, they cross the Big Ten Curve behind the small town of Rocky. Erik is amazed at how the train swings to the left, backs up, turns a large circle of 180 degrees, rolls west again, and finally seems to turn right. "I don't understand what the train is doing here," Frank says as he squints out the window. "Well, the main thing is we're getting somewhere." So, the two see the train's long ribbon of curves several times over.

Now, the train stops and makes no move to continue. "It must be the Moffat Tunnel," says Erik, who is leafing through the railroad book he bought at the Denver station.

"Why? Is the tunnel overcrowded?" asks Frank.

The next train has to wait when one has just passed through. That's what it says here," Erik says, holding up the book. "Computers measure the air quality in the tunnel. Between ten and 20 minutes must have passed before the next train is allowed to go in while the fans are blowing." After fifteen minutes, a freight train passes the "California Zephyr," and afterward it can leave. The "Zephyr" approaches the village of "Tolland" from the east at the portal of the "Moffat Tunnel," which passes under the mountain massif here.

"Frank, the story of David Halliday Moffat is fascinating. This tunnel is named after him."

"What makes him so special?"

"Moffat was a railroad pioneer from Denver and was eager to connect the city to the national network," Erik says. "First, he was a teller at a bank in New York at age 12, then he moved west. At 21, he moved to the fledgling city of Denver, Colorado, to open a bookstore." Apparently, there was still money to be made in bookstores back then, Erik thinks; at least Moffat must have believed so, or he wanted to fulfill his literary dreams. The bookstore didn't do well, and Moffat went back into banking. "And he became passionate about railroads," Erik says. First, he got involved in a few rail lines with business friends and tackled a transcontinental link through the mountains.

"Listen, I find this tragic now: he invested his entire fortune in constructing this railroad in 1902. In fact, he already wanted to construct the tunnel but had no more capital for it." Erik recounts how Moffat had a circuitous, steep route built over the pass so the train could run at all. "At a whopping 3560 meters above sea level, the "Moffat Line" finally crossed the "Continental Divide." That's got to be somewhere above us here."

"I don't suppose it will have done that if the route is so circuitous?"

"No because the new line ended halfway to Salt Lake City because he ran out of money. He traveled to the East Coast to recruit new financiers. The cost of keeping "Rollins Pass" open in the winter ate up the few profits. He failed in New York, where he had once started as a messenger boy. He died in March 1911 at the age of 72 while still negotiating. There's no question about it: after his death, the railroad company had no choice but to go bankrupt." Erik hadn't even realized the fates that could lie behind rail lines in the west.

Only a new company with new funding could connect the rail line to Salt Lake City and build the new tunnel, which was named "Moffat Tunnel" for the sake of the visionary. The 6.2-miles long structure through which the train now rushes went into operation in 1928. In the middle of the tunnel, Erik feels a click in the air, like in an airplane when the pressure changes. "What was that?" asks Frank. "That must have been the gate at the west end opening now," Erik says. "It's for ventilation, and now the air pressure has changed so that the locomotives in the tunnel get enough oxygen. And us, of course."

"What actually happened to the route over the pass?" asks Frank. "The tracks were dismantled after the tunnel opened, and the little towns with restaurants along the route became ghost towns," Erik says. "But a road was opened on the pass that is said to have enjoyed some popularity for many years, with mountain bikers and '4x4' off-road riders. The small tunnel collapses caused the road to be closed. There's probably not much left up there on the mountain today."

You have just gotten used to the darkness when it suddenly gets light again: Directly after the western tunnel portal, the ski resort "Winter Park" follows. This is where the train stops. They are just two hours away from Denver. The mountain world surrounds them as they step off the train. The ski resort of Winter Park is right in front of them. No wonder a "Ski Train" runs up here from Denver every weekend in winter, as the attendant reports.

After a few minutes stop, the train continues on its way. The train winds its way between the mountains through valleys, which sometimes close in on the track, sometimes leave a little room for a river, and sometimes recede wide. But always, they surround the green pine forests that gently decorate the mountains up to the tree line. Frank notes that this is the most beautiful part of the drive from Chicago so far. The two are lucky, having switched to the observation car after Winter Park and found available seats. Again, Erik is overcome with a desire to look closer at the landscape and its sites. The more beautiful it gets outside the train window, the more he feels the urge to get off and ride through the mountains on foot, by bike, or even by car. You could just sit back and relax, he thinks. But you're just traveling through this landscape; you see it as a backdrop and can't participate. It doesn't help: Erik says you must build in stops with train journeys of this length.

The next stop for them is supposed to be Reno, Nevada, which is just outside California. There's time to look at the Rocky Mountain scenery, stroll through the train, and travel between the "coach" seats and the panorama car. Because they're traveling in "economy" class, they don't have meals included. "You could soon be over the sandwiches available for purchase in the lower deck," Frank says. But they'll have to suffice for the one day to Reno.

Erik muses, then has to ask Frank what he thinks. "Say, we Europeans like to ride trains. Americans don't? "

"What do you mean?"

"Well, we're traveling through a foreign country on another continent. And in doing so, we set our own European standard."

"Other countries just happen to have different customs, different means of transportation."

"That's exactly what I mean. Everyone likes to drive, and it's convenient, after all. But shouldn't people take more trains in the context of climate protection?"

Frank replies: "We have found the counterexample in Denver. The city has a very revitalized downtown again. So there's a trend going in exactly that direction." While enjoying their lunch of soft bread topped with ham and cheese, they talk with two young women from Chicago who have sat next to them in the panorama car.

They take the train to visit relatives in San Francisco. Erik asks why they are taking the train instead of flying. "Why not?" replies the black-haired, petite American woman, around 30 years old. "The price is ok. It takes longer, but why not?" The thought that there are people who use this intercity train like a "normal" means of transportation had not yet occurred to Erik. So far, he has perceived the day-long train ride either as a "rail cruise" for people with a lot of money and time on their hands or as a mode of transportation for those who can't afford to fly, like Frank and him, for that matter. Neither applies to Mary and her friend Anne. They could fly, but they don't, nor do they want to take the bus or even get behind the wheel themselves.

"Look," Mary says, showing her smartphone. "It takes us two days and four hours by train."

"Well, you have continuous seats," Erik replies.

"Why, you don't?" she asks in amazement.

"We had to take a one-night break in Denver and stop in Reno."

"When did you book?"

"The day before we left."

"That's a lot of short notice, don't you think? We booked this trip a month ago. Besides not having space problems, it's also a lot cheaper."

Yes, there it is again: the "penalty fee" the two pay because they thought they could just spontaneously drive across the continent. When Erik tells the two of them this, they have to laugh out loud. "You can't tell me it's any different in Europe," Mary says.

"No, but we thought that with you guys in the U.S., you could just hop on the next plane."

"Sometimes you can. It just depends on the demand from the major airlines. And you just got unlucky. But look here, that would be much worse."

She holds her smartphone in front of his nose. "You would need 32 hours by car, theoretically anyway, if you drove day and night. You'll need three days if you only drive ten hours daily, which would be enough. For that, it's always along Interstate 80, from Chicago to San Francisco. And don't you think you could easily go crazy there?"

Erik agrees with her. "Sitting and chatting with you on the train is really nicer."

"You wouldn't come through Denver but Cheyenne in Wyoming. But didn't you like Denver, too?" Erik reports that the hostel was lovely, and Eline and Drake's story impressed him. They like the story, too, "Only love matters, huh? That's romantic."

But the two are not just on the train because they enjoy it. During the conversation, it turns out that Anne has a great fear of flying. "There's a reason for that," she says, looking at the mountains. "As a child, I had to be there when our plane had to make an emergency landing. It was horrible. Everyone was screaming in panic. Thank God nothing happened to us. I didn't understand what happened until my mother told me the plane touched down pretty hard because of an engine failure. But now when I have to sit in an airplane, first my hands get sweaty, and then I get terrified."

"Yes, that's the real reason Anne is on this train, and so am I," Mary admits. She glances at Anne and adds encouragingly, "But it's fun too, isn't it? Chatting with those two Germans?"

Anne regained her composure. "Yes, it's fun and better than driving."

Anne and Mary return to their "coach" seats a little later. Frank does the same, for a nap, as he says. Erik strolls through the train. At a crossing between two cars, he meets a group of men. One of them asks him if he's enjoying the train ride. He is a little older; Erik estimates him to be around fifty but well-trained. "Yeah, it's great, but it's also a little slow," Erik says. The undertone of his counterpart becomes slightly aggressive. "Of course it's great, this train is fantastic, isn't it?" he throws back. It didn't occur to Erik that the man and his cronies were simply looking for a fight. They were probably bored with the train ride.

Another of the group, a bit younger, tries to smooth the waters in his own way. "I don't like Germany," he says with a grin. "You're a country that David Hasselhoff thinks is good." Well-informed, the man, Erik thinks. "How can you guys be into someone like David Hasselhoff?"

Fortunately, Erik has the hot coffee from the cafeteria with him. So he says he has to go. "Yes, you Germans, always on time," the first man teases afterward.

"I can't stand people like that," Frank says a few minutes later after Erik tells him about the encounter at the square. Frank would respond much more to the provocations, Erik notes. Good thing he wasn't there earlier.

Frank and Erik meet Anne and Mary again in the panorama car in the evening. It's "happy hour" here, and there are cocktails from plastic cups that you can get in the cafeteria on the lower deck. Outside, the sun is setting, and the shadows in the valleys between the mountains are lengthening. The two women from Chicago seem to know the entire drink menu by heart: The four unerringly drink from one cocktail to the next in response to their recommendations. This begins to have an effect: They start laughing at ridiculous jokes. Erik later doesn't even remember what they were talking about.

But Frank and Erik are only really gobsmacked when Anne fetches another round of cups full of Coke from the cafeteria. Then, in the observation car, she takes out her water bottle and pours a good shot into each of the glasses. She rounds that off with a "cheers," raises the glass, and toasts. "You've got it going on," Frank says, and Erik is impressed, too. "We just know how to help ourselves. Vodka in the water bottle, I've got that handy."

The train has already reached the Salt Lake City plain, as shown by the lights that can be seen from the windows of the panorama car. The next stop will be Salt Lake City. The coach service attendant joins them. "We'll be pulling into the new station soon," he explains. Salt Lake City has three stations. Erik hopes it looks different from Omaha. No, it's not quite that bleak, says the attendant. He knows them all. "We used to go to the Union Pacific Depot," he explains. "That's a big structure on the west side of downtown. But starting in 1986, the 'Zephyr' rolled into the Rio Grande Depot. That was much nicer and more magnificent, with great glass facades. Finally, in 1999, the new station opened, and the Rio Grande Depot became a shopping center."

The new station, "Salt Lake Central," is on the edge of downtown. The new suburban railroads cross here. It's called an "intermodal hub." "But plenty of people think it's a shame because the Rio Grande Depot was a real station with a great reception building, and the 'hub' really just has a couple of platforms," the attendant says.

The train slows down and stops at the brightly lit platform cast from concrete. A suburban train pulls in opposite. It has become half past eleven at night. Erik is walking up and down the platform when an announcement comes: The "California Zephyr" departure has been delayed. The attendant says, "You can take your time with the walk." Erik asks him what's wrong. "The locomotive is broken; we can't go on," he says in a lowered voice. "Amtrak is now trying to find a replacement locomotive."

You rarely experience that, Erik thinks. It could have been a quiet stopover. If his "friends" hadn't shown up. Once again, the man with the short-shaven head is the ringleader. "How fast are your trains in Germany," he wants to know. Erik thinks for a moment. "Well, the fast trains, they go about 100 to 120 miles, something like 200 kilometers per hour." That's too much for him. "Is that how fast your trains are supposed to be?" His cronies burst into a torrent of talk, which Erik understands next to nothing. Then Mary steps next to him and pulls on his arm. He asks her what the men are talking about. "That's just nonsense. You don't even want to know. There will be mischief if I tell you. Come back on the train right now," she says quickly but quietly. With Mary, Erik disappears into the train car.

Frank says it "smelled" like a brawl in front of the train, shocked. He suggests: "First, we stay in here. Second: We stay among people. And third, we go for a drink."

Although it's already midnight, they get another round of Cokes in plastic glasses in the cafeteria. Of course, Anne has her water bottle handy, so she can pour a round of vodka to go with it - which helps Erik calm down. What was going on out there in front of the train, he doesn't know, but it seems safe in here. The train starts moving again. Exhausted and quite drunk, the two sink into their coach chairs, and the vodka doesn't miss its mark. He immediately falls asleep and drifts off deep into the land of dreams. Fortunately, he is not dreaming of the men, but of a service attendant who pours him one vodka after another with her water bottle.

CANDICE FROM MONTANA

The train conductor gently nudges Frank and Erik. "We'll be in Reno soon; that's your stop," he says. Erik is half asleep and realizes that all the evening's drinks have left him with a hangover. But they must hurry and pack their things because it's already close to eight o'clock and the stop is not far. They have left the Great Salt Lake and the highlands to the west behind them in the darkness. In the early morning hours, Erik recalls the train once stopped in "Elko" in Nevada, and he had again felt this strange desire to get off and see the small town. However, it was still dark outside, and the train had time to catch up, so the stop lasted no more than a minute. In truth, there is little to see between Salt Lake City and Reno except small towns and flat rolling countryside, which he only got a little of at night.

The two women from Chicago don't see them again, so quickly, the train arrives in Reno. They probably slept through the morning. They grab their luggage and get ready to leave the train. Fortunately, the dark, large suitcase is still in the storage compartment, just as it was yesterday when Frank had stowed it there. Nothing is happening on the platform as Erik and Frank leave the "Superliner" and head for the exit. The two roaring locomotives at the head of the train sound their horns, the conductor calls "All Aboard". Then everything happens quickly. A man in a leather jacket is waiting for them at the exit just as they are about to enter the street. He, too, wears sunglasses, Erik notices, seems 45 years old, and has something Italian about him, with his dark hair full of gel. "There are Paul's friends," he notes with a broad grin. "And they kept their word and brought the suitcase." Frank holds up the suitcase. "Here you go, completely intact, just like in Denver."

"I have no doubt about that." The man pushes them both out through the exit onto the street. "Let me check the locks.

Yeah, even the numbers you set are right there; you didn't tamper with them," the man in the leather jacket says. He reaches for his wallet and pulls out three $100 bills. "Here you go, for your vacation. Enjoy it." Then he takes the suitcase from Frank's hand and quickly disappears downtown. "There you go," Frank says, "Everything's fine, and we're $500 richer."

"Yeah, if the FBI doesn't jump on us right away," Erik counters. "The way he checked the position of the numbers on the lock. The other guy in Denver must have given them to him. I guess that was his way of showing us how smart he is. Better put the money away, and then let's find a hotel."

Erik tries to forget the matter and be happy they have three days to see this region in the "Sierras." Because Lake Tahoe and Reno are one in terms of tourism, they agree to forego car rental and take buses. The train stopped in the middle of town, which is convenient, especially when "downtown" offers some hotels.

"In gambling towns in Nevada, you shouldn't have trouble finding a hotel," Frank says. "If it has a big casino, the prices should be acceptable for the room, the drinks, and maybe the food." Frank is satisfied; they find reasonably priced accommodations. In the evening, in a shopping center that is a large casino, they visit a large gold mine made of plastic and steel, built as a tourist attraction. Around it are bars with live music, connected by bridges to adjacent hotels. "It may be convenient in the winter," Erik says, "and it's air-conditioned in the summer. But somehow, it's also nonsensical. It's just a touch of Las Vegas." He notices that some casinos are offshoots of the well-known Las Vegas chains. Reno has its own charm. In this respect, the slogan "The Biggest Small Town in the World," printed on a neon advertisement stretching across one of the roads, fits well.

❄

"If we really feed the one-armed bandits now," Frank says, "we'll be lucky to make so much money that we'll just have luxury for the rest of the trip." The two ponder what that might be. "We'll go to every hotel without thinking about how much it costs first," Erik says. "We'll visit every bar and only order expensive cocktails," Frank notes. "We could spend local rounds," Erik says, glancing around: plenty of gamblers sit at the tables and bar, individuals in cowboy hats, well-groomed and not-so-well-dressed couples among them. "Or not, and keeping it all to ourselves." The two realize it would be a little luxury they could buy - should they win.

"We could lose everything," Frank objects.

"Yes, and then we wouldn't have enough money for the return trip and have to try to have something sent from Germany."

"Or we do win a lot."

Erik remembers that Frank didn't dislike gambling at all. He had been to the casino with him a few times: In Travemünde, for example, when there was still a "real" casino. Or in Hamburg at the Dammtor and in the Schenefeld casino. What worried Erik sometimes was that Frank had always won relatively much. He didn't believe his friend would let go of the gambling tables in Reno. But at the same time, it had been his idea to make a more extended stop here. "Let's leave it at these Budweisers for now," he tried to get Frank's mind off things.

It was to be a memorable evening. Because it was the evening on which Erik met Candice - who was to become an important person in his life. What he, just as little as she, could not have guessed. Looking for a "paaarty," as Frank put it, they wandered the casino corridors and adjacent hotels. Finally, they sat down again by the giant paper-mâché mine in the center of the complex. While Frank was thinking about how to initiate a conversation with a group of girls, Erik decided to get another drink. He goes to the counter and orders two "Wheat" beers, which are supposed to be some kind of Bavarian wheat beer and taste remotely like it.

With the "Wheat" beers in his hand, he turns around in front of the packed bar counter, doesn't pay attention for a second, and runs into a woman who, in turn, has two cocktails in her hands. The "Wheat" beer spills all over her dress just as her cocktails sway and spread all over his shirt. She groans loudly, then apologizes.

"What the hell happened? I have no idea; please forgive me!"

"No, no, it's my fault," Erik says. "I wasn't paying attention; I was just looking at this beer and not seeing what was happening around me." He and she look into each other's eyes for a second. She has long brown hair and eyes, a similar shade of brown that seems to shine a little despite the "accident." He estimates the attractive-looking woman to be in her mid-thirties. Something unfamiliar flashed through him. Later, he asked Candice what she had been thinking at that moment, and she said that his eyes had fascinated her. It must have been the same for both of them at that moment.

"Hold on, I'll fix that," Erik says, setting his glasses down and returning to the bar. If he could have napkins, he asks the bartender. To his amazement, he has a whole bunch of paper napkins. He had already seen himself on the way to the restroom and he would have found that more or less embar-rassing.

"Look, I may have bumped into you and your cocktail, and you got my beer, but at least I organized a stack of napkins." The line wasn't that original, but it must be chemistry. She's pleased and gratefully takes half the stack. Then she turns around, dabbing with the napkins while Erik rubs at his shirt. Not that he thinks it will do any good, but since she does the same, he doesn't want to stand around. Grinning, she turns again.

"The mishap is already taken care of," she says, tugging at her dark dress, which is still wet from the beer splashes. My, she's a brave one, Erik thinks.

"I'm Candice. And who are you?" Erik introduces himself. "Tell me, with your accent, you're not from around here? From Nevada or from California?" Erik always thought he didn't have such a strong accent, but that seems false.

"I'm from Germany, along with my friend back there," he says, waving to Frank, who is watching the action from his seat.

"That's interesting," Candice says. "I'm from Montana. I went to San Francisco because my sister lives there. We both went to Reno to see the gambler's town."

"So, are you playing? Is it worth it?"

"No, we kept our hands off the machines. Are you guys in on the gambling, then?"

"We considered it because we could invite everyone to a local round. But once you think about it, you conclude that you shouldn't play after all."

"You're at least as sensible as we are," Candice grins. "Now you're sitting in this tourist bar, just like us."

"Isn't everything in Reno touristy?" asks Erik. "Even the beer seems to have been brewed for tourists."

"I thought that was a specialty here."

Erik is struck by a flash of inspiration. Without thinking about it, he asks Candice, "What do you think? I'm going to the bar to get us some new drinks. What would you like? The same?" By his standards, he sets quite a pace with that.

"Yes, that's good. I'll have the same: Two mojitos, please. And then, why don't you both come to our place if you like?"

It's not that hard to spot Candice's sister. She looks just like her, except she seems a little younger. The two sit further back at a table with chairs. Erik fights his way over to Frank.

"My goodness, what are you doing? You go to the bar once, and already you're picking up the prettiest girls in the whole place," he says. "When you're not spilling beer on them."

"Oh, Frank, it gets even better. I'm about to get four mojitos, and then we'll sit with them."

A little later, when they are seated at Candice and her sister's table, they have a great conversation. At least Erik and Candice do - they seem to have a connection. One word gives the other, and they chat animatedly about their lives. Candice from the mountains of Montana, that sounds reasonably romantic to Erik.

"Oh no, it's not that romantic. I come from Kalispell, which is on the edge of the mountains. And I work in an industrial plant. But we have Flathead Lake, and it's gorgeous. It's a big, blue lake in the middle of the Rockies."

Erik tells Candice in short form that they come from Hamburg. Respect, he thinks; she's heard of his hometown and knows it's in northern Germany. Just not by the sea, like San Francisco. While the two are engrossed in their conversation, he looks at Frank. He, too, is having a brilliant discussion with Candice's sister. But that was just a sideways glance as he looked at Candice again, gazing into her pretty face with brown hair; she pointed her head briefly in their direction and nodded. She has grasped the situation.

"But where was I? I wanted to tell you about Hamburg on the Elbe," he says. Frank suddenly says, "Oh, you know what, I'll get us another round." So, there is something in the air, and Erik notices that Frank wants to continue their meeting. This is just fine with him, though, since he's engrossed in a veritable waterfall of a conversation.

When they say goodbye late at night, Erik knows much

about his new acquaintance. What impresses him most is that she is from Montana and a science fiction fan. How she can talk about her books of alien worlds is something he hasn't experienced before, at least not with a woman. "Oh yes, I'm glad you had a nice evening. I think Michelle is so nice, too, though. She's pretty hot," Frank says, not very ambiguously.

Plans to take the bus to Lake Tahoe had evaporated an hour earlier. Candice and her sister Michelle also want to go to the lake. They drove up from San Francisco in Michelle's car. Candice flew there from their little town in Montana, whose name he can't remember now. When he told her what the two of them were up to, there was no question in her mind that they were going - while Michelle gazed into the air. Erik likes the fun-loving woman from the little town. He thinks the name began with a "K" in Montana. Her eyes flash when she talks - about her little town, her family, her place, and the Rocky Mountains. And, of course, but that came after the third mojito, about her science fiction novels. He's not a fan of her favorite genre but has occasionally peeked into a science fiction novel. When he talks about the train trip, Candice listens spellbound. I wonder if she then thinks the same way, "My goodness, he's got a thing for train travel." But when she smiles, it looks sincere. This is how he imagines a "country girl" from Montana, even though she's not from the country but from a small town.

The four sneak up on Lake Tahoe from "behind." They make a big turn south in the car, across Carson City, then drive toward the lake from the east. If it were up to Erik, they would go directly from Reno to the lake and then along the shore. But Michelle thinks this route is faster. Yet the road by the lake is one of the most beautiful routes Erik can think of in the United

States: You can constantly look down on the blue-green waters - sometimes into sheltered bays, then again into longer stretches of shoreline where the wind churns the water into waves. Pine forests are everywhere, with pretty houses in between, ranging from simple "Holiday Cabins" to large estates. On the horizon behind the lake stretch the mountains with their green forests and gray peaks, the "Sierras", where the hikers are in summer and the skiers in winter.

Erik had been there once before, many years ago, during a family vacation. He had come from Los Angeles but by plane. Back then, they had gone to "Squaw Valley" to ski in a former venue of the Winter Olympics. The lake had taken a fancy to him, so there was no question: Frank, who would probably have preferred to drive straight through to the Pacific coast, had to be persuaded to make a stop-over if they were already going to get through here by train. As he thinks about it and laughs, the Amtrak counter clerk was right. His laughter does not escape Candice, sitting in the back seat beside him. "What are you laughing at?"

"I, uh, was just thinking about Lake Tahoe."

Frank intervenes with a grin; he can't help it. "This man here told me you must stop in Reno because they have the most beautiful girls you can meet. Now look at him." As if he can read minds, good Frank, Erik thinks. It's not him who blushes, by the way, but a red shadow flits across Candice's face.

"You know what? The counter lady at Amtrak confirmed it, too. There, you see what we got from Reno," Frank adds.

Michelle laughs behind the wheel. "My big sister, my clever big sister," she says.

Behind the pass, the big lake flashes in the mountains. "My goodness, it's huge. It's almost like Flathead Lake. Maybe even bigger?" says Candice. Erik didn't remember the body of water being that big. They're headed to Harrah's, again a giant casino.

South Lake Tahoe is a well-kept, almost "harmless" resort on the California side. There are restaurants and gorgeous houses between the main street and the lake shore. At the border to Nevada, the gambler's paradise begins: "Stateline" is the name of the continuation of the town in Nevada. Right here, the big casinos stand next to each other. The closer to the border, the bigger they look. Also, the vast building of "Harrah's", which they head for. In front of it, the four of them pass the cable car that leads to the "Heavenly Mountain Resort," where there is a lot of activity, even in summer. The parking lot is filled, and a tiny line has formed in front of the entrance to the cable car.

Directly at the "Stateline" there are beside the "Harrahs" the "Harveys", the "Hard Rock Café and Hotel", the "Ballys" and others. In the "Harrahs" they get rooms at a favorable rate again because it is a casino hotel. The receptionist gives them a small package: coupons for gambling parlors, buffet dinner, and tourist bus excursions. Of course, a brochure about the paddle-steamer trip on Lake Tahoe is not to be missed. Erik watches Candice cradle the boat brochure in her hands and leaf through it with interest. So this seems to be something for her.

On the one hand, a boat trip on the lake would appeal to him, but on the other hand, Erik thinks the journey on the paddle steamer is quite expensive at $99 per person. You fish off the gambling crowd from the California part of the shore behind the Nevada border. The lake is divided in two: The west belongs to California, and the east shore, somewhat shorter, has been assigned to Nevada. Behind the small casino town, by the way, not much follows. Abruptly, the town stops after a few hundred meters along the road. It is just a gambling annex for "South Lake Tahoe".

Why do they find themselves in a hotel that looks exactly like the one they stayed in last night in Reno, Erik wonders? Where they can hear the slot machines ringing in the lobby?

Where they once again have to consider whether they shouldn't risk a few dollars? He knows the answer: Exactly, because of the low prices and because he wanted to go to Lake Tahoe, just like the two new acquaintances.

Firstly, they move into their rooms. "This is perfect here again," Frank says. "If you keep chatting with Candice, I can turn on the giant TV here."

"Maybe you can talk Michelle into a movie night," Erik says.

"Who knows what kind of movie night this is going to be. Do they have spicier movies here?" Erik has to shake his head. Frank would actually do that: Inviting his new acquaintance to his room, where "spicy" movies would then be playing on the hotel TV, quite accidentally. That would certainly not be Erik's style.

Later, they meet Candice and Michelle for a walk along the water. They leave the casinos on the left and march down the road to the lake, where a small marina is on the shore. The weather is friendly; the sun shines from behind a few clouds. The marina is bustling, with small motorboats whizzing in and out on the lake. The group of four gets into a conversation with a man sitting relaxed at the stern of his motorboat. It's a nice boat, Erik thinks: about six meters long, with wood and an American flag on the stern. It makes an old-fashioned impression, like one of the well-known Riva boats from Italy. The man doesn't look particularly striking with his baseball cap, beard, T-shirt, and shorts. But the 50-ish man seems to know his way around. He asks where they live and what they've seen of South Lake Tahoe so far. Erik confesses that they have only just arrived.

It turns out that he owns shares in one of the casinos. "It's a profitable business," he explains, "and it doesn't eat up my time. We just invested wisely twenty years ago. There weren't that many casinos here then. But the business has become very big. We're in on it," he says candidly. He is hospitable and offers cans of "Bud" that he pulls out of his boat's cooler. "The ladies, too?" he asks. Michelle extends her hand and comments, "Cheers, Bottoms up!"

"Actually, I wanted to go out fishing today. But then it was too windy. So I stayed in the harbor, and now I've had a few too many beers," he says. "But it's more fun in a company, so I'm buying a few rounds." The four join him on board and settle in with the ice-cold drinks in the cockpit. Erik says he'd like to tell him something exciting about his industry. Still, he doesn't know much about casinos in Germany under state supervision, except that they had also visited some of them between Travemünde and Garmisch-Partenkirchen. But the boat owner says: "Sometimes I also like to gamble. But my investments with my wife are also an exciting game."

"Speaking so frankly," Frank says suddenly, "do the casinos have anything to do with the underworld?" Erik might not have asked that so openly, and Candice looks shocked. But he just smiles, "Not really here at Lake Tahoe, they're all legal companies. It can be different in Reno. It's different in Las Vegas. But the days when the mob ran the casinos are gone. These are big companies that are very hard-core. It's just a branch of the entertainment industry, like Disney, but for adults." Erik remembers reading once that the casino industry wanted to become more family-friendly in the 1990s, so it built many new attractions in Las Vegas. The trend declined in recent years that gaming was something for adults and that "Disneyization" didn't work. "True," the man notes, "except that it never caught up in northern Nevada. You guys have seen Reno: Does that look anything like Disney and family-friendly entertainment?" Not really, Erik agrees. Now Michelle is getting more curious: "Is there really nothing to the stories that the Mafia ran the casinos?"

"Well, there might be some truth in that," he says mysteriously. "When you say Lake Tahoe, you must mean the Calneva Resort. That was, or is, at the north end of the lake. Right on the California-Nevada border, like here on Stateline." He points his arm north.

"This has a long history that started back in 1926," says the host on the boat as he buys another round of Budweiser. An early real estate speculator on the lake, Robert P. Sherman, had the resort built as a hotel and casino. But the guest who would put the property on the celebrity map didn't arrive there until 1951: It was Frank Sinatra. His trip made headlines, however, because "Franky Boy" took a hefty dose of illicit pills here, which other guests tattled on to the sheriff. Nevertheless, he liked it so much at Lake Tahoe that he returned. He also performed there in a jam session with prominent band leader Harry James and singer Betty Grable. By 1960, it was clear to "Franky Boy": I'm buying this resort. He shared the property with Hank Sanicola and Paul "Skinny" D'Amato, and Dean Martin was among the other shareholders.

The only problem was that the chic resort, with its main house, pavilions, and lakeside swimming pool, also had a silent partner: none other than Sam Giancana from Chicago. The Italian-born "businessman" had become the Mafia's "Chicago Outfit" boss in 1955. No wonder, he had enough liquid assets to help Frank Sinatra buy the casino. However, the "mobster" is also said to have had connections with the CIA and, more seriously, with John F. Kennedy, whose presidential candidacy he is said to have supported. On the beach at Lake Tahoe, that was a long way off, and the new part-owners decided to open the casino year-round. Sinatra built the "Celebrity Room Theater" and installed a helipad on the roof. There are said to have been Prohibition-era smuggling tunnels under the property that were converted: Through these tunnels, carpeted, one could get from the chalets to the main building without being seen.

Allegedly, the Mafia used this possibility to stay undetected in the resort.

This, however, called the FBI to the scene, which put the hotel under constant surveillance. The federal police were concerned about Mafia involvement at the "Calneva" and a prostitution ring. Marylin Monroe spent the last weekend before her death at the resort in late July. She is said to have attempted suicide there, with pills, but still called the reception herself - and was saved, even if only for a few days.

The 1960s were characterized in the "Calneva" by extravagant parties with celebrities such as Judy Garland, Liza Minnelli, Shirley MacLaine, Sammy Davis Jr., Tony Curtis, and others. "Franky Boy" really lived it up: In significant mood swings, he received guests sometimes warmly and invitingly, sometimes insultingly and brusquely. Incidentally, his silent partner, Sam Giancana from Chicago, was banned from the casinos in the state of Nevada. Sinatra generously allowed him to stay at the Calneva Lodge.

After Giancana was publicly spotted on the premises, the Nevada Gaming Control Board canceled the license. That's when Frank Sinatra backed out: the constant bad press because of his casino and the suspicion of illegal activities got to him, and he gave up the resort. Sinatra tried to sell the property to the multimillionaire Howard Hughes or "Caesars Palace" from Las Vegas. Still, finally, it went back to the casino operator from Reno, who had already owned it once. The following decades were only a relic of the great times. Although the resort was expanded and rebuilt, changed from one real estate investor to the next, it was no longer a meeting place for celebrities at Lake Tahoe.

Mixed into the narrative is this unique blend of the casino world, the underworld, and the glamour of the big wide world that the place experienced through Frank Sinatra and Sam Giancana - which ultimately became its undoing. The boat owner tells it all in a relaxed manner, but in between, his eyes flash - as if the story didn't play out so far from him.

Suddenly, a man comes walking across the dock to the boat. It flashes through Erik's mind: it's the man who had been waiting for them at the Reno train station. It's absurd that he's wearing his sunglasses again now, Erik thinks. The man stands beside the boat and says, "Hey, boss, that's great. You've got our couriers from Denver on board."

"Oh, isn't that right? You are the two who brought me the package from my friend Paul? Thank you very much for that," says the boatman.

"What was in it?" asks Frank.

"Oh, a great old statue that Paul brought me back from a trip. I wanted to get it as soon as possible and not exactly entrust it to a courier service."

What did he say, Erik ponders? He was just a businessman, who had invested in casino holdings with his wife. He had kindly introduced himself as Bruce. But whether that's his real first name?

"Well, if you've helped me so well, you must be reliable characters," Bruce says. "Why don't you go play a game? What did you come to Lake Tahoe for?" Erik wants to object that they need to keep their money together. Still, unexpectedly, Michelle says, "Oh yeah, gambling, we could try that for a round. Couldn't hurt." Candice gives her sister a dirty look. "Well, you see," Bruce says, "the lady is right. She thinks you should test your luck sometime."

"I really like playing poker," Michelle adds. Candice shakes her head.

"What?" says Bruce. "So come on, you want to play and did me a huge favor. I'll give you the change you need. Then you can head off to the casinos." Erik doesn't like hearing that at all. But

Bruce continues: "Today is your lucky day. I'll give you $4,000 to gamble with. If you win, you can pay me back. And if not, we'll find a way." Erik thinks, "No one could be that unreasonable to accept this." But Michelle is thrilled. "It's a great deal, huh, Frank?"

Frank doesn't want to disappoint his new acquaintance; Erik senses that. He also has a weakness for playing the "man of the world." "We shouldn't miss out on that," says Erik's friend.

"What about you and your girlfriend?" says Bruce, addressing Erik.

"No, thank you, that's out of the question for us."

"Really? That's a one-time offer. Johnny, look what you've got," Bruce says, addressing the man in the sunglasses.

"Sure thing, boss. Here, look, I brought some chips." He pulls a plastic bag of colorful chips out of his lapel straight from one of the casinos in Stateline. "Well, that's swell. You can get right to it," Bruce says. Erik has noticed that his tone has changed. He sounds different now, kind of cocky. Michelle's eyes widen. "Frank, we have to do this."

"Sure, now we want to get a feel for "Lady Luck"," says Frank, who also puts on a somewhat cocky voice as Erik notices. Within seconds, the mood on board seems to have turned around. It's as if a gold rush has broken out. Bruce takes the plastic bag from the man in the sunglasses and thrusts it into Frank's hand. "These are from the Stateline Casino, which is a neat place. It's fancy, and it's always busy. You can really go for it now. Oh, you know what? Just say you're from Bruce's when you get to the bar. Or Johnny, why don't you go down there with them? You'll get a lot of free drinks." Bruce's wink is so wry and seems so fake that it turns Erik's stomach. But Michelle and Frank can't be stopped. "Come on, let's do it," Michelle says.

The four get up and step off the boat onto land. Candice

shakes her head. "Erik, you can't do that," she hisses. "It's not a good idea," he says. "No, it can't. I'll tell you why in a minute."

"Have a good time at the casino," Bruce says as he begins to gather things on board. "And if you two change your minds, just ask Johnny if he has anything for you, too."

"Yes, uh, thank you," Erik stutters. Then, they go ashore over the jetty.

On the shore, Candice holds Erik while "Johnny" walks with Michelle and Frank toward the glowing casinos. It almost seems like he's leading them there, it flashes through Erik's mind. "See you around, Erik," Frank calls out, waving to the two before they walk away quickly.

"Erik, you can't," Candice says as they stand on the shore.

"No, that's crap. You're right." He tells Candice how they brought the package from Denver to Reno and got $500. And how excited Frank was about the operation.

"The critical thing is that Michelle has a gambling problem. You saw the way her eyes lit up, right? She was all over it when that boat owner offered them the money."

"Yeah, I noticed that. What do you mean she has a gambling problem?"

"A few years ago, she lost quite a bit of money at a casino in Las Vegas. She had gone there with friends I didn't know. Then, finally, our father had to bail her out because she had gambled away so much that I couldn't come up with it. He was so pissed, and now if something happens again ..." Erik recounts Frank's gambling adventures in Germany, but they had gone well so far. "I should have guessed he'd grab it right away."

"Erik, we need to find these two as soon as possible and stop them. It's not normal for someone to slip them money."

"Yes, we'll do that right now. What was it called again? Stateline Casino? Let's go there!"

Candice and Erik go to Stateline and start roaming the

casino. But they have no luck in the gambling facility: neither in the vast rooms with the slot machines nor in the rooms where poker is played, where there is blackjack, or where the roulette tables are, can Candice discover her sister and Erik, his friend. Erik thinks it all looks chic and glamorous: The casino areas are in light, heavy wood, and the seats and benches are upholstered in soft red leather.

But the glamorous atmosphere doesn't quite come through. Instead, the two have the feeling of being inside a gambling machine. The guests are predominantly older, wealthy-looking, perhaps a little better off than in Reno. They obviously like moving from the buffet to gambling and the bar in just a few steps.

"They're not here, anyway," Erik notes when they return to the casino lobby. "So let's go to the next one," Candice says. Diagonally across the street, they go to the "Hard Rock Café and Hotel," where the theme of rock music runs through the hall, the bars, and the casino areas.

"This is the former Sahara Tahoe," Candice knows. Sahara, Erik had heard that before. Now it comes back to him: "I have an album, Isaac Hayes live at the Sahara Tahoe".

"That's where music history was made," Candice says. "Especially because Elvis Presley performed there regularly in the early seventies. They had built a big theater attached to their casino and brought the stars there."

"Why can't they just go see an Elvis impersonator instead of going to play?" notes Erik. But here, too, they are unsuccessful: there is no sign of Michelle and Frank. The tour continues to "Harveys" and "Ballys," the other large casino hotels which radiate more solidity, similar to "Harrahs". Dark colors are the order of the day in the interior areas, walls with clinker made of natural stone, with splashes of orange in between - from the interior decoration, it's all top-of-the-line.

As Candice and Erik settle down at the bar in their hotel, they are on the verge of giving up. It must have been hours they've now spent wandering the gambling establishments. "I'm on the verge of going to the sheriff," Candice says.

"But that could lead to questions like, what did we do with the package?"

"What was in there? What do you think?"

"So definitely not a statue from a trip. I'm afraid it must have been something to do with drugs. They gave us far too much money to bring a suitcase to Reno. I think we took quite a risk there."

Erik and Candice have been talking at the bar for half an hour, and it must be close to midnight when Erik's phone rings. "That's Frank's number," he realizes and picks up.

"Erik, I'm glad I got a hold of you. The whole thing went a little wrong."

"Frank, where are you? We're worried about you."

"We are in the Stateline Casino in a back room. Can you come here? The money is gone, and I'm supposed to pay!"

Erik tells him they're about to leave. Candice shakes her head. "That's the way it had to go. It took them one night to come through with the money? And we've been looking for them all this time to no avail?"

"The whole thing must have taken place in a back room. It must have been set up, so we wouldn't find them."

When Erik and Candice arrive at the Stateline, Frank is standing at the casino's reception desk with a red head. The place is still bustling, with many guests coming and going, but Erik immediately spotted his friend in the crowd. "Where's my sister?" Candice yells at him.

"She's still in the back room. Erik, we need to find the money."

"What actually happened to you guys?"

"This Johnny maneuvered us into the casino with the chips and then asked us into the back room. There was supposedly a "poker party" with exclusive guests. We were still happy that we could join in. The drinks were free."

"That worked out great for you," Candice notes with biting irony.

"Yes, we did; we played really well the first few rounds. We were winning pretty good. Then we should have stopped."

"Let me guess: My sister was unstoppable."

"Yes, that's right. We kept playing, and then we lost it all. All four thousand dollars, Erik. It's all gone. And then this Johnny guy came and said we'd better stop now and pay up."

"I have to hand it to him: At least he made you stop. You could still have gotten into trouble," says Erik.

"In the red?" notes Candice, "You guys are totally in the red. The $4,000 was just borrowed. You've gone so far into the red. Who was actually gambling? Was it my sister? No, then you would have gone broke much faster."

"Yes, it's true, it was me. That's why we have to get the dough somehow now, Erik. But from where? I'd have to put it all on the credit card."

"I want to see my sister," Candice says.

"Can't," Frank answers. "She's sitting in the room behind the door in front of the grinning Johnny." Erik looks again and sees the guy from the pier and the train station in Reno on the other side of the lobby, nodding at him with a grin.

"Let's think about that for a minute," he says to Frank. The three of them walk outside the casino, and Erik lights a cigarette, something he rarely does. Although, he could have smoked right there in the casino lobby - you can still do that in the state of Nevada. But they wanted to get a cool head. Erik blows the smoke into the air. Frank's hands shake with tension. And Candice looks reasonably desperate.

"So, pay attention," Erik says. "It's one o'clock here now. In Germany, it's ten o'clock in the morning. I'm going to call Peter now. You don't want to drag your parents or siblings into this, are you, Frank?" He shakes his head. Peter is a friend of theirs, a lawyer, and Erik is sure he can help them out.

The situation is surreal, Erik thinks. He stands in front of the glittering entrance to the large Stateline casino, where women in evening dresses and men in cowboy hats disappear. He holds the phone to his ear and explains the situation to their friend Peter in Hamburg. To do this, he is already smoking the next cigarette in the night air. Then he hangs up.

"Peter thinks we'd better pay. He believes the whole thing is a signal to us - that's why they're holding your sister. And, of course, we've fallen for a nasty loading. Peter thinks we'll be lucky if the package doesn't come out. So it's better not to go to the police. Especially since they really didn't force us to play."

"And where are we going to get the money now?"

"There's a store back in Lake Tahoe that's open all night. And it has a counter for a wire service, Western Union. Peter can send us the money there, and we can pick it up immediately in cash. But Frank, one thing is clear: he's lending you the money. You'll have to pay him back, too."

"Yes, of course. The main thing is that we can pay here first."

"Well, let's go then."

The Seven-Eleven store is a fifteen-minute walk away. They cross the state line and re-enter California. Candice whispers as a patrol car drives by, "I'd like to pull that one over now."

"I think so. But what are we supposed to say? That Frank and your sister can't pay their gambling debts?"

When Erik presents his ID at the store counter, stating the money's country of origin and the amount of 4000 dollars, the cashier releases the transfer. Between hot dogs, machines stirring a red sugar drink, and a plethora of candy, Erik picks up the money at the counter. Peter must have been really fast, he thinks. Frank is still standing behind, a little confused. "Here, I'll give you the money now, and then we'll go back, and you pay."

Back in Nevada, in the casino lobby, Frank gives the grinning Johnny the 4000 dollars; after that, he wordlessly opens the door. Behind it, Michelle sits alone at the table where the poker game had been going on hours earlier. In front of her is a battery of empty glasses, which had obviously been served to her to shorten the wait. Candice rushes in and hugs her sister. Frank looks apologetic at Erik. "I messed up. I'll stand for it. Now let's get out of here." They leave the grinning Johnny again and leave the "Stateline" to get to their hotel. Frank and Erik sit at the bar while Candice and Michelle go to their room.

"Okay, Frank, you couldn't have guessed how much Candice Sister likes to gamble. But you shouldn't have taken that $4,000. Thank God that somehow turned out okay."

"Yeah, we got ripped off pretty good. I would have liked to have done something with Michelle tonight other than bail her out of a back room."

"You really only think about the one thing," Erik says, shaking his head. "I really wouldn't have thought of that now."

"It's over now, after all."

"I could use a change of pace right now, after last night's experience," Erik says in the morning. They've slept late, and the sun is already high above Lake Tahoe, which they can see out the side window of their hotel room. "Now I'd like to experience the real 'Wild West' for once. With cowboys, western towns, and, of course, railroads. We can go to 'Virginia City' after all."

"What, that's really supposed to exist? I thought the town only existed in 'Bonanza'."

"The NBC TV series is set here at Lake Tahoe. Think about the opening credits: There was a burning map with Virginia City drawn on it."

"Then the card went up in flames, and Lorne Greene introduced himself as Ben Cartwright and his sons."

"The whole thing is right around the corner here. The Ponderosa Ranch and Virginia City."

"Forget it," Frank says, turning over in his bed. "No such trips with me today. I'm going to lie here and mourn my $4,000."

"That's not going to make it any better. You should distract yourself a little."

"No, I'm staying here. Why don't you ask Candice to come with you? And feel free to tell Michelle I'll knock on her door later if I've forgotten all about it."

Erik leaves the room. The situation is precisely the same with Candice next door: Michelle is in bed and won't leave it. "She's having a real hangover from last night," Candice says. "And won't budge today. But I'd love an outing as a distraction." Michelle hands her the car keys, and Erik and Candice head for breakfast. Afterward, they drive off. Later, Candice confides in him that her sister spent half the night "crying" to her. "I have sympathy for her, but also only limited. It's not the first time she's lost at gambling. At some point, I've had enough, too. That's why I'm glad to be out with you now and to gain some distance."

They come to Carson City. With a population of just under 60,000, it's a small state capital. But it's a pleasant city, Erik finds: The administrative buildings are low, have a lot of greenery, and there are tiny houses in between. They drive outside the town to the stop of the "Virginia & Truckee Railroad," the museum railroad dedicated club members have built true to the original.

They park in front of the station building, and a passenger train is ready to run with three cars and a puffing steam locomotive. The line ran directly to Carson City and even as far as Reno. The first section was built in 1869 to haul ore, lumber, and supplies for the Comstock Lode silver mines. But when things went downhill in the 1940s, closure followed, Erik reads in his brochure. Much of the track was torn up and sold, along with locomotives and cars.

"My, but you read the brochure carefully," Candice interrupts him. "Yes, it says all that. Exciting, isn't it?"

"Well, not uninteresting. Would you find it interesting if I told you as much about the science fiction book from the Alpha Prime series that I'm reading?" What should he answer, he wonders. "But of course, I can't wait," he says with a grin.

"But how did it become a museum railroad now?" asks Candice. It was thanks to an enthusiast named Robert C. Gray, who had ridden on one of the last trains and dreamed of reviving it, which he eventually did with the help of other enthusiasts. Meanwhile, the company has at least five steam locomotives in its inventory. Standing by today is number 18, a Baldwin 2-8-2 of the "McCloud River Railroad" built in October 1914. It is to pull the three open cars of the train. The railroad also has six diesel locomotives in its inventory.

"Would you like me to tell you about the Alpha Centauri-class star cruisers sometime?" teases Candice. "I think I'd get at least as much detail together."

"Oh no, let's get in and enjoy the ride. Because you can't do that with your star cruisers."

"Excuse me? Your old locomotives are supposed to be more interesting than star cruisers?"

"Yes, because they can pull three-car passenger trains over an old railroad."

"The star cruisers can carry a thousand people through space."

"But space is cold and dark, and here the sun shines."

"We could head for a planet where the sun is shining."

History is one thing; the present is another, Erik thinks. It makes him happy to hear the deep puffing of the steam engine as it begins to pull the wagons. It displaces the unpleasant experiences of the previous night. Candice probably feels the same way. A primal force emanates from the locomotive, saying, "Pulling three little cars up a mountain in Nevada - I can do that just as well today as I could 100 years ago." It takes an hour and a half to drive through this "Western landscape," where the railroad winds its way along the mountains in gently sweeping curves. "You guys are lucky," says the museum conductor on the train. "Last weekend, we couldn't run the Baldwin. So we had to take the diesel locomotive as a substitute." Erik would have been okay with that, but part of the attraction, of course, is the snorting of the steam steed at the head of the train. Not only is the ride an experience, he thinks, but it's not expensive at all. A paddle steamer ride on Lake Tahoe would have cost twice as much.

"So look, we're being frugal with our vacation experiences," Candice notes. "When we're not entering a casino where we're playing hardball."

"Yes, actually, we should be thrifty. But you see how Frank has kept it with the thriftiness."

Erik notes that the ride's destination, Virginia City, is exciting. It is a "semi-ghost town" that has been given a new lease of life with the help of tourism. The town took off in 1859 when the first significant silver deposits in the US were discovered here. By the mid-1870s, 25,000 people lived here. From 1862 to 1864, the writer Samuel Clemens, who first used his new pseudonym "Mark Twain," also worked there.

But then, the "output" of the silver mines began to decline, and the people moved away bit by bit. Now, just 787 inhabitants are living in Virginia City. The main source of income is now tourism. Many of the residents own businesses. As the four stroll down Main Street, they pass antique stores, saloons, and other stores. The "National Historic Landmark District" has an air of lost glory. Many facades are crumbling, paint peeling on the walls. The result is a charming mix of renovated tourist establishments with a fair amount of ghost town, attracting more than two million visitors annually.

Erik and Candice are standing on the street. They lean against the wooden sidewalk railing in front of the houses. "Is this the Wild West you were looking for?" asks Candice.

"But yeah. It's great. Does it look like that in Montana?"

"Well, not quite. My hometown is a modern town, compared to this museum. We don't have wooden houses with antiques and wooden sidewalks in front of them."

Candice tells Erik about Kalispell, Montana. "My dad has a building supply store just on the edge of downtown. He's really into the store, which is doing reasonably well. His favorite thing to sell is snowplows."

"Snowplows?"

"Yes, snow plows. He has a whole department for that. 'Built to put Mother Nature in her place,' he has written on a sign above it."

"He wants to put Mother Nature in her place? That only happens in Montana," says Erik.

"There's something else behind it. If you like, Mother Nature didn't mean well with him. The fact that he's so infatuated with the store is also because my mother died a long time ago."

"That's sad."

"She died when I was ten years old. It took us a long time to get over it, my sister and me. Our father threw himself into his business. His sister took care of us, coming to the house every day. She did the housework, helped us with our schoolwork, and cooked dinner. My sister and I were very close, though. We took care of each other. At least as long as we could. Today, I can't really understand what's going on with her sometimes. Like when there's a gambling episode in her life. At the same time, she and I were two to 'steal horses' back then."

"Did you guys do anything like that?"

"No, we didn't steal horses. But we sometimes secretly drove around in our father's car while he was in his store. No one noticed, or so we thought. We didn't drive far, just out of town and back in again. He had noticed, though. But it was his sister who finally confronted us. We got a hell of a thunderstorm."

Candice looks down the street as if she's looking into the past. And she grins at the thought of the forbidden car rides with her sister Michelle. Then she turns back to Erik. "So how did you grow up?"

"Me?" Erik falters. "I have experienced similar things to you." He hesitates. Then he looks at Candice.

"I grew up with my aunt and uncle. Because my parents and brother died, too."

"Erik, this is terrible."

"Well, I haven't experienced anything different from you. It's just that everyone was gone from me, from one day to the next."

Erik does not find it easy to talk about this. He also can't "switch gears" as quickly as Candice can. He has the impression that she is better at talking about her past.

"I was even a little smaller than you." He looks into Candice's brown eyes. "I was only six years old, and somehow I didn't really notice." They had been on their way to the ocean, his mother, father, and brother three years older. Erik had stayed with his uncle and aunt. Then, on a country road in Schleswig-

Holstein, in Dithmarschen, there was a collision, Erik reports. Allegedly, they were all killed instantly - the car had swerved out of a curve and into oncoming traffic, where it collided with a truck.

"At first, my aunt told me they would not return. But then my uncle explained me the whole story. Do that to a six-year-old. I'm told I didn't speak for days."

Candice looks at him sympathetically. "At least I was lucky that they were both very understanding people. They tried to give me a home. I didn't thank them much," Erik says, his face contorting.

Then he tells Candice how he rebelled, even as an eight-year-old. In school, he dragged his feet. "I knew I could do better, but didn't want to. After all, they made sure I went to high school. But even there, I only did the least to slip through." Things only became really critical when 17-year-old Erik met the wrong friends. "I had never really made friends at school. But then I got into this group. They met in a pub in Altona, in a somewhat rundown neighborhood. They drank beer."

"At seventeen?"

"In Germany, you can do that from 16," Erik laughs. "We screwed on mopeds and later on motorcycles. We roared through Altona and St. Pauli all the time. And we also got a little off the rails."

"What, you've become criminals? I can't imagine that with you at all," Candice says. "Last night, you were such a paragon of sanity. I loved how you set things up with your lawyer friend."

"You think so? I don't think I really wanted to be a criminal, either. But I got carried away. We didn't think it was big stuff, even if it got us off the rails. We broke into kiosks and stole the merchandise. Once, our leader even robbed a store. That scared the hell out of me. Although the group suddenly had real money, I was afraid that we had gone too far. I got out."

"How did you manage that?"

"My uncle knew about it. Or he suspected it. In any case, we had a long talk one night, just between men."

Candice grins slightly.

"He did that well without any reproaches. He told me that as a youth, he also belonged to a gang that made the streets in the north of Hamburg unsafe. And that they had been "caught" one day. His parents gave him hell. But it was my aunt who had put him on the right track because she had fallen in love with him, and she counted for more than all the fuss with his gang. Then he asked me, "How do you want to go on?""

"He sort of gave you a choice?"

"Yes, exactly. He left it up to me. He would stay out of it, he told me. When I realized I had a choice, I thought about it for days. And then I just started studying and always went to school on time. I didn't see my friends from the gang anymore. And because I had no other friends, I had a lot of time to catch up properly at school. I graduated from high school and studied, all with good grades. And then I became a journalist."

"That must have been it: Erik's miraculous transformation to goodness," Candice grins. "And here he is in front of me, shown again how to solve problems, even if it's in the casino."

Candice becomes thoughtful for a moment. "I missed my mother despite everything. You probably felt the same way about your parents?"

"Yes, that always hovered over me like a shadow."

Erik had become a somewhat cautious person, especially in relationships. He was always on guard against loss. He thinks that Candice seemed to have recognized that from how she looked at him. At the same time, he admires her easy-going and robust nature. After all, she has suffered a similar loss, yet she seems better able to cope.

The hours pass in Virginia City as they stroll through the

streets. Then, the steam train takes them back to Carson City. Later, they stop in the small capital. They visit a steakhouse in one of the casinos. "I'm sure they have cheap food there," Erik says. "Cheap should already be with you from now on," Candice says. "But now you can take an American girl, out for a good time." They have steaks served with vegetables. The restaurant revels in seventies charm, Erik thinks. The casino is all retro. No, it's even the original decor. There's a lot of brown and a wildly patterned carpet. But the food is excellent, and they are invigorated for the drive back to Lake Tahoe.

Later, when they get to the bar at Harrah's, they meet Michelle and Frank there. "Hello, you two," Frank says by way of greeting. "We spent the afternoon at the pool."

"So, was that it?" says Candice to her sister.

"Well, and we messed around a little, well, a little," she giggles.

"Michelle, what do you call that?" says Candice in a reproachful voice, but one that seems a bit played, Erik thinks anyway.

"Oh, nothing; I just showed Michelle the TV program once." Erik knows precisely what program his friend showed Michelle, and she bursts out laughing. The two seem to have had a few drinks already.

"Well, at least you can still laugh after what happened," Candice says.

Michelle replies, "Sis, it doesn't help. What happened is what happened."

"The main thing is that you two have learned your lesson from this."

Frank talks about travel plans and says they have tickets on the next Amtrak train from Reno to San Francisco. "We had to stop here on the way there because the train was full. But now we could keep going."

"Now you're stuck with the schedule," Erik says. "I might as well stay here for a few more days."

Erik looks over at Candice, and she takes the initiative. She convinces her sister to drive them to the train station tomorrow morning. "Thank God," Erik thinks. A glance at the bus schedule showed him that it would have been almost impossible to get there by bus before the train's departure.

THROUGH THE SIERRA NEVADA

On time, Erik and Frank stand at the platform in downtown Reno. "I can't wait to get out of here," Frank says.

"Why is that? You had fun at Lake Tahoe, you and Michelle," Erik notes wryly.

"Yes, but I think every moment, this guy with the sunglasses comes around the corner again. He's really cost me a lot of money now."

"That's right, Frank. But what are you going to do? Get the FBI involved? I'm afraid you don't have enough on that."

"Maybe Peter in Hamburg still has an idea," says Frank, looking at the lawyer, who sometimes presents astonishingly creative solutions.

The following "California Zephyr" arrives, and again, a coach attendant greets them at the entrance in the lower deck of the "Superliner". They both "trudge" up the small staircase to the second floor and push their way through the row with their luggage until they find the two seats. The fellow passengers look tired, huddled under blankets in their reclined seats. After all, they've just had the night out of Salt Lake City. Erik and Frank flip a coin to decide who sits by the window, because the view through the Sierra Nevada promises to be eventful once again.

He has Candice's phone number on a piece of paper. He has a chance to see her again once they get to San Francisco. Because

Michelle and Candice want to stay at Lake Tahoe for two more days. Erik is excited. He enjoys being on the road with Candice. As the train rolls through the suburbs of Reno, Erik reflects that he finds her very interesting. He doesn't know the answer yet whether he finds her more than nice. Frank, on the other hand, is now silently looking out the train window. He must have been affected by the experience; even Michelle couldn't change that. The two of them got into something, and Erik is glad not to be in the shoes of his friend, who has obviously had contact with the American Mafia. Frank shouldn't be going into a casino so soon, he thinks.

They are again traveling along the route of the first transcontinental railroad through the USA. The railroad had already reached Reno in 1868. Erik is not sitting at the window but at the aisle. At first, he thought, "too bad," but then he got to know his seatmate Kennard, who is leaning back in his "coach" chair on the other side of the aisle. Kennard is from Sacramento and seems to know his way around railroads. "Once a year, I drive this route all the way to Salt Lake City, visiting relatives," Kennard snaps him out of his thoughts. "I usually do it in the summer, but sometimes in the winter. Because especially when it snows, the drive through the Sierra Nevada is quite wonderful." Then he points his arm outside, "Look, there's the second track, right by the Truckee River. This is where the trains can get out of the way." Squeezing through the valley are the freeway, the highway, the river, and the two rail lines. "Our track still comes from the first railroad to run across America," Kennard says, and you sense a bit of pride resonating.

The Central Pacific Railroad Company of California built 680 miles east from Sacramento to Promontory Summit in Utah. The Union Pacific Railroad built 1080 miles from the eastern starting point at Council Bluffs west to Promontory Summit. Kennard had been there before - but not by rail. That's because the line has long since taken a shortcut across the Great Salt Lake. The point where the two railroads were connected is now isolated to the north. At least the "Golden Spike National Historic Park" is there, including a small museum railroad line. The line runs a few miles in one direction and a few in the other before its track gets lost in the desert. On it run replicas of the historic locomotives that were there when the last golden nail was hammered in. "It's worth it, just for the little museum. But it's an hour and a half drive from Salt Lake City, and you can only get there by car," he says.

But now, the train is approaching the small town of Truckee. The landscape looks as one imagines it in the Wild West - or more precisely in the image conveyed by Westerns and series such as "Bonanza": Rolling hills and steeper mountains, thickly overgrown with green pines, with large and small wooden houses in between - that's the Sierra Nevada. The most common tree you see here is the "white-stemmed pine," Erik thinks it gives the mountain region its distinctive character: trees as far as the eye can see stretch up the gently rolling hills.

The little town of Truckee is the tourist spot of the area, and that's not just because of the railroad but also because of its location on the Interstate, which makes it quickly accessible. Truckee is the gateway to the eastern shore of Lake Tahoe. There's a respectable little downtown on Donner Pass Road at the station: behind the flat station building is a row of multi-story brick buildings with saloons, cafes, a hotel, and many small stores. "Looks like a picture book here," Erik tells Kennard. "Oh yes, Truckee is a beautiful place. Every time I think I'll get off here once - and I haven't for twenty years," he replies with a laugh.

One attraction is the "Northstar" ski area, one of the big ones around here, and it's supposed to be only about ten minutes from the station. But unfortunately, the stop doesn't last five minutes. Already, the "Zephyr" jerks up again. Further up, another ski area is at "Donner Summit" at "Boreal Mountain". But they won't see it because the railroad passes under the summit in a tunnel.

"Do you know the story of the Donner Party?" asks Kennard. Yes, Erik had heard of it before - but that doesn't stop Kennard from giving the gruesome story in great detail. "Once upon a time in 1846, the railroad didn't exist yet, a group of settlers headed west," Kennard continues. The brave families followed the "Oregon Trail" with their covered wagons, and they started in Springfield, Illinois, between Chicago and St. Louis. At that time, such an expedition took between four and six months. But the Donner Party was delayed after deciding on a new route called the "Hastings Cutoff," which bypassed the familiar trails and traversed the "Wasatch Range" of the Rocky Mountains. The desolate and rugged landscape and the difficulties they later encountered traveling along the Humboldt River in what is now Nevada resulted in the loss of many cattle and wagons, so quarrels arose within the group.

At the beginning of November, they had reached the Sierra Nevada and thus the last 100 miles of their route. But this is also the most challenging section, and the settlers were too late. They were trapped in the middle of the mountains by an early, heavy snowfall near Truckee Lake, now called Donner Lake. The group had broken up into several sub-groups, each consisting of their own families. However, they found shelter in three cabins that had been built there by hunters a few years earlier.

But too quickly, they ran out of food. A man named Eddy managed to kill a bear, but his hunting luck ran out. They were also unable to fish in the frozen lake. A few brave people set out on foot in mid-December to get help. It was on this trail where shocking incidents of cannibalism are said to have occurred - Kennard knows the gruesome details. Still, Erik deliberately tries to push them out of his mind. After all, some rescue parties made it to an Indian settlement after hardship-filled marches, during which some died. There, they were taken in and cared for. But that winter, there wasn't much help that could be sent into the mountains to track down the remaining "Donner Party": the US was at war with Mexico, and most of the soldiers from the nearest fort had been withdrawn for the fight for Santa Barbara. Just three men set out on the rescue expedition. It was not until mid-February 1847 that help arrived at Donner Lake, nearly four months after the wagon train had become stuck. Of the 87 members of the party, only 48 survived the ordeal. They were then brought to California in three rescue efforts.

The fate of the Donner Party became known throughout the US at that time, and the newspapers reported in great detail the gruesome incidents in the Sierra Nevada mountains. This and the war with Mexico caused the flow of settlers who dared to cross the mountains to California to diminish tremendously. For historians, the tragedy of the "Donner Party" is one of the most fascinating episodes in the settlement of the American West. The story's appeal, says historian Kristin Johnson, is simply that the events focused on families and ordinary people rather than individuals. The events are "a terrible irony that hopes for prosperity, health, and a new life in the fertile valleys of California led many only to misery, starvation, and death on the rocky threshold there." Kennard is also fascinated by the story. Erik thinks, "This is really creepy, as we hear it from him on the train.

By the way, it could get quite uncomfortable here in winter, even in the recent past. On January 13, 1952, a train carrying 222 passengers and crew got stuck on the track 17 miles west of

Donner Pass. The "City of San Francisco" train was heading west when a snowstorm hit, preventing the locomotives from moving forward or backward. The passengers and crew were stranded for three days until the nearby highway was cleared enough to transport them to the nearest lodge.

The railroad ran over Donner Pass since 1864 in a series of small tunnels and galleries that kept the snow out in some places. The Sierra Nevada has a unique geography: to the west, it rises steeply; to the east, it falls flat. Erik and Frank have virtually taken the flat "ramp" with their train, now crossing under the pass and looking forward to the part where the track winds rapidly downward.

The mountains here have names like "Rattlesnake Mountain". It goes through the "Emigrant Gap" valley, the gap in the hills through which the emigrants moved. To the left and right of the train, pine trees continue to stand close to the slopes, and between them, the view falls on the Interstate and the vast land behind the Sierra Nevada. Then the valley opens, and they roll past a small, blue lake. "We're finally home," Kennard says. "It's all flat from here on out, and the landscape is without obstacles." The train seemingly confirms this by picking up speed. With those mountains gone, the last hurdle is cleared; they're rolling toward the flat part of central California.

In the pretty town of Colfax, the "Zephyr" stops again a good two hours after it left Reno. Only a little is happening on the small platform, so the journey continues quickly. The hills have become even flatter; they have almost reached the plains. And then the greater Sacramento area begins, where the suburbs stretch out far. At a quarter past two, they pull into Sacramento, the capital of California. The train took a good six hours to get here from Reno. It was entertaining, which was due to the exciting landscape but also to Kennard's stories. He gets off, and they continue the journey without a well-informed companion.

The first transcontinental railroad initially ended in the city because one had to continue by paddle steamer from Sacramento. The capital is still connected to San Francisco Bay today via the "Sacramento Deep Water Ship Channel." That sounds interesting, Erik said. But Kennard had made the trip once before, on an excursion steamer now moored downtown. "It wasn't quite as exciting as I thought it would be. The canal runs straight, and you can't see much on the bank," he had reported. The railroad didn't reach Oakland until 1869, another year later. The train ride is now dead straight. For the next two hours, the "Zephyr" travels much faster. The two "passengers" pass the time with sandwiches in the observation car.

The end of the line offers two stations: In Oakland, the "Zephyr" stops at Jack London Square, the modern station of the city. Trains have never continued directly from here, as the bridge over the Bay was built for automobile traffic. To get there, the "Zephyr" takes fifteen minutes to the Emeryville station. In the past, some ferries took travelers directly to San Francisco from a long pier where the cars stopped. Today, people transfer to a bus in Emeryville.

"I'm so glad we made it west. The trip has had its pitfalls, but the ride has been comfortable," Erik tells Frank. So they say goodbye to their service attendant again. The station is modern. Apartment buildings have been built close to it. They are still on the bus for a good half hour, crossing the "Bay Bridge" with its spectacular view: In front of them, the big city, on the right, the wide Bay, and also on the left, the water. Erik finds it especially nice to go from the first bridge into a tunnel on the rock of Yerba Buena Island and then on the second bridge into the city. Erik and Frank reach the "City by the Bay" almost on time at 5:30.

❄

The two stay in San Francisco for a week and browse the city from its northern end, Fishermans Wharf and the Embarcadero, to the hip Mission District with its bars and clubs in the south. Frank and Erik occupied a small hotel close to the Pacific Ocean in the "Outer Sunset" neighborhood. The giant ocean is clearly noticeable there, and the fog moves coldly up from the beach into the city in the morning. Every day, they take the streetcar from there to the center. Then, they do the whole program that travel guides virtually impose on tourists. Erik already suspects that he wants to take the next trip to the United States without a guidebook; the "sightseeing" with its eternal checking off of "top sights" is not at all his cup of tea.

So it's all the nicer when, after three days, he picks up his smartphone and dials Candice's number.

"What's new with you?"

"We made it back to San Francisco from Lake Tahoe. You guys, too?"

"Well, sure. We're in a little hotel near Golden Gate Park. You know how economically we Europeans can organize our travels."

"Frugal above all, huh? Just don't let a ticket expire."

Erik grins over at Frank. Now he takes heart: "What would be nice now is spending some time with you."

"I feel the same way. Michelle is already back at work, and I'm alone in her apartment."

"Well, I'll be glad to distract you a bit."

"Oh, come on, don't sell yourself short. You're more than an escape. You're a mildly entertaining distraction."

"Thank you. I'll take that as a compliment."

"You should. It's the best I can do without admitting I like you."

"Ah, you like me. That's good to know."

"I never said that. I just said you were a little entertaining."

"Right, right! And what's the next level after mildly entertaining? Moderately amusing?"

"I don't know; maybe we should consult the dictionary of
dating terms."

She said, "Dating terms," he thinks with a grin. "Oh, that
sounds like a dangerous book."

"Why? Are you afraid to discover that you're only slightly
more entertaining than watching paint dry?"

"I thought it would be at least as entertaining as watching
me wrench on a moped."

"Oho, your gang past comes through. You should put that
on your resume."

"Ha, maybe I'll do that. Skilled in the art of moped
wrenching."

"I'm confident this will impress all employers."

"Hey, you never know. I might get a job as a mechanic in
Kalispell."

"That's precisely the right cue, isn't it?"

"You guys live near Golden Gate Park. I wanted to see that."

"Well then, let's go see the Park. Maybe as early as this
afternoon?"

"There's nothing to keep me in this apartment."

"So it's a deal!"

Frank can take care of himself, Erik thinks, because he may want
to stop by Michelle's apartment later. Until then, his friend wants to
settle in the hotel garden, equipped with a few beers and his music
player. Erik makes his way to Golden Gate Park, where he wants to
meet Candice at the portal. He recognizes her from across the street:
Long brown hair blowing in the wind. She sees him, too, and smiles.

"Where we meet again like this?" says Candice in greeting.
"How lucky for me to have you as a distraction." The park is a
natural attraction. What's more, it's enormous: over three miles

long is the green space is in the middle of San Francisco. So you should be careful where you go in, Erik thinks, and consider what you want to see beforehand. With Candice, he walks toward the "Murphy Windmill," located near the beach.

"I haven't seen a windmill like that yet. Is this what windmills look like in Germany, with you in Hamburg?"

"Yes, a little. It's a little slimmer than a German windmill. They have a rather thick tower. By the way, Holland is the land of windmills. But that's not so far away from Hamburg."

"So not only do you know about railroads, you know about windmills."

"Well, but not so good with spaceships and stars."

They continue walking through the park. "There are plenty of lovers around here, though," Candice notes. "Yeah, and look: we're in San Francisco." They pass a mismatched couple: one wearing a business suit, and the other authentic '80s shorts and a mesh shirt.

Candice grins. "Do you like me too?"

"Yes, you know that. You're a big distraction to me, even if I'm only a little one to you."

"That's not true at all. Here and now, you are an excellent distraction."

"But that's really a compliment. From moderately interesting to outstanding."

She laughs, and they walk enthusiastically to the second "Windmill", close to the Pacific. It looks as little like a Dutch windmill as the first, with its slender, round tower. But it is called a "Dutch Windmill.

After the long walk, the two go to the "Beach Chalet Brewery and Restaurant," as the pub at the end of the park is called. It's not a chalet but rather a giant, chic restaurant on the beach. From their table by the window, they can look out over a street, with the sandy beach behind them, where the ocean waves break.

"This is a fancy place. You've chosen well, even if," she glances at the menu, "it's not exactly inexpensive."

"Well, it doesn't always have to be while we're here."

They spend hours in the pub into the evening. Candice and Erik still have a brilliant conversation. He learns about Kalispell. Candice tells him that it is even possible to take a train to the area. Candice likes living in the mountains. But she likes these days in San Francisco so much that she can understand why her sister moved here. "But guess what? Not only do we have bars, we even have a record store in Kalispell."

"Really, you mean vinyl records?"

"Yeah, right. I have my dad's old record player, and I already have a nice collection."

Erik is surprised that science fiction fan Candice, who listens to modern electro music, has a record collection. The two don't see eye to eye when it comes to musical taste: Her techno music is miles away from the jazz Erik listens to. But records are big on both sides of the Atlantic.

In the late evening, Erik takes Candice to the streetcar. It stops on the other side of Golden Gate Park. It goes back to her sister's apartment. Furthermore, it must be one of the last street-cars of the evening. As the car rumbles away, and he sees Candice waving, he wonders if he should have let her go. Or if he shouldn't have asked her back to the motel for another drink. But sometimes, Erik thinks, one acts inappropriately practical at such moments. This chapter ends at the streetcar stop in San Francisco, in front of Golden Gate Park; he realizes that much. He could catch a ride to the airport - but he doesn't. Frank and Erik leave after two more days of sightseeing. They check out the hotel and go to "SFO International Airport" with their luggage.

Erik looks down at the Bay from his window seat as they take off in their giant Boeing. He looks at the screens and waits anxiously to see if he can tell if the plane is taking a route over Montana. But the plane is already flying further east to the north, so he can't catch a glimpse of Flathead Lake from above. Erik thinks: This airplane cabin is the actual tin can in which a traveler is trapped. He can't leave it for the next many long hours, even if it takes him to another continent.

He travels back home reluctantly; that is clear to him. After all, he had met some interesting people. Somewhat saddened, Erik puts the seat back and thinks about his work in Germany, his employment, and his work for the magazine. "I'm not really that wild about returning," he says. "I'm happy to fly back to Germany," Frank, on the other hand, says. "This is not for me." On the other hand, Erik consoles himself with the thought that he wants to return. That lifts his spirits a little.

CHAPTER 3

The Empire Builder

This year, in March

The setting sun is reflected in the windows of the buildings opposite. Slowly, at a walking pace, the big train leaves Seattle's King Street Station. It is bitterly cold out there; white smoke rises from chimneys, but the sky is clear. In the evening light, Erik leaves Seattle on the train. In a cozy, warm compartment in front of which the city's houses pass by. The train disappears in a long tunnel under "Downtown", the city center. It comes out again northwest of it, directly at the "Waterfront", to drive along the "Puget Sound" in front of Seattle. Especially in the last sunlight, Seattle looks beautiful from the compartment window; Erik thinks the apartment blocks with a lot of glass and balconies, modern office buildings, in between a lot of green, which now, in spring, still looks rather gray. Nevertheless, you can admire a picture in dark colors on the other side of the pane.

He is relieved because the train left on time. As Erik has heard, King Street Station looked terrible before being rebuilt. The waiting room had suspended ceilings; the paint was peeling, and rusty heating pipes ran along the walls. The architectural "masterpiece" of that reconstruction was from 1967 when the Northern Pacific railroad company more or less tried to give the station a modern look – probably to make it resemble an airport. In the process, all the 1906 decorations disappeared behind plaster and plastic cladding.

But fortunately, that has changed: The station was renovated as early as 2013. The waiting room shines all in white; the stucco on the ceiling and the decorations on the passages had been meticulously repaired. After all, the trains to Chicago, the "Empire Builder," run from here, as do the trains to Los Angeles, the "Coast Starlight". Finally, there are trains to Canada and Portland, the "Cascades". Still, Erik wondered just before departure, there was nothing to buy, no newspaper, no snacks. The station needs to be more significant for a kiosk.

Erik felt that he was hungry. He took his ticket out of his travel bag and twisted it in his fingers. It said something about "meals included". So surely, there will be something on the train, he thought. Then, he reconsidered how he had gotten here. Eight months had passed since he had met Candice in Reno. The trip across the US on the train from Chicago to San Francisco fascinated him. Especially after he had returned to his surroundings in Hamburg. There, he often sat on the balcony of his apartment and looked up at the sky. There, he sometimes saw the jets flying out into the world.

But his publisher had a thing for salaried journalists who wanted to go out on a limb and could do it. In retrospect, what he was doing at the magazine seems surreal. The workdays continued to be endless. He didn't write articles but planned and edited texts, piece by piece. A particular highlight was at least being able to choose the photos for the stories that ran across many magazine pages. That might be fun, Erik thought back.

But the magazine had already reached the base economically, which everyone knew. There were barely enough staff in Hamburg to keep the operation going. They had a budget that was far too small for the photos they needed, at least if they wanted to maintain the quality of the pages. He took some comfort from the fact that, on paper, there was a collective bargaining agreement under which they were paid. Given the long workdays, overtime included, that was really little more than wastepaper. The "Cookie Monster", as the publishing manager was known among his colleagues, constantly worked to increase the pressure. Although the workdays didn't start until 10 am, they didn't end until 9 or 10 pm either. If Erik hadn't experienced it differently, he might have thought it was normal. His colleague and ex-girlfriend Andrea didn't seem to have any problems with that. At least, Erik watched her as she liked to move on to the next bar at 9 pm with different colleagues. But he believed he could make it professionally, and everything would improve.

One weekend evening, Erik was out again with Frank and Peter, the lawyer who had bailed them out in Lake Tahoe. There he was again, talking about his professional woes. "I don't understand that," Peter said. "What happened to the rebel who once roamed Altona on his moped? Have you now become a fully automated office robot? Erik, you didn't have to go quite that far."

"Well, you're not exactly rebellion personified as a lawyer."

"That may be, Erik. But you know what? My workdays are shorter than yours. And I earn a lot more money than you," Peter said.

"And more than me, too," Frank added.

"I guess there's something to that," Erik had to admit.

Even though he often thought back to the Rocky Mountains and the Midwest, eight months passed before he could travel there again. That's because of the limited annual leave he has available. Candice he had written to regularly. The two had sent emails to each other, so no letters, but no short messages either. Erik found it was an in-between way, and they had included photos with the emails. So he was up-to-date: He knew about her job at the industrial company where she worked as a service technician and also about her sister, who had already left San Francisco again and moved to Los Angeles because there was a better job there. It's funny how different they are, Erik thought. Candice held on to Kalispell; Michelle did as many Americans do and moved after the job. He didn't realize until much later what a special person Candice was. She kept in touch with him from far away Europe, even though he was returning to the US many months later. He thinks he might have flown back sooner and not taken until spring. But at the time, he was tied down by work more than anything else. He had comforted himself by the fact that they could keep in touch "electronically."

So Erik had traveled by plane again, this time to Seattle. He was traveling alone. Frank stayed in Hamburg, preferring to go skiing in the spring instead of traveling to North America. "Don't you think that's kind of cowardly," Erik had asked him directly. "Yes, I do. But I also have no desire to fly to the US again. After all, I took on the whole $4,000 back then. Now I want to stay here."

"And wouldn't you like to see Michelle again?"

"Yes, but that's not why I'm flying halfway around the world. Erik, I'm just different from you. If you want to travel to the US to meet Candice, that's something different. You are much more serious than I am. You also take your acquaintances with women much more seriously. I'm sure you're more important to Candice than I am to Michelle." So that was Frank, back to being the party boy he saw himself as Erik thought. He planned to travel across the northern US and Canada from Seattle.

He wondered: The name is already funny, "King Street Station". Could there be a central train station in Seattle? Yes, there is, on the other side of the tracks, just a few hundred meters away. But no train leaves there anymore. Seattle Union Station had already been closed in 1971 when passenger traffic in the USA was reorganized. Today, the "Union Station" is a magnificent building with a lavishly renovated waiting room that houses the administration of the region's mass transit system.

The day Erik took the "Empire Builder" east had been exciting - and exhausting, so he sinks back into the soft cushion of the seat with relief. Just 24 hours ago, he had landed at the "Seattle / Tacoma Airport" and taken a bus into the city. For a European, a train journey in the US begins with a long-distance flight. In his case, it went via Amsterdam to Seattle. Erik preferred to avoid the long flights. He finds it a pain to "endure" for hours, especially when squeezed into a cramped seat in economy class. He was lucky, though: the plane had new seats equipped with large video monitors for the entertainment program. So it was simply a matter of holding out for twelve hours - interrupted by occasional breaks in front of the galley, which he forced himself to take to keep his circulation going. The entry could have been more swift and inconspicuous.

The most interesting part was the bus ride into the city: Erik was the only passenger on the bus going "downtown," and the driver was chatting. Would he be from Hamburg? That had rarely happened to Erik. Americans would guess "Munich" or "Frankfurt" for a visitor from Germany. In Seattle, it was different: Here, people knew Hamburg. That's because of Boeing, the region's largest employer in the Pacific Northwest, and its competitor Airbus. So even the bus driver in Seattle knew the aircraft plant in Hamburg-Finkenwerder.

"You build good fliers in Hamburg. We have to watch out for that," the driver attested. As if he and Erik were competing to see who could offer the best jets. But he wanted to be friendly and returned the compliment: "Yes, but you also build pretty good planes. I just got here in a Boeing from Amsterdam, and I have to say, that was a good flight, with state-of-the-art equipment." After this exchange of compliments, both Erik and the bus driver seemed satisfied: the latter because the visitor appreciated the quality of aircraft construction at Boeing, and Erik because the driver knew Hamburg in the first place and knew about Airbus.

Cheerfully, Erik got out and walked to his hotel. It wasn't a very cheerful affair, though: The house, which belonged to a large chain, was in a state of renovation. But as he plopped down on the plastic-covered sofa in his first-floor room - it was dark red plastic of the cheapest variety - something whizzed by outside the window. Curious, he looked: The "Seattle Monorail" ran outside the room. Fascinated, he watched the train rattling back and forth on a concrete track since it was a monorail. This is something for future retro fans, Erik thought, because this is how people imagined the traffic of the future in the 1960s. He has a thing for that. It's good that it was still running in Seattle, even though the network was never expanded. It only connected downtown on one route with the "Space Needle," the observation tower on the "Seattle Center" exhibition grounds.

Due to the time difference, he woke up early the following day. Erik wanted to complete an extensive sightseeing program: First the tour of downtown in the early morning, then the ride on the monorail, a visit with a coffee break on the observation tower "Space Needle" and finally, he could not get enough, a ride on an excursion boat on the Puget Sound. This trip was a memorable experience because it went from downtown first out onto the Sound, that is, out to sea, then through the lock "Ballard Locks" into Salmon Bay, and on to Lake Union, which is located behind downtown. From the ship, he could marvel at the houseboat settlement. It was laid out as early as 1900, as the "tour guide" reported over loudspeakers. In the meantime, the houseboats have been dressed up and lie in long rows along the shore. At that time, however, it must have been a rather rough settlement where the woodworkers had built their own homes on the water. Erik thought it was a pure necessity; now, it stood for an original lifestyle that ranked somewhere between being a hippie and the noblest home decor. The tour guide reported that prices like a million dollars for a larger house were quickly paid for here. The settlement spread a cheerful atmosphere With its bright colors and many different types of homes, from small to huge, from one to several stories. No wonder the houses had formed the backdrop for the romantic movie "Sleepless in Seattle".

Now, it went briskly by cab to the hotel. Otherwise, it was no longer manageable in terms of time. Erik picked up his suitcase and drove to "King Street Station". Because of the nine-hour time difference, he was pretty flattened after this excursion program when he could finally take a seat in his compartment. "That would have been enough for two or three days," he says. Now, he doesn't usually travel through foreign countries in "tourist mode on steroids." But he had worked out a schedule beforehand back home in Hamburg, which provided for precisely one day in Seattle. Erik wondered whether he had to organize his life according to a schedule. But hadn't it worked out all at once: downtown, Monorail, Space Needle, Pudget Sound? Even the cab driver thought that was a bit ambitious when he had told him.

Outside, darkness has fallen as the train makes its way north before turning east. Erik had planned the trip through Montana to Minneapolis, where he wanted to turn around to go back via Canada. That was the plan: once through the Rocky Mountains, then through the prairies, turned around, and back through the Rocky Mountains. In his small compartment, however, the urge to explore takes hold of him. First, he inspects the "roomette" thoroughly. Roughly speaking, there are three classes in all long-distance trains that travel west of Chicago through the USA. There's the "coach," the regular seats, in a wide-body car.

There is the "Roomette," which is a type of "couchette" for one or two people. The "real" sleeper compartments are considerably larger and can even be booked with their own sanitary facilities. Accordingly, they are also expensive. Erik found the "roomette" quite suitable for himself because at least you get a real bed there on which you can stretch out. But now he pulls open the sliding door and makes his way through the train. There's not much going on in the observation car; no wonder, outside, it's just the night passing by. In the dining car, people are busily dining. But behind them is his goal: he wants to take another look at the "Coach" cars. He takes a seat in an empty row and sinks into thought. This is the environment in which he crossed the continent last year. Now, the coaches have been given fancy blue lighting that fits perfectly with the night. As a European, he is surprised again at how spacious the seats are. Not only can you recline this seat enormously far back, but the distance to the next seat should far exceed airplane business class. It's pretty comfortable here, Erik thinks.

The sleeping car attendant who had assigned him the "roomette" when he boarded the train in Seattle approaches. "Oh, there you are," he says in amazement. He has indeed searched the train for Erik and now seems surprised that "his" guest from the compartment has made himself comfortable in the "coach" car. Erik tells him he wants to reminisce about past train rides. "But your dinner is ready; you can go to the dining car." Now Erik is surprised because he is unfamiliar with the dining car as a former "coach" passenger and because the attendant has searched the train for him to tell him that dinner is ready. "That's very kind. I'll follow you." It's a first, which is very welcome tonight because, first, Erik senses he's hungry because there's nothing to buy at the Seattle station. And second, he's looking for entertainment.

The dining car is pleasantly furnished, Erik finds. The seats are made of plastic again. Actually, they are four-seater seats made of white plastic with blue cushions. But each table is set, and fresh flowers are in a small vase. The lighting here is also dimmed, which he finds pleasant. Moreover, the dining car attendant has provided entertainment: he's dining with a Tacoma businessman traveling to the Midwest.

"I do enjoy traveling by train in Europe," Erik says. "But once I think about being on the road in your huge country: Business and trains - do they go together?"

"Not really," replies the man, who introduces himself to him as Paul. "But I like to travel by train. You can organize it that way: That's when I take a stack of documents with me to read at my leisure on the train. Then I'm prepared when I arrive."

So the whole thing without plugging in a laptop, he asks?

"Yes, I do, but I don't use it on the train. There's no Wi-Fi here," Paul tells him. The country is enormous, and you can't expect Internet coverage everywhere on this vast continent. So Paul prints out everything he takes on board on paper in the old-fashioned way.

Erik and Paul drink beer, and the food is served. "Wait for the famous Amtrak steak," Paul still said. Indeed, Erik thinks this steak, with beans and potatoes, must be one of the best he's ever eaten - perfectly fried, a little "well done," just the way he likes it. The fact that you can also have an excellent meal on a train is rare in Europe, he explains to Paul. "So you travel to get from A to B?" he asks. "Yes, that's right, you're traveling fast, but it's not that pleasant."

"Well, if the trip lasts, you might as well get comfortable," Paul counters, ordering two more beers. The two chat. Erik learns that Paul likes to take the train because he enjoys the peace and quiet and time to himself. His wife, and here Paul briefly grimaces, had already moved on years ago after the divorce. That's why he has more time now. But he doesn't want to dwell on the subject. In Minneapolis, he plans to rent a car and visit his customers; he has a job in the agricultural sector. He will return the car a few days later and return to Tacoma by train. "That makes sense," Erik says, "and eating and drinking well in between?"

"Exactly, that's a wonderful way to use the time." Outside, beyond the dining car windows, there's a hiss. "That's the Cascade Tunnel," Paul explains, "it takes us to Mount Howard, right in the middle of the coastal mountains." The train is not yet in the Rocky Mountains, but it is passing through a mountain range - these are the "Cascades," or simply the "Cascades."

"The Cascades Tunnel was built after a serious avalanche accident on the old route," Paul reports, sipping his beer. "The old tunnel was much higher up in the mountains. It can get as hot as 35 degrees here in the summer and as low as minus 30 degrees Celsius in the winter."

"So, a pretty tough area to build a railroad, right?" asks Erik.

"Yes. The route was planned by John Frank Stevens, who later became the Panama Canal chief engineer."

"Oh. And what was wrong with the route?"

"It could hardly be kept clear of snow in the winter. In February 1910, three trains were stuck in the town of Wellington, somewhere up there in the mountains." Paul points to the window into the darkness.

"That's when an avalanche broke loose and hit the trains. Ninety-six people died." He shakes his head. "Then finally, the railroad realized it couldn't go on like this and planned a new tunnel under the whole massif."

"I've read that past Denver at the Moffat Tunnel before."

"Yes, it was something like that. Except this tunnel is 7.7 miles long instead of 6.2."

Their "Empire Builder" rushes through the tunnel; nothing can be seen outside in the darkness. "Hold your breath," Paul advises him.

"Seriously, now?"

"Trains used to run electric here because of the exhaust fumes. But in the 1950s, the railroad company took down the wires."

"And then?" Erik notices that Paul knows the route well.

"When a train passes through the west portal of the tunnel, a door is closed at the east end. Fans then blow air into the tunnel," Paul explains. "The door opens again when the train gets within a half mile of the east exit. The train can go through and exit the tunnel. But now the door closes again, and the fans run at full power for 20 to 30 minutes to clear the masonry of exhaust fumes."

Erik shakes his head. "Did I understand that correctly? But there was an electric line, wasn't there?"

"Yes, but they wanted to save having to re-harness the locomotives." Paul also explains to him that the crews of the trains that travel here carry oxygen tanks in their cabs - you never know if the train might stop.

"So we can only hope in our dining car that the fans are doing an outstanding job."

"Don't worry, they do. You don't have to seriously hold your breath," Paul laughs. A unique sense of humor this man has, Erik thinks.

After the tunnel is behind them, the two say goodbye. Erik goes to his compartment and pulls open the door. The sleeping car attendant has converted the "roomette": The two seats mounted by the window have become a bed. It is freshly made, with white sheets, a thick pillow, and a comforter. Upstairs, there would still be a folding bed for a second occupant in the roomette. But for him, as a single traveler, the lower bed is sufficient. He draws the blue curtains of dense fabric and thus locks the night out of the compartment. Erik has to yawn. The time difference, the day of sightseeing in Seattle, the beer, and the rattling of the train do not fail to have their effect. He falls asleep immediately.

So he doesn't notice when the train stops in Spokane, the second-largest city in Washington state. If he had been awake, he could have seen the "Empire Builder" extended: A second section is attached to the train. One starts in Seattle, and another, shorter, in Portland, Oregon. In Spokane, both parts continue their journey to Chicago together. But Erik doesn't notice more of that than he does of the dark Rocky Mountains. In the morning, he wakes up to a loud noise. He sees that the train is going through a tunnel again. This was the second-long one on the route: the "Flathead" tunnel, almost seven miles long. It had only been inaugurated in 1970.

But now it's time to get up and stock up on coffee, Erik thinks. The next stop is only 28 miles away from the portal. It's a good thing there's plenty of coffee for the passengers: Outside the aisle is a large container with a lever for filling paper cups.

WHITEFISH IN MONTANA

A huge man in a cowboy hat stands on the platform of the small town of Whitefish. He approaches Erik and extends his hand in greeting. "You must be the guy from Germany who rented my car," he says in a low voice, emphasizing the "my car" as if there were only one car in Whitefish, or at least at his rental agency.

The station is relatively quiet, even though it has a considerable building artfully constructed of wood. So it was easy for him to spot Erik on the platform. The man with the cowboy hat is friendly, as Erik finds out: They both drive the little Ford to the nearest café - "much better than anything served on the train" is the breakfast, the man in the cowboy hat assured him.

Over dinner, Erik learns a lot about the area. Starting with the fact that the car is brand new. The protective film on the sun visors had yet to be removed. But summer in Whitefish is still to come, he explains, and he just didn't have any rental cars there. His contract, however, requires him to be able to offer a car if someone asks for one. Erik is almost uncomfortable with this; after all, he could have asked for another rental. But the rental company doesn't find that unusual at all. He says they'll buy one if there's no car in stock; that's the deal.

He gives tips for a round trip through Montana: The "Glacier National Park" is, of course, worth a visit, as is Helena, the state capital. Then, one could drive a circle to Flathead Lake with its beautiful shore road. If Erik was interested in railroads - he probably deduced this from the fact that he got off the train - one could make a detour to "Somers". That's a place on the lake from which a branch line led to the water, where you used to be able to transfer to the paddle steamer. Sounds excellent, says Erik. They say goodbye, and the man returns to his Ford dealership with its attached car rental.

Erik knows approximately where Candice lives in Kalispell.

She had described it to him: It's on a side street close to downtown. "Without my smartphone, I wouldn't be able to find it," Erik says as he drives down the country road from Whitefish. Now, he had a brand-new rental car, too. Although Candice and he had only been friends so far, he had looked forward to seeing her again.

Erik stops, and Candice greets him with a warm hug and a smile. They stand on the porch of the small but cozy house on the side street. In the US, many people live in houses, unlike in Europe, where she would probably have an apartment, Erik thinks. It feels to him like hardly any time has passed since they last met.

"Do you want to see Flathead Lake now?" asks Candice as they sit in her living room.

"After all, you've often told me how beautiful it should be."

"Beautiful doesn't even begin to describe it," Candice replies with a grin. "And the drive there is just as breathtaking."

They set off, windows down despite the spring cold, and with loud music playing. As they approach the lake, Erik is amazed: the crystal-clear water glows turquoise blue and stretches almost as far as the eye can see. "You're right, it's at least as big as Lake Tahoe," he says. "Except for the casinos, you must do without those here. How is Frank, by the way?"

"He's just his old self. Always looking for a party to take his mind off his office job."

"You know what? I'm not surprised one bit that he didn't travel with you. And I think even Michelle would be surprised if he showed up."

"Yeah, that's Frank - a little shallow already."

"Unlike you, huh?"

"Yeah? Hopefully... How's Michelle doing, by the way?"

"Well, I think she's fine. I'm not sure what she learned from what happened in Lake Tahoe. She could be been playing again.

She won't tell me, but I have a feeling about what my sister is doing."

"I hope there's no trouble there."

"Well, we can't quite rule that out. But I believe that you could also use a distraction from your magazine job for once."

"The whole thing doesn't make a good impression. The job is getting tighter and more exhausting. It can't go on like this eventually. Especially not with this boss." He looks at Candice and feels guilty. "I'm sorry I haven't come here in so long."

"You wrote to me, after all. I can understand you. I am all the more pleased that you are here. Now I need a change of pace in Kalispell."

Candice and Erik spend the day walking and lounging on the lakeshore. It's comparatively warm weather for mid-March in the Rocky Mountains. As the sun nears the horizon, they pack up for the evening. "That was a really nice afternoon."

"Me too," Erik says. "Now we're going to town?"

"Which city? Oh, you mean the big city where I live here? Well, it should be good for a stroll. Let me show you my favorite place."

They drive downtown, park, and visit an Italian restaurant on Main Street. "You're a science fiction fan, too, aren't you?" asks Candice.

"You think? I thought you'd think I was more of a rail fan."

"Yeah, but Solaris is playing at the movies tonight. How about it?"

"I didn't expect to be able to see a movie like this in Kalispell, Montana," Erik says. But he likes the idea of going there with Candice. In the middle of downtown stands the cinema, which sometimes includes classic films in its program alongside the box office hits, as Candice explains.

Erik thinks the flick is enjoyable, but not as fascinating as he had thought. After all, that evening, there is the remake by

Steven Soderberg from 2002, which is somewhat more pleasing than the Soviet original from 1972. After the screening, it is evident that Candice likes the film. She is downright enthusiastic. Erik doesn't find the spectacle exciting and realizes he's not a George Clooney fan, either. But he doesn't want to spoil her joy and discusses the film with her in great detail. Secretly, he plans to drag her to a railroad movie someday, should the opportunity arise.

"Let's go on an adventure tomorrow," Candice says. "We could go to Glacier National Park." "Are we taking your car or mine?" asks Erik. "Oh, you have such a fancy new Ford. Why don't we drive that and not my old Chevy?"

Erik had taken the precaution of reserving a motel in Kalispell. After taking Candice to her home, he heads for the "Motel 6", located just outside the center on the main road. The rental car is parked in front of the door, the room on the second floor has a sitting area, and there is even supposed to be breakfast. At least some kind of breakfast, as the receptionist explained: "I serve fresh coffee. And at that vending machine, you can get your favorite chocolate bar and eat it with your coffee. That's our breakfast." Erik is a little surprised that you eat a chocolate bar for breakfast in the land of mountains and forests. But the hotel's price is so reasonable that it doesn't matter.

He gets in the car with Candice the following day, and they drive northeast for hours. Most of the sparsely populated state of Montana is not served by rail. The main cities are too far south from the route of the "Empire Builder." The first thing they do is roll over the pass that was again built by the engineer

Stevens, who was the first to come to the region to scout out the route for the "Great Northern".

"I've driven along this pass virtually before," he says.

"What does that mean, virtually driven along?" asks Candice.

He confesses to her that there was once a computer game, the "Train Simulator," in which this line was recreated: from "Whitefish" you could ride the train to "Glacier Park" and on to "Shelby."

"Ha, you might be a train nerd," Candice interjects. "The worst kind, if you even drive trains on your computer screen. I'm nothing compared to that with my science fiction bent."

Erik rows back. "It wasn't that fascinating. The train was running on the screen, but I didn't spend entire evenings doing it." That wasn't true, he thinks. He had spent whole evenings shunting trains on the screen. But he didn't have to tell that story, he thinks to himself. "The most fun I had was turning up the music, sitting back, and watching the train roar through the Rockies."

"All right, then, you're more of a Rocky Mountain Man than a railroad nerd," Candice says.

"What actually impressed me: If game developers have spent this much time and effort recreating 'Maria's Pass,' then there must be something to this corner of Montana."

It is a sunny day again. The roads are winding, and the views of the mountains and forest make the drive a pleasure. When they reach the national park, they are overwhelmed by the mountains that shoot up here, unlike in the Whitefish and Kalispell areas. They see peaks, clear lakes, and dense forests. Then, Candice and Erik park and take a short hike to see the scenery up close. On the "trail," the mountain air is pure and clear. It's a bit of a challenge, but worth it, they agree - and not just for the views. They stop in the forest, and

Candice is sure she has seen a deer among the trees. Erik, however, can't spot any wildlife in the undergrowth. They are delighted with their "outdoor interlude" when they return to the car.

They continue to "Great Falls" in Montana. Erik says he has no idea what to expect in the little town, and Candice has never been there. But it sounds good. "Great Falls, I expect huge waterfalls there, and maybe it's as pretty as Whitefish." The roads are almost empty, and they both keep looking left and right, marveling at the beauty of the surroundings. The landscape changes as they get closer to Great Falls. Flattening hills surround them, and only scattered forests.

The town seems more extensive than they thought. They drive off Interstate 15 and navigate through streets with beautiful homes until they reach the waterfalls of "Great Falls." After all, the Missouri River flows here. The falls consist of a weir with a concrete wall over which the water masses flow. They can take a short walk from the shore and take a look, but after a few minutes, Erik states, "I think we can keep going."

"Yeah, let's move on," Candice agrees. They could be more impressed. Hadn't the car rental guy in the cowboy hat raved about Helena? Isn't it just a good two-hour drive to get there? Although it's getting darker, the two begin the final stretch to Helena, where Candice and Erik spend the evening in a small hotel near the center.

He feels a bit insecure as they stand in front of the reception. But for Candice, the only option is a shared room, which she quickly tells the receptionist. However, when they unlock the door, the newly renovated hotel room has two beds. "Pick the one you like better," Erik says. "Well, sure, I'll take the one by the window." They make themselves comfortable. But they don't push the beds together, even though Erik had briefly thought about it. But so the two good pieces stay apart, and each stays on his side of the room, so to speak.

Erik is later very taken with Helena: The city has only 30,000 inhabitants, which means it is only half the size of Carson City in Nevada. It is the capital of the state of Montana. The streets around the massive Capitol, which towers over the city, are wide, with old trees and beautiful houses. The Cathedral of Saint Helena stands on a small hill. Candice says the Catholic church in the "Gothic Revival" style is modeled on a church in Vienna. She also knows that Helena, which was once a mining town, was initially called "Last Chance". However, the residents found the name too gloomy, so they changed it to Helena. The gold rush brought the town great prosperity in the 1880s. "At one time, most millionaires in the world lived here," Candice says of her capital.

Today, Helena has become a slightly dreamy city, or so Erik feels. It has left its great days behind, but as the capital, it has an essential function for the state. And then there's a "dinky" pedestrian zone with old houses downtown. The two also find a nice little restaurant near the hotel, where they have dinner.

While waiting for their order, Candice tells Erik about a few weeks ago trip to the mountains. "Just what you do here in Montana." She said she felt great when arriving at one mountain peak near Kalispell. "I couldn't stop smiling. Walking into the sunset, I felt a sense of accomplishment I've never experienced."

"That sounds profound," Erik says.

"Well, you know, I'm a pretty practical person. It's not like I ponder the meaning of our universe, even though I love reading science fiction novels." Erik has to laugh. Candice really is a hands-on person. She continues, "But that was different. That's when I felt everything in life had a purpose."

"I'm convinced of that."

"Well, then you should try that too: Up to the top and very close to enlightenment," Candice returns as the food is served. They have both ordered a steak and are drinking beer with it.

Erik looks at Candice and thinks that they both have a connection. He feels it clearly. But at the same time, he suspects that they are not in love with each other. It's a strange feeling to be so close to someone and yet so far away. Is she thinking the same thing now, he wonders? I don't know what she's thinking, he admits as they enjoy their dinner.

Candice tells him that she has always been attracted to the unknown, the unexplored corners of the universe yet to be discovered. She is curious, he thinks. After all, he is also on a quest, practically exploring North America. The long day and the effective time difference have tired him after dinner.

When they are both back in their hotel room, he gives Candice a long kiss, which she returns. But then she turns away and crawls under her covers. Erik wants to say something but lets it go. She looks at him briefly. Then he undresses and crawls under his covers as well. "Good night, Candice," Erik murmurs, realizing he's pretty tired. "Good night, Erik," she whispers back. He would never have thought it: he was sure he wouldn't be able to sleep at all with Candice in the bed next to him. That he would be constantly tempted to slide over. He would hear her breathing and not be able to sleep a wink. But as he is still thinking about it, he falls asleep. Candice has stayed on her side of the room "by the window".

The next day, some snow has fallen. The streets of the small-town look even more beautiful, Candice thinks, as they walk around the Helena Capitol. The houses are enormous, Erik notes, and because there are rarely fences there, it feels like a giant park. "If you want more railroading in Montana," Candice tells Erik, "you'll have to convince the congressmen here. Here and in Washington, of course. A very active initiative, the Big Sky Rail Authority, is trying to do that. They want to boost tourism and reconnect places like Billings, Bozeman, Helena, and Missoula to rail."

"That does sound like a good plan."

"Yes, but they still have a lot of promoting to do. My state is more sparsely populated than others. The largest city in Montana is Billings, which has only 117,000 residents. Kalispell also only comes in at 24,000 and ranks right after Helena."

"But I think it's an impressive state with great scenery. And I like the people, too," says Erik.

They continue by his car to Missoula. The route leads curvy over a pass. They can stop at a parking lot called "Lookout" and let the eyes wander over the mountains, valleys, and forests.

In Missoula, they briefly roll past the train station near the center of town. The town even has two stations, but they stop at the one where there are still tracks today. Erik didn't know what a stupid idea that was: while he looks at the platform, where nothing stops anymore, a golf cart drives by. In it sits a female police officer, who can thus roll through the entire city center without having to walk herself. And she unceremoniously sticks a hefty parking ticket behind his windshield wiper.

"So you're not even allowed to park in front of the former train station?" Erik asks her. "No," is her curt reply, "you're not allowed to park here." There's no discussion there. He feels pretty stupid because his railroad nostalgia is now costing him money. She doesn't seem to care, preferring to press down on the gas pedal of her golf cart and roll away with a low hum. A short time later, Erik understands why: In the beautiful city center with its many old buildings, there are a few corners with stores. Still, they are so far apart that apparently, no law enforcement officer would think of walking through Missoula.

In the center, Erik and Candice find a store that still offers CDs. "When I'm in a strange place, I enjoy wondering what kind of music people buy here," Erik says. "Once, when I had to fill up on the Southside of Chicago, I picked up a soul album from the checkout counter that was good - and a great fit for

Chicago." It's even easier for him in Montana: even if he's not a country fan, John Denver fits in well here. Erik buys a double album, which he returns to the rental car. Because the Ford still has a CD player built in. Candice protests a little at first because it's not her taste.

They head straight north, toward Flathead Lake. Then John Denver pleases them quite well. The mountains rise steeply on both sides of the road, which is also little traveled. There are some leaves on the dark asphalt. It's getting lonelier; there's no one else on the road here, Erik thinks, while "Rocky Mountain High" sounds from the CD player. He tells Candice that he had met a couple in Denver who had made the song their life motto. They had succeeded in doing so, he says, since they moved to the Rocky Mountains. She is impressed. Above all, the view of the lake is spectacular: the great body of water stretches on either side by slopes filled with forests. "I didn't promise you too much about Flathead Lake, did I?" asks Candice. "No, you really didn't."

A mountain range rises to their right, drawing ever closer to the lakeshore, until the road follows the ridges with many curves. He wouldn't have imagined this to be so lonely, Erik thinks. On the map, the region around the lake looked lively, at least compared to many other areas of Montana. Via the towns of Woods Bay and Bigfork, they finally reach Somers at the north end of Flathead Lake. This is said to have once been the site of the railroad ferry that brought wagons and locomotives from north to south to provide a link between the two major lines through Montana. Erik thinks it's a shame, but traces are barely visible; the ferry is long gone.

They pay another visit to Whitefish, the place with the train station, in the rental car. The eastbound "Empire Builder", with which he wants to continue, stops once a day, early in the morning. So they have plenty of time and want to check out the ski area. Erik has heard that many passengers come to Whitefish by train to go skiing. After all, that's a good idea if you're coming from the West Coast or the Midwest.

The road winds up the mountains at the picturesque "Whitefish Lake". They reach the ski resort of Whitefish. "It's quite a construction site here," Candice notes. "In the middle of the season, there's hammering and carpentry everywhere." Indeed, Erik thinks, there are legions of men in high-visibility vests and helmets working. Next to them, the ski area is in full operation, even in this weather. They stop and watch the men in their vests and red flannel shirts. Erik loves skiing. Even from Hamburg, they regularly went on skiing vacations in winter and spring. No wonder, he wants to take a look at the ski area in Whitefish in March, and he would have loved to go to the ski rental shop right away. But Candice can do nothing with it. Even though she does not live far from some respectable runs in Montana, she has yet to be on skis. It hurts Erik's soul to turn away from the snow-covered slopes.

He looks at the construction work. "How's it going?" he asks one man. "We're pretty busy and barely keeping up," the man explains. "The owner said he still wants to expand the porch." The carpenter is wearing one of those handy belts that hold all the standard tools Erik has always admired. Very American-look-ing, he thinks. "It's nothing special," the craftsman counters when Erik asks him about it. "I have everything handy there." He takes out a large hammer and drives in some nails. Erik notices that there's not much else for visitors to discover. After a tour of the downhill slopes and the rows of stores, they return to the valley.

Whitefish is a beautiful place, and the hotel fits the bill. It's built of big logs like the buildings are clad in wood from logs. But there is an attraction. On a terrace, right on the mountain river that flows from here into "Flathead Lake," there are several "hot tubs." Erik says he likes these hot tubs because they are so hot in the USA. So he invites Candice to come to the hotel with him - which she finds exciting. They visit the hot tubs on the terrace together. The temperature of the bubbling water is 40 degrees Celsius, plus there's a bit of sleet and, in between, a cold dip in a cooling pool. What the sauna is to northern Europeans, Erik thinks, the whirlpool or "hot tub" is to Americans. In this case, the "hot tub" on the terrace, close to the steep bank of the river, is worth it. It's just right after the round trip, and they both relax in the hot water. To do so, they tell each other stories and, sip by sip, empty the beverage bottles at the pool's edge.

Late that evening, Erik takes Candice back to Kalispell to her cottage. So she didn't stay overnight at the hotel by the river. "Promise me we'll do this again soon," Candice says with a grin as they hugged goodbye. "Promise me it won't take you eight months to get here again."

"Of course," Erik replies, feeling a sense of warmth in his heart. "And hey, who knows? Maybe next time we'll fall in love." Candice looks a little affected, blushing slightly. Now Erik blushes too, he feels. The wrong sentence slipped out of his mouth. "Stupid me," Erik thinks. "What am I talking about?" Another hug, then he climbs into the Ford as she waves goodbye. Darn it, he realizes. This reminds him of the goodbye at the streetcar stop in San Francisco.

The following day, he is up early. But that's a good thing because the train is scheduled to leave the town at 7:26. He is sitting in the breakfast room of the large hotel, where he is the only guest at this time. Some friendly person, whom he can't see and doesn't make an appearance, has done an impressive job, though: The buffet is fully stocked. The offerings range from fried eggs, sausages, and bacon to fruit, cottage cheese, and a waffle machine where you can make your own waffles to eat with sticky maple syrup. It seems almost surreal: A small town in Montana, it's still dark at 5 am, he's sitting alone in a dining room, and there's not a person to be seen in the entire hotel.

He doesn't have to check out at all, as he was assured the night before. Now, he drives to the station in his rental car and leaves it in the dark - the key simply goes into the glove compartment. Candice sends him a short message: whether he made it to the station, she asks. Or if he didn't want to stay? Erik thinks the situation is not happy: Why did he leave? Then, out of the darkness emerges the big train that is now supposed to take him to Minneapolis. The wagons squeak to a halt in front of him, and the service attendant opens the door. He greets him in a friendly manner and asks for his name. Erik puts the smartphone away, gets on, and pushes aside thoughts of parting. The train starts and rolls out of the station, heading for Maria's pass. Again, it's away from Candice for Erik. He has the feeling that he won't necessarily get another chance.

EDMONTON, CANADA

December 28, Today

It is the end of December, and we are back in the hospital in Edmonton. There, where our story had begun. I think of how Erik told me he had taken the train to Montana and Minneapolis this spring. I could understand him: Things hadn't "clicked" with Candice. At the same time, it must have been hard for him to continue his journey as if on a schedule. It wouldn't be my case, I told him.

Now it's December, just after Christmas. I am back with my sister Amelia. She is lying in her bed and looks pale. No wonder, with the surgery she has to endure. But she is happy about the visit from me. Most of all, of course, she is glad that her boyfriend Erik is with her. The two of us sit in the visitor's chairs. Outside, the snow is sweeping across the campus of the university hospital. This has already become a routine: I stop by Amelia's when I leave the office. It's the same for Erik.

"You've got it pretty good with railroad tunnels. Earlier, the Moffat Tunnel near Denver, and then Paul tells you all about the Cascades Tunnel," Amelia says to Erik. She puts the book's manuscript down and reaches for the paper cup with the latte on the nightstand beside her bed.

I admire Erik a bit: he wrote down the whole story of his journeys through North America. Amelia literally devoured the manuscript. No wonder it's the story of the two of them. Her eyes sparkle bright and clear when she talks to Erik. I'm so grateful he's with her. It's essential that he's here while Amelia still has time. How long that will be, the three of us don't know.

Erik had the manuscript printed at a copy store in "Strathcona" that I had recommended to him. Amelia's printer stopped working long ago, but what does that matter when there's a copy store down the street. He experimented a bit with the fonts and finally chose a nice, large font with pretty serifs - I must say, it makes for good reading.

"Why did it actually take you eight months to return to North America?" asks Amelia Erik.

"At the time, I wasn't sure what I wanted. I didn't really know what was important to me. And in Germany, I was too involved in work. I thought ..." he hesitates, stroking her hair, "I thought work was the most important thing in my whole life, and everything else was just an accessory. How wrong I could have been, especially considering what it has brought me." Now, he has a bitter tone about him. What happened to Erik there - I don't wish for that.

Amelia looks at Erik seriously. He gives her a kiss on the forehead. How affectionate the two of them are with each other.

"Oh, come on," he then says. "Germany doesn't really count. In fact, it doesn't matter. There are more important things in life."

"And in Montana, you had met Candice again?"

"Yes, but as you just read, There was nothing between us."

"If you can get to know someone like Amelia, then you don't need a girlfriend in Montana," I tease Erik. "Even though, yes, you've been through quite a bit together. Especially in Lake Tahoe."

"Well," Erik says, "Amelia, you and I didn't know each other then. I liked Candice. As much as you like someone you're friends with. So I went to see her in Kalispell, but then I moved on. I felt really lonely after that until I ..."

"... Until you came to Jasper," Amelia adds. "You know what, I think I'd like to meet Candice sometime. She seems like a fine person. So if ..." She falters, coughs a little, sinks back onto the pillow. "Well, I mean, well, you know what I mean."

"I'm sure there will always be time for that. For that and for everything else," Erik tells her.

She contorts her face somewhat in agony. Then, she regains her composure. "I'll read on now. After all, I want to know how you got to Edmonton."

"You're brave."

"Oh no. I'm dying to know the whole story."

"Don't worry. There are still some railroad tunnels coming up."

While they laugh, I discreetly withdraw from the room and leave them to their own story.

Drive to Minneapolis

Montana, in the spring of this year

It continues in the spring, with Erik leaving Whitefish and settling on the train to Minneapolis. At this time, he was busy moving back into a small "roomette" at the Empire Builder and putting thoughts of Candice and what might have been but wasn't out of his mind. For the first time on this trip, he has daylight on the ride and inspects the small compartment as the mountains roll outside. There are two seats covered with blue fabric. Because a small device with controls is installed in the upper right-hand corner next to the backrest for the head, including a reading lamp, the seat has an almost retro-futuristic appearance, Erik thinks. It's also quite broad. Next to it is a shelf where he could place his travel bag. At the top, above the sliding door, you'll find a knob that lets you adjust the airflow a bit.

The small compartment could stand for train rides in the golden age of the North American railroad. It's big enough for that, and Erik likes the view from the second floor of the "Super-liner" type of car. It doesn't look modern either; more retro-futuristic. He remembers that the color scheme was recently orange-brown in the design of the late seventies. Now, the plastic has been dyed or painted from brown to white in an unknown way.

He looks out of the window. Now comes "Maria's Pass". The train crosses the Rocky Mountains at 1589 meters above sea level. The rail line is double-tracked towards the wide pass, framed between widely curved mountain ranges. Next to it, the US Route 2 road follows the tracks. The "Empire Builder" has hardly slowed down when the powerful diesel locomotives pull it up to the crest of the pass. Now, it also crosses the "Continental Divide", which is the North American watershed. Whereas previously all the rivers flowed to the Pacific, they now flow to other seas: namely, to the Arctic Ocean or to the south, to the Gulf of Mexico, and further east, finally to the Atlantic.

The places have names like "Bison Creek" and "Rising Wolf" and are primarily small settlements with wooden houses. Erik thinks the names really sound like "Rockies." The train travels along the southern border of the national park. At the station "East Glacier Park," it stops. Whitefish is two hours and ten minutes behind. That's the station before the big national park that Candice and he visited by car. There is a fancy hotel and some vacation homes there. The mountains have already moved further into the background here: Behind the dark brown station with its wooden beams, the impressive skyline of the mountain massif moves to the horizon. On the left, you can still see the Rockies; on the right, it's already getting flat.

After the stop, the train slowly starts up again, and after a good five miles, the Rocky Mountains are over. Behind "Glacier Park" the prairie begins, and the railroad line runs dead straight. The following towns are called "Browning", "Cut Banks" and "Shelby". But this prairie is not entirely flat, as Erik notices: Again and again, the train passes significant cuts in the landscape on bridges. Rivers wind their way through these valleys. But the "Empire Builder" speeds up as it travels through eastern Montana. Erik notices himself starting to get a little restless in his compartment. The spectacular scenery has passed, and the flat fields with individual snowdrifts seem monotonous again.

Erik sets up his laptop on the small table in front of the seat and is pleased it can be folded. "It's really ergonomic," he notes. Yet he knows that he's actually bored. Because only a little is happening, the train has no Internet connection. So, he switches the laptop off again. The trip to Minneapolis will take a good 25 hours. Erik thinks about Candice in Kalispell again. He could have stayed there one more night. Then, he would have just gotten on the plane to Minneapolis and arrived just as quickly. That would have been nice. But wait: This is a train ride, Erik tells himself. He can't "cheat" and dream of planes taking him across the prairie in a few hours. He stretches out and reminds himself to appreciate the comfort of the train. "Get a grip," he tells himself, "there's train riding now." He muses a bit about "pulling yourself together." Pull yourself together had become his motto while working in Germany. Pull yourself together, he told himself when he said goodbye to Candice. Now, he should pull himself together again?

The ride turned out to be quite pleasant after all due to a few walks through the train. In the basement, he discovered the shower compartments. They are quite spacious, with a stack of fresh towels in the corner.

This was again accompanied by lunch in the train restaurant, which was included in the price, and dinner, which was quite excellent. On top of that, Erik had the company of an elderly American couple who told of many trips across the continent. He went to bed early in his "roomette." But at night, Erik did not sleep well at all on the train. It sways violently. The "Empire Builder" seems to have increased its speed further and is now racing through the night. But the rails don't make it easy for him: it rattles and wobbles like no other train Erik can remember. At one point, he startles himself at night, thinking the train must derail. Fortunately, it doesn't. The blue night lights shine in from the aisle, and it's quiet except for the clacking of the cars on the tracks. But the train leans to the left and right, so you might think you're on a ferryboat. "Am I perhaps not as train-suited as I'd like to be?" he wonders. "First, it takes so long, and I'm already dreaming of a plane ticket, and then it sways so much that I can't sleep."

The next morning, however, the sleeping car attendant tells him many travelers feel the same way in this section. The best place to sleep would be between Seattle and Whitefish, where the train would not travel so fast. That calms him down a bit. He visits the small washroom on the lower deck. Erik notes that the faucet has the unpleasant property of working like in an airplane: While you press the lever marked red or blue, water flows. As soon as you release it, it stops flowing. So you have to fill the sink with the right temperature, which means a little rhythm of pressing hot, cold, tapping cold, hot again - until the temperature is right. It's awkward, especially when the draft fluctuates. But eventually, he finds what he wants: a bowl of perfectly tempered water that sloshes nicely from left to right.

At just after half past eight, Erik is ready: The train pulls into the newly renovated Saint Paul station. "Saint Paul-Minneapolis, Minnesota Union Depot" is the facility's name. Previously, the twin city was served by the so-called "Midway Depot," located on the connecting road between the two cities. Erik had heard about it at dinner the night before: it was a relic from the 1980s. Like Saint Paul's, Minneapolis' big train station had been decommissioned. Instead, a concrete purpose-built station had been erected between the two cities - again, of course, with a low-hanging ceiling, neon lighting, and equidistant from both centers. But at least the two towns decided they could use a "real" train station again. The choice fell on smaller Saint Paul for tangible reasons. When Amtrak took over rail service in 1971, Saint Paul was no longer served, and traffic was concentrated in Minneapolis. However, the Minneapolis Great Northern Depot station continued for only seven years. In 1978, construction workers razed it to the ground to make room for the main building of the Federal Reserve Bank of Minneapolis.

But impressive is the revival of the Saint Paul station, which was not on any demolition list but was simply used by the US Postal Service all these decades. So this station could be reactivated. This is because the new streetcar, some bus connections, and, on the extended platform, the "Empire Builder" have stopped there again since 2014. The introduction of a new train connection to Chicago, the "Great River", is in the starting blocks.

He checks into a large hotel right in "downtown" Saint Paul. It belongs to a chain, and he finds it distinctly faceless. It is a concrete colossus, even though it has a glass atrium and he has a nicely furnished room. He finds it pleasant that he can walk there from the train station. The hotel also has a swimming pool under a glass roof, circular in shape and of considerable dimensions. Erik recovers from the previous night's bumpy train ride by taking a few laps. But Erik also notices that he feels lonely.

His smartphone rings. A number from Germany. That can't be true: The editors are calling him. They're asking about articles that should be stored somewhere they can't find. "You guys realize I'm in the US, right?" asks Erik. "Oh, what? In the US? Then you can still help us with the articles." He does, leaving the call costs out of it for once. Because what helps against loneliness, Erik thinks? Right, the feeling of being needed, for example, at work. Although he suspects it can't be completely normal here in Saint Paul to be happy about a call from the editorial office because you think you're lonely.

The Twin Cities have a lot to offer. But he feels Saint Paul clearly got the more minor "cut of all the Twin Cities attractions." Erik thinks he should have thought so, given the difference in hotel prices. People here boast of "skywalks," a connection with glass bridges leading from one skyscraper to the next. Pedestrians can use them to march through the city in the freezing cold of winter or hot summer with relative peace of mind. But in reality, the "skywalks" in Saint Paul instead lead from one high-rise building to the next, from office portal to office entrance, interrupted by a few small stores.

Now Erik is drawn outside. What a difference awaits him after riding the "Green Line," the light rail to Minneapolis - a long ride through the typical arterial streets that connect Saint Paul and Minneapolis. The train crosses the Mississippi River on a large bridge just before reaching its destination. The city looks busier throughout: Houses are taller and newer, and stores are on the street level. There are also many more people outside. In the heart of the city, at the "Nicollet Mall", he gets off.

Minneapolis has a similar "skyway" network of pedestrian bridges running through the office buildings as Saint Paul. But outside, there's more life on the "Nicollet Mall." There are book-stores, fashion stores, and chic cafés. He takes a seat at a Café to drink a large "Americano" – espresso with hot water, which is also called "Verlängerter" in Austria. This way of serving coffee from Italy has made it to the US. Now it has come back to Europe, such "Americanos" are also available in Germany.

Erik walks toward the Mississippi River at Nicollet Pavilion, where live events are to be held in the summer. On the great waterfront, it's colder than in the city because an icy March wind sweeps across the river. But it fills him with a certain majesty to stand on the banks of the mighty river, so far in the cold north, so far from the warm Gulf of Mexico, where the Mississippi flows into the sea. The river is 2350 miles long. It is almost 500 miles from here to its source.

The large warehouses of the former flour mills stand on the waterfront. Some have old neon signage that has just come on. On the roof of the adjacent wheat silo, the neon sign "Gold Medal Flour" shines in yellow, and on the other bank, "Pills-bury's Best Flour" shines back in red. On the frosty day, the neon lights that spread warmth fit in relatively well.

Erik takes a brief look at the "St. Anthony Falls". They are more of a barrage than waterfalls, but here, the river rushes over a wide ramp and thus virtually changes its height. The ware-houses, the old bridges, and the concrete, which already has rusty spots, make it look like industrial romance down here. But the many new apartment and office buildings that have sprung up along the riverbank catapult the visitor into the present day. The river offers a fascinating urban picture here.

But city planning and sublime Mississippi aside, Erik feels lonely as he walks along the river on this cold afternoon. He feels abandoned. Close to the riverbank stands a historic train station, which today is simply called "The Depot". It is the place from which the "Milwaukee Road" trains once departed westward and also to Chicago. Today, the former station houses an event center with a chic "Mariott" hotel. However, chic is relative, Erik thinks: A multi-story, square building has been added to the old train station, but architecturally, it looks rather banal. In the station, you can walk through part of the former hall covered with marble. But the actual hall of the station is now a ballroom or event hall, which is closed. So that station doesn't have any potential to brighten it up.

He decides to look for a bar or a restaurant. A few places are in the "Gateway District" on the river. But more activity exists between the "Nicollet Mall" and First Avenue. And so he ends up in an "Irish Pub", which looks a bit sterile from the outside but highly cozy from the inside. A lot is going on here. He is only dog-tired when he sits at the counter and looks at the menu. But there are many people in the bar, and as he drinks his first beer, he starts a conversation with other patrons. Asked about Minneapolis, he usually gets a similar response: "It's cold here," a twenty-something at the counter tells him.

"Yeah, really icy. The whole stupid winter hardly stops, even though it's March," adds his friend.

But what are the Canadians who live even further north supposed to say, Erik asks. "What, someone lives there," is the ironic answer. Suppose you live in a country as big as the US, with warm cities like Miami or San Diego. In that case, you obviously want to live in the south, Erik thinks, if you come from a "cold city" like Minneapolis. Now that he's also from the north, likes to travel to Scandinavia, and doesn't find cold climates so bad, he thinks you can stand it here after all.

"Yes, you can stand it, unlike the rest of Minnesota, where nothing is going on at all," they agree with him. "It's just like Scandinavia," Erik says, "away from the cities, there are few inhabitants and mostly nature. If you like that, it's wonderful up there."

"Yes, Minnesota has some beautiful spots, too. But the prairies aren't as interesting," they report. If he had the time, he'd have to drive up to Lake Superior; he might like it there. After all, he doesn't have the time because he has his plan and goal of going to Canada.

With dinner, steak again, and beer and company, Erik stays up much longer than he thought he would. It's not until "11 pm" that he leaves the friendly pub and heads for the light rail, which he then returns to Saint Paul. Fortunately, his hotel is close to the stop. That, Erik finds, is then no different than in Germany, when you sit after a few beers in a neon-lit train and go home.

The next day, he looks at the "Mall of America". He decided to buy some new clothes. Because in his travel bag, he had not taken so much at all. He also doesn't like the old pieces from Europe he carries with him anymore. The mall had caught his eye on the map. The name sounds very pompous, Erik thinks. The Mall of America! It's not the most prominent mall, but it is, he marvels, the most visited, with over 500 stores. The planners must have done much right: The center doesn't suffer from vacancies. It doesn't mind "shopping malls." On a cold day in Minneapolis, it's an excellent place to warm up, after all. The "Mall of America" is located in a suburb behind the airport, but at least it is connected by light rail.

So he can drive back to Minneapolis, change trains, and

arrive briskly at the mall. One could spend hours strolling through the many floors that wrap around an atrium inside. There's even an amusement park. In the past, it was supposedly dedicated to the character "Snoopy," but no agreement was reached on the license fees. Now, it is simply an amusement park without a mascot. The crowd at the mall looks affluent and fashionably dressed, Erik thinks. No wonder whoever goes here must have financial reserves because he will surely leave much more money here than he intended.

Erik browses through some stores and looks at what they have on the shelves. When men shop for clothes, they usually take a determined approach and want to "check off" what they need. Erik is no exception. If he even checks off a trip according to a schedule, why should buying clothes be any different he thinks. This time, he has time. Plenty of time until the evening, when he continues his journey. It's snowing outside, so he doesn't want to wander the streets of Minneapolis.

On the other hand, he likes the pieces he's looking at. Finally, he notices the reasonable prices. That may be because the dollar exchange rate and the clothes aren't expensive.

In a huge jeans store, he rummages. Piece by piece, he sets aside until a saleswoman joins him. She must be around twenty, looks nice, and addresses him with the typical phrase, asking if she could help him with anything.

"Yes, I'm looking for these jeans in a size that fits."

"What size are you looking for right now?"

"I frankly have no idea."

The saleswoman looks at him scrutinizingly, then takes the stack of jeans he has already picked out.

"But that's not going to happen with them. Unfortunately, you've miscalculated; they're all too small. Much too small."

"Oh, I didn't realize that. I must have put on a little weight."

She laughs. "Just a little, I would say. These jeans run small;

we've heard that over and over again from customers. Hang on, I'll get the right ones."

She returns with a stack of jeans for Erik to take into the cubicle and try on. He thinks that the fitting rooms are enormous in this store. He's used to small holes in Europe, but this one looks grandiose. He pulls aside the curtain.

"That looks great," says the saleswoman waiting outside. "Yes?" asks Erik, a little uncertainly. "Absolutely, the style suits you."

Ultimately, Erik has four new pairs of jeans, which he likes so much that he wants to take them all. "You men like to buy in bulk, don't you?" the saleswoman asks him. "Yeah, we have such a tendency to check things off. But I like all the jeans."

"Are you from Europe?" she asks him, "I hear an accent there."

Erik tells her he is from Germany and traveling across the northern United States.

"And in Europe, do you all wear these clothes?" she asks him with a smile. Erik is taken aback. "What do you mean?"

"Well, if I may say so, your clothes have a shabby charm. I'm sure it was once high quality, but now it looks a little worn and old."

"You think so?", Erik looks down at himself. He hadn't experienced that before, a saleswoman saying something about his old clothes. But it doesn't bother him.

"Don't get me wrong," she says. "It's not like everyone here is wearing fancy new clothes. On the contrary, when you're picking out so many jeans and wearing, well, such old clothes at the same time, you want to re-dress. I've noticed that." She smiles disarmingly at that.

"I don't know why, but I don't like my clothes anymore," Erik replies. He usually wouldn't speak so openly. But she seems to understand him, and he has confidence in her. That's probably because she seems to be very stylish: she wears jeans, of course, along with a colorful patterned blouse and a scarf. It all fits together perfectly, Erik thinks. Yet she doesn't have a model figure by any means; on the contrary, he thinks she's a bit portly. That's not much different from him.

"Watch out, we only have jeans here. But down the hall, there's a store with many other pieces. You should like that if I judge correctly. That's where my friend Rosanne works. I'll take you there; she'll get you everything you need."

Erik is quite taken with it. "And what's your name?"

"I'm Cathy." Erik gathers his courage. He thinks about the whole long day he has left to spend in this mall. So he tells her, "And when I have all my new clothes, can I show them to you?" Cathy laughs happily.

"What are you saying?"

"Well, can I buy you coffee later, after I get my new pieces?"

"Yes, why not? I'm on my lunch break, so we can go to the café at the south entrance. It's nice there, not as crowded as the ones at the food court. How about at one pm?"

"I'm glad."

So Cathy takes Erik to Rosanne's store, which Erik realizes has something to do with "nautical." The fashion at least has a nautical style. Erik likes it at first sight. Then Rosanne advises him in all facets. She lays out many sweaters, shirts, and T-shirts before him. Erik tries on the pieces. After an hour, he has his things together: The four pairs of jeans have been joined by three sweaters, four shirts, T-shirts, boxer shorts, socks – everything a man needs when traveling. The bill at the checkout is lower than he feared. Rosanne has laid out a few pieces from the "take two, pay one" section and pointed them out to him. He says goodbye cordially and heads off to the café.

"Hello Erik," Cathy greets him, "someone has made a big purchase. Now you fit right in at this mall."

Erik lugs around his travel bag and quite a few huge paper bags. "Yes, your Rosanne had exactly the right nose, as do you," Erik replies. They both order coffee at the counter; Erik pays for his "Americano" and their "Latte Spice Pumpkin," and they sit at a table with two wing chairs.They look through the glass façade where it is snowing heavily.

"You have good taste," Erik says. He thinks Cathy can pick out the perfect clothes.

"Thank you. It's my job, after all. Actually, my part-time job while I study."

"I didn't even notice, but my old parts really aren't that great anymore."

"Oh, I didn't mean it that way. They're fine, just, you can see their age. You men rarely go shopping."

"I guess that's true. That's why I wanted to take the opportunity."

"Which is what you've done now. Most people would have gone to an outlet for a big purchase."

"I definitely wouldn't have been as well advised there," Erik says.

"It wasn't that expensive, was it?" Erik tells her he didn't expect to pay that much at all. "Rosanne and I know what we're doing, not with every customer, by the way. But if we like someone, we get the pieces we think are good and on sale. Otherwise, we do it the other way around," she laughs.

Cathy talks about her life in Minneapolis. About the cold winters, of course, but also the warm summers. About her architecture studies and her family. Erik finds her very relaxed. He enjoys the conversation. He's never done anything like this: ask a saleswoman out. He is pleased that it is such a nice meeting. So he immediately gets two more coffees. "I'm about to get a caffeine jolt," Cathy says, "but what the hell." Erik is very open with her. He'd heard before that sometimes people confide more in strangers precisely because they are strangers. This clearly must be such a case. "I had the idea this morning that I need completely new clothes. Just like I don't like my life in Germany anymore," he confesses to her.

"That's a clear-cut case. We solved the clothing part pretty well, don't you think?"

"Yes, we managed that well," Erik enthuses.

Unfortunately, he is not on a date, as he thinks. He would probably like a date with Cathy very much. But their lunch break is over in a few minutes. "I'm sorry, but I must return to the store", Cathy says. "Why don't you give me your email if you like".

"I'd love to; I'll write you what else happens to me on my trip," he replies. They exchange emails and look at each other briefly, then Cathy turns around and disappears into the mall, waving.

Erik, however, realizes that he now has decidedly too many clothes. He can't possibly travel like this, With all the paper bags and the extensive travel bag, which is already full anyway. So he asks at an information booth for an old clothes container. To get there, he has to leave the mall and walk through the snow until he finds a large container on the side of the parking garage. Then Erik takes piece after piece out of his travel bag and throws it into the big flap. He is still thinking that it would be a shame to throw away clothes. But when he looks at his things now – the tattered jeans, the shirt with a tear, the old boxer shorts – no, it can't be a pity about them, so off to the container with the things. It feels to Erik like he's leaving part of his past behind. He then packs the new clothes into his travel bag. It's a perfect fit: the load feels lighter than before.

Back in the warm mall, he notices a chain store he knows. He walks into the gift store that carries a lot of funny and useless stuff. But these stores have excellent massage chairs. You can try them out. If he really wanted to buy such a chair, which he seriously didn't, he would have to try all the models: The small, rather inconspicuous ones, but also the thick, big, and bulging ones that would definitely disfigure any room. But they have a remote control with plenty of buttons and massage the back wonderfully. As Erik lolls in the faux leather chair, he notices a lanky salesman pacing the chairs. Just then, an elderly lady gets up and leaves the store with a flushed face. The salesman has already reached Erik.

"Sir," the man says, "you've been using our massage chairs for quite a while now. Are you planning to purchase one of these?" Erik feels caught off guard. "Uh, yes, if it fits," he stutters with a noticeable accent. "Or are you just planning to try out the chairs?" the salesman asks him. "In that case, I'll have to ask you to leave our store."

"It's okay," Erik says quickly, "I'll go." As he turns toward the exit, he can still hear the sales clerk making a move on the next occupant of the chair. Erik actually feels caught. He feels like he's been kicked out of the store. Well, serves him right, but half an hour of free massage has finally earned him that.

NORTHBOUND TO WINNIPEG

The "Saint Paul Union Station" is busy in the evening. Erik is relieved. He would not have liked to spend waiting time in a deserted station. But the hall is full of people waiting for the "Empire Builder". The train is scheduled to leave at 11:15 pm. They are mainly younger passengers who have gathered here hours before. Many train riders are older, Erik thinks, simply because they have time and money. The many backpacks pushing their way through the hall with their porters paint a different picture. Many younger people wait here, traveling alone or as couples. Just across the street from the station is a restaurant that welcomes guests until 11 pm. He strolls through the station for the last few minutes until departure. A magnificent bridge leads over the tracks, from which stairs descend to the platforms.

When the "Empire Builder" finally arrives, it would actually have had a fifteen-minute "break". But because it is running late, the train stops for only five minutes. This time, he is not in a roomette but in the upper deck of one of the "Superliner" cars with "Coach" seating. The car is full to bursting. But the overnight trip should only last six hours. The doors are closed, and the train pulls away, leaving behind an empty platform in a far too big station. The coach attendant comes by, checks his ticket, and attaches a small strip to the seat. It says where he has to get off: in "Grand Forks," North Dakota, at 5:34 in the morning. He leans back. So now he has six hours in this warm car, but what follows? What's it going to be like up there, in North Dakota? Will I get to town? Erik wonders? What will I do then? As he ponders, he falls asleep.

Erik is woken up by the attendant ten minutes before arrival. Well, nothing can go wrong, he yawns. Not that he would suddenly be in "Whitefish" in Montana, possibly without a ticket. Apart from him, a few passengers are getting ready to get off the train. It is pitch-dark outside. Then, the "Empire Builder" brakes audibly and loudly and comes to a halt in the middle of a curve. He enters the lower deck, exits the train through the door – and finds himself in a cold, hostile environment. The wind whips around his ears. "There's no station here at all," he mutters. The train simply stops at a curve bend. Of course, Grand Forks had a "real" train station. But it's in the middle of town and hasn't been used for many years.

But there is a station house. Yes, Erik recognizes that Amtrak has put one of its seventies concrete places here. It's not big, but the door can be opened. Inside, the waiting room is brightly lit and warm. What a relief. Besides him, a young woman with a large cap enters. He asks her if it would be possible to walk to the bus station from here? "No chance," she explains, estimating that Greyhound would have to be at least an hour and a half walk away – because the bus stop is downtown. "Unlike the train station, of course, which is outside," he adds. "We're lucky to have a stop at all," she says, walking over to one of the telephone handsets on the wall from which you can hail a cab. She advises him to order one as well. But while she's still talking, headlights appear outside. A cab driver tries to take advantage of the "favor" of the train stop and pulls up in front of the station. Erik lets her go first and calls his own cab.

What is he doing in "Grand Forks" anyway, Erik wonders. Apart from the place's name sounding interesting again, he has to change from the train to a bus. After all, he could ride the "Empire Builder" almost two-thirds of the way through the night. But now the train is heading west, and anyone who wants to go further north will have to find another way. In the 1950s, as many as three trains with names like "The Winnipegian" connected Minneapolis to Winnipeg. Those are history. Good thing there's a bus, Erik thinks. But it doesn't leave for another five hours. So he has ample time to spend with Grand Forks. This is now the time he has been dreading: He has to sneak through an extinct city at night and wait hour after hour in the freezing cold for the bus.

He has been lucky: Sometimes, there is a bus from Grand Forks to Winnipeg, sometimes not. There was one once, then there was none again for years. When Erik arrives, "Jefferson Lines" has a bus running again. His luck, but later, it drops out again. He has to look up such critical connections beforehand, he reminds himself. Otherwise, one could easily get stranded on the prairie in North Dakota.

The cab pulls up, he gets in, and it rumbles away toward the lights, the city. He explains what he's up to to the cab driver in his plaid shirt – and he has the rescue. "There's a café just diagonally across from the bus station. They're nice; you can go there," he advises the visitor who has made it to his city at night. Which the cab driver also finds quite exciting. And above all, he doesn't find the plan to change buses here to Canada so absurd.

He enters the café, which is already brightly lit at this hour. Erik goes to the long counter and tells the lady there that he wants to stay a few hours until the bus leaves. He assures her that he will also order breakfast. "Don't worry, honey," she says. Even if he only had coffee, he could make himself comfortable on a bench for as long as he wanted. Erik finds that very hospitable, so he immediately orders coffee and a breakfast of "pancakes," finds a cushioned bench, and settles in with his things. "Great, I won't freeze to death. I don't need the extra scarf and hat," Erik says happily.

Four old farmers have settled down at the neighboring table. They unpack their things, order coffee, and then hand out playing cards. The whole thing wouldn't be unusual if it weren't happening at this hour: it's just six in the morning, and it's still dark outside the door. Apart from Erik, the four gentlemen are the only guests. They play, they joke, they talk about this and that. This must be some kind of "daycare," he thinks. A friendly meeting place, where they're open early and let the guests have their way, even if they only order a little.

Erik strikes up a conversation with them because they noticed him with his luggage at the next table. They, too, find a visitor from Germany interesting. After all, these states in the north of the US have a high proportion of people of German descent. One man, Erik estimates him to be 80 years old, has white hair and a well-groomed appearance. He finds it quite impressive that Erik is passing through here. "From where to where are you traveling?" he asks.

"I came by train from Minneapolis, and now it's on to Winnipeg," Erik replies as if it's the most normal thing in the world.

"What, the train is still running? I wouldn't have thought so," he replies – which shows the role the train must play in their lives. "I know the train," says his neighbor, who appears to be a bit older. "I used to go to sporting events in Minneapolis with my son and my parents. I think it's great that the train still runs. I didn't think it would." But from downtown, the train just disappeared, they know. Where would it stop?

"There's a little station at the bend, just a little house," Erik enlightens them. Suppose the train is no longer visible, as it is at the station in the city center. In that case, the whole world apparently believes it's no longer running. The third person in the group immediately adds: "The train is going to Canada? That can't be. Nothing goes there any more unless you take the interstate."

"Yes, there should be a bus there in a few hours," Erik replies.

"What, the bus is still running?" now asks the fourth of the sprightly card players. "I don't think so; the bus to Canada hasn't been around long."

So, one thing is clear: If he had relied on these four gentlemen, he would only have tackled the route with a rental car. "Yes, I just read it on the Internet," says Erik.

"It's good that the bus is still running," he replies. But now, no memories of a bus trip to Canada come to mind, as they did for the previous speaker.

Erik notices that people in Grand Forks are hospitable. The gentlemen tell him to visit the university, which has a beautiful campus – but he replies that he'll have to take the bus immediately if he's going. Then he turns his attention to the next coffee, which the waitress pours while slowly getting light outside. The café is also getting a bit more crowded and busy.

Erik reads a bit, only to be surprised to find that the time is up. That was quicker than expected; he must have been sitting here for around four hours. Erik gets up, says goodbye to the card players, pays, and steps out onto the main street in front of the café. Sure enough, a Jefferson Lines vehicle has stopped diagonally across the street. He thinks it must be his bus, drags his travel bag across the street, and goes to the bus driver. It really is a bus to Winnipeg. It's not that empty.

The following person Erik encounters is a Canadian border agent. She is not as friendly as the bus driver, the lady in the café, or the Amtrak attendant. She is not friendly at all. On the contrary, she is suspicious. She doesn't understand why he now wants to travel to Canada after a few days in the US. She says it haughtily, as if he wants to enter the land of God on earth just like that.

"Listen, your great Canada isn't so great," Erik wants to tell her. But he doesn't say that because there would definitely have been further difficulties. He was the only passenger to leave the bus at the border crossing and face questioning in the border building. But he keeps his nerve and patiently explains that he is taking a train trip through the Midwest and the Rocky Mountains. He says he wants to return to the West Coast through Canada instead of the United States. The unfriendly female officer has a crush on him for some unknown reason. Ultimately, the officer flips his passport shut, hands him back the document, turns away, and leaves. No "Thank you very much for putting up with my extremely unnecessary, unfriendly, and artificially protracted questioning," or at least a "Thank you very much, sir." No, she just walks away. He returns to the bus. "Don't worry about it," says the US bus driver, "it happens here all the time. Passengers get called into the den there and questioned at length."

The coach continues its journey, and the scenery looks the

same beyond the four-lane road as it does in the USA. The fields aren't much different, nor are the towns. A maple leaf can occasionally be seen on street signs, flags, and advertising posters. Finally, the suburbs of Winnipeg approach. People on the bus are silent, staring out the windows or "daddling" on their smartphones. The capital of the Canadian province of Manitoba, with just under 750,000 inhabitants similar in size to Minneapolis, is getting closer.

The car stops at a bus station in the west of the city. This is a disappointment for Erik. Because he had chosen the hotel near the train station in the east, thinking he would also arrive there. Now he has to walk across the city center with his bag. It's Sunday noon, but only a few people are out and about here. Okay, the weather may not be after that, it's windy and freezing cold. Isn't that a shopping center to his left? There are no pedestrians there either. In that center, the stores are closed. Downtown streets remain deserted. "What a comparison to Minneapolis," he mutters, where the center was bustling. He approaches the concrete building that, no doubt, must be his hotel. The advertising even promised "direct access" to the "skywalks." So here are the same pedestrian bridges between skyscrapers as in Minneapolis and Saint Paul. Except that on a Sunday lunchtime, these access points show what they can do: little. No people are walking here when the offices are closed. Which confirms his suspicion that the "skywalks" are only for office workers.

The hotel is getting on in years, but that has rarely bothered him. May the carpets also be worn, the windows at the entrance portal no longer entirely clear, the reception counter a bit scratched – he doesn't care because he has a hostel in the drafty city. Especially since he got a reasonable price. The friendly lady at the front desk asks if he wants a high or low room. "Are there people who want a low room?"

"Oh yeah, some people don't like to live that high up."

"Perhaps you would have a room at the top?" he asks, looking forward to enjoying the view of the empty city from a safe distance. He does indeed get quarters on the highest floor.

Erik sits at the top, looking down on empty Winnipeg. The wind whirls up sand, dust, and leaves in the streets. He had imagined it differently; it is not an uplifting feeling at all. He feels left alone. Furthermore, he is staying in a vast hotel in downtown Winnipeg on the weekend as one of the few guests, staring down on an empty city from the 15th floor. Erik hopes to find some distraction in the hotel pool. The facility is aging, and the tiles in the pool are peeling. The swimming pool smells strongly of chlorine. But the water is warm, and the pool is surprisingly large. He swims a few laps as the only guest. But that only lifts his spirits a little.

Later, Erik sets off for the city once again. There must be something he could look at that would give him a feel for the town. In fact, there's nothing he can discover. Sunday evening in Winnipeg – nothing is going on there. Are the people all at home in the suburbs, in front of their TVs, he wonders? What else is there to do on a cold, rainy day? Erik spots an open pub, goes inside, and orders his dinner. "No, nothing is going on downtown on weekends," the innkeeper confirms. "Sometimes a few patrons stop in, though, so I'm open."

But Erik senses that there is actually another reason why he feels so lonely in Winnipeg. Could it be because of Candice? Why did he ditch this lovely woman in Montana to continue his pre-booked train ride? Why did he "stick to the schedule" instead of doing what he wanted? Erik ponders: You plan something, which is then worked off, leaving no room for diversions and extra trips. At least he could have stayed with her. But no, he traveled across the Midwest and then fought his way north. Now he sits here, the train traveler, the passenger, all alone in an extinct-looking town on the Manitoba prairie.

Erik becomes melancholy. Why am I driving alone through the north of the USA and Canada, he asks himself? Didn't he already have this thought when he left Whitefish? He thinks whatever he's looking for – he is still determining exactly what it is. If he found it, could he go for it? Is he fearing it would turn his life upside down if he took the next step? Erik thinks of the Dutch woman and the American he had met in Denver. They had dared to do something together. Shouldn't he do the same?

Now, he has a complicated trip across North America planned. But wouldn't he have stayed with her if he had found what he was looking for with Candice? Did he really make the wrong choice? What he is looking for in Winnipeg doesn't seem to be there. He doesn't really feel better now. On the contrary, he feels miserable as he sits back in his hotel room after dinner, looking down at the dark city with its lights. He can't find any sleep.

Erik has always loved traveling. Because, at least for a while, it had also become part of his job. He found it exciting to discover new places and meet people there. It was a different way of traveling than when he took a vacation. Erik was interested in something other than taking vacations to relax, but to discover. In the process, he usually recovered all by himself. As soon as he got to grips with a new place, everything else receded into the background: everyday life, worries, whether private or professional, whether about a relationship or money. That suddenly seemed far away, at least physically. By putting distance between himself and everyday life, much of what otherwise bothered him disappeared. He gained additional distance from his daily worries by meeting new people: the encounters broadened his horizons. The fact that he could make this his profession had made him delighted initially. He was able to work as a travel journalist, but not as one who merely researched the beautiful sides of travel, as can be read in vacation reports, but one who dealt seriously and critically with his destinations. That's also where his attitude towards travel guides came from, which provide you with the best tips.

He could "go on tour" and discover and research simultaneously. He could then write up his collected notes on a magazine story that he hoped would be exciting and provide readers with new insights. "Enlighten and explain" was his motto. It had been his motto because, for the past few years, he hadn't been enlightening anything at all, just tied to his desk. Instead of experiencing something himself, he had to edit, organize, and plan the texts of others. The happy years were over for him professionally, he realized.

But this misfortune was familiar to him. Now that he is standing at the window in this hotel on the prairie, Erik is surprised that new feelings have crept into his journey. Feelings that he had not previously associated with travel in this form. The fact that a tour poses such problems for him emotionally as this trip did, he did not know. Whether he was in Europe, North America, or even Asia – when Erik was on the road, he usually felt good the whole time. This time was different.

Could it be the inconvenient train journey? But that's what attracted him: He wanted to discover North America by an entirely different means of transportation. It would have been easy to buy a plane ticket to Montana, visit Candice, and then drive around in a rental car. No, Erik wanted to follow up on his travels where he had done research. That's why he wanted to move by train: He hoped it would give back some of the discoveries of earlier years. Instead, he felt lonelier than ever.

Erik pours himself a drink from the minibar. He holds the

glass in his hands and looks out the window. He should look ahead now. After all, there may be something, or someone, he wants to find in the vastness of the prairie. As Frank once said to him? "You've got to do what you always do, what your nature is: keep going, keep going." He wonders if that's the right prescription here. Shrug your shoulders and just keep going? Without reflecting on it? It won't help him that night; that much is clear. So Erik tries to look ahead.

From Winnipeg, he wants to take the "Canadian," the big train that the Canadian Amtrak counterpart "Via Rail" runs between Toronto and Vancouver. It is the northern counterpart to the "Empire Builder. The train has fancy, older carriages made of lightweight steel, which look attractive. However, unlike the Empire Builder, it only runs three times a week. It is a hefty bit pricier, at least if you book a sleeping compartment. However, it has an even bigger disadvantage: it won't leave Winnipeg until Monday evening.

Erik thinks about whether his low mood could be used as an excuse to go to the airport and take the next plane to Vancouver. "Pull yourself together. You would rather not cheat. Do what you always do: keep going," he tells himself. It's not about speed here. Besides, he wants to ride the Canadian.

So, the following day, Erik finds himself in a museum where Native American art is displayed. The exhibition is well done, and the exhibits are effectively staged with light cones. It's open, as is the mall on Monday, although it remains pretty deserted. He wanders through the "skywalks," bustling with office workers.

In the afternoon, he looks at the "Canadian Museum of Human Rights," built on the train station's other side. The idea came from Izzy Asper, who had built up the "Can West" media conglomerate of TV stations and daily newspapers based in Winnipeg. After his death, his daughter completed the project.

Erik finds the structure's architecture, which opened in 2014, impressive: a concrete base connects it to the ground, a ribbon of glass floats on top, and a spire juts out from the top. Admission is free, and you can stroll through the building on long "walkways" and learn about human rights. It's a mix of "showing respect" for indigenous heritage, cautionary displays, and multimedia exhibits, he finds. Among other things is an area in the hall where people pass each other while being captured by light cones. If two get too close, the cones of light merge into one large one. What symbolism, Erik thinks, as his cone of light strides alone across the surface. Should he now realize that he is lonely? Ultimately, they should "celebrate hope," climbing to an observation deck at the museum's top. All right, he wants to celebrate hope. But he doesn't feel like celebrating when he reaches the top via a staircase and stands at the very top.

Perhaps he also lacks access to such a museum. Do human rights even need a museum? Shouldn't they be ubiquitous? Well, if the place helps grow respect and tolerance for one another, it has served its purpose, at least for the Winnipeg residents who visit.

Erik finally returns to the hotel lobby, where he spends the early evening. He leans back in an armchair with a book. He relaxes. There's coffee there, too, and cake later. Amazing, Erik thinks, but in the hotel's seventies lobby, in an armchair, he regains some equilibrium. The gnawing feeling of loneliness subsides – coupled with feelings of guilt toward Candice.

ON BOARD THE "CANADIAN"

When evening comes, Erik moves with luggage to the nearby train station. After all, Winnipeg has a large station, even if a train only comes through here occasionally. The gigantic building is well maintained: The concourse is neat and clean, and a counter is open where he can "check-in." A dome arches over the hall with its marble floor. Actually, there is also the "Winnipeg Railway Museum" here, which houses an exhibition of historic steam locomotives, but for some unknown reason, it is closed. The station only offers a little else, no stores, restaurants, or kiosks, just an empty but well-kept station concourse and a passageway to the tracks.

Very slowly, however, the hall fills up. Passengers start to arrive. Most of them are elderly people, married couples, and some are single travelers. They all crowd into the tunnel under the tracks. Finally, the time has come, the train rumbles overhead, and the "Canadian" pulls in. He climbs the stairs and stands on the platform in front of the large, shiny silver train with the blue stripe under the windows. He looks for the carriage to his booking. But the sleeping car attendant has a problem: Erik is not on his list. So he would prefer not to let him on the train at all. But since his "papers" are in order, he inevitably has to. So Erik is allowed to board and is assigned a compartment. A few minutes later, the attendant comes frantically into the compartment and makes it clear to him that he cannot stay. "You shouldn't be on this train at all," he says irritably. After a few minutes, he knocks on the door again: Erik may stay. But he hears no trace of friendliness.

Once again, the feeling creeps over him: "You're not welcome in Canada." As the train rolls away, he inspects the small compartment, the "roomette" for one person: It is a touch larger than its US counterpart. The seats are upholstered in gray leather, probably plastic. The lighting is pleasantly dimmed, and the single-level car is much higher. Only the toilet bowl opposite his seat, he does not like it so much, although it may indeed be convenient. It is closed with a thick cushion on a hinge, so you can use it as a footrest. But does it have to be a toilet bowl in the middle of the compartment, Erik wonders? He would have preferred the one outside in the corridor. But what does it help? The train is warm and cozy, and hurtling westward.

Later, in the dining car, Erik has company and an excellent meal on the table. There's steak again, just like in the USA. As there, it is perfectly prepared. The couple with whom he shares the table is not very talkative. The two prefer to have their meal mainly in silence.

Fortunately, he is proven wrong an hour later. He strolls through the train. Nothing is happening in the "Dome Car" with its glass observation dome. No wonder it's dark, and there's hardly anything to see on this train except for the occasional passing light of a signal. But behind the "Dome" is a lounge, and a very entertaining group of passengers has gathered. He joins them. There is no alcohol, the bar has already closed, but there are hot drinks. So Erik treats himself to one fruit tea after another while the train rushes through the prairie.

The sleeping car attendant who assigned him his compartment earlier is also standing there. Now, he turns out to be a friendly, open-minded fellow. "I'm sorry, the stress of the incorrectly assigned compartments got to me earlier," he says. "But in itself, our trains are very nice, aren't they?"

"Yes, I think it's great here. The compartments are big," says Erik.

"You can travel the whole country with them."

However, Erik also learns from the attendant that each passenger is supported by the Canadian government with almost 500 dollars on his journey in this train, so high are the operating costs of the "Canadian".

"Travelers like you cost us dearly," Erik hears a man beside him say. But a younger US couple intervenes. "Isn't it worth it to you guys to bring tourists into the country, like us, for example?

We came all the way from New York by train," the woman replies.

A lone traveler, an elderly man from Toronto, agrees: "It's good if tourists can ride our train and visit Canada that way."

By the way, attendant Samuel doesn't think much of the US trains: "They're much more run-down than ours. Maybe we don't run as often, but the cars are well-maintained. And we intend to expand our network."

Erik keeps to himself that he has found the Amtrak trains better, even if his image of Canadian trains brightens. Hour after hour passes during the ride through the night, and no one wants to leave the group, which passes the time here animatedly. A few guests join them: Another couple, this time from Vancouver, and two young women traveling across the country who remind him of hitchhikers. They talk fast and excitedly. Each entertains the round with his story. It must have been after three in the morning by the time the game slowly disperses, and passengers head for their coach seats or compartments. While the "Canadian" rocks gently and doesn't shake as nervously as its US counterpart south of the border, he falls asleep in his room.

Erik sees very little of the city of Saskatoon early in the morning. With the first morning light, he looks out of his compartment window onto the prairie covered in clouds and snow. Half asleep, there is a knock on his compartment door. The attendant wants to know if he is the "passenger from Chicago". Word has obviously gotten around, perhaps from his colleague in the lounge last night. He is the passenger from the US, but not from Chicago. "Breakfast is ready," he says. Just before the dining car, Erik again meets the attendant from last night.

"Man, do I have a headache," he groans. That was too much for him.

"But we didn't drink alcohol, just tea, half the night," Erik tries to cheer him up.

"Yeah, but that was enough for me. It doesn't have to be alcohol at all for you to get a 'hangover,'" he notes. He's also been up early again to care for the train and its passengers.

Breakfast is again as good as dinner. Erik is pleased that "VIA" does without some plastic packaging that is so popular at "Amtrak". The coffee can also be drunk from a cup instead of a paper cup. Noon and the afternoon offer him time to wander through the train, from his compartment to the "Dome Car," whose panoramic deck provides a beautiful panoramic view of the flat prairie during the day. Then, he continues through the lounge to the end of the train, where there is another observation car. Every seat is taken: Passengers enjoy the view to the rear from the panoramic windows at the end of the train, where the seats are garnished in a semicircle. Erik still strolls through the "coaches," i.e., the large-capacity cars. The audience there is younger than in the dining car or the lounges. But the ticket prices here are also more affordable. Between mountains of backpacks, blankets, and pillows, students traveling west by train have made themselves comfortable.

Erik notices that the cars in the US are roomier, with wider seat spacing. The Canadian cars may look stylish after all, but he notices from the furnishings that they are older. He doesn't necessarily want to spend four days from Toronto to Vancouver in these seats. But he doesn't have to because his compartment with a built-in toilet is still available. The train approaches Edmonton in the evening, and he has to get off. The train there is again wholly booked. He finds this astonishing, but the trip through the Rocky Mountains attracts many travelers, even at this time of year. Erik only hopes to feel more comfortable in Edmonton than in Winnipeg.

Slowly, the train is pushed into the terminus on the city's outskirts, leaving the main line for it. Edmonton, unlike Winnipeg, no longer has a "real" station. In the center, the tracks were torn out at the end of the 1990s to build new offices – although one of the main offices of the railroad company "CN", Canadian National, is in the center. But this meant that the city's train station, which is topped by a 110-meter "International Style" skyscraper, no longer had a siding. Instead, a spur track on the city's edge was provided with a platform, and a station house was built there. Not exactly a very attractive prelude to a visit here, he thinks. On the other hand, the other passengers stretching their legs outside bid Erik a fond farewell, as did the attendants he had met on his journey.

This time, he doesn't hesitate: The next bus stop from the train station is one mile away, so he lets a cab take him into the city. To be more precise, he drives beyond it, to the southern side of the North Saskatchewan River, to the Strathcona district. This is a good six miles from the station, but it was a tip from the Canadians on the train. They had assured him that something was going on in Strathcona, that there were bars and restaurants and also lovely hotels.

Indeed, he is pretty taken When the cab stops in front of his reserved hotel. It's on a long street but lined with stores and eateries. The "Strathcona Farmers Market" is also around the corner, an indoor market that is an attraction around here. He likes this much better. People on the street here don't look like office workers on their way home. His hotel is housed in a square cube on a pedestal slightly twisted to the street front.

They're friendly at check-in, too, and when he strolls down 82nd Avenue a little later and finds a small eatery, Erik finally feels at ease again. "Aha, so there are also nice cities in the prairies" he says to himself.

The neighborhood is still beautiful down the street: along an avenue, he can stroll and admire original little stores with handicrafts. Later in the evening, Erik pays a visit to a lively bar. There, he strikes up a conversation with two Canadian women studying at the University of Alberta, just a few blocks away. They both like living in the city. One of them, with green eyes and a charming smile, has taken a shine to Erik. He realizes that he is literally hanging on her lips.

"The question up here is not 'Winnipeg' or 'Edmonton,'" she tells him, "the question here is 'Calgary' or 'Edmonton.'" These two major cities are only a few hours apart. One, Calgary, is a little closer to the mountains and the town of Banff. The other, Edmonton, is to the north, and the nearest mountain town is Jasper, still a good four hours away. Erik ponders if that could fit Hamburg and Berlin or Bremen, but Calgary and Edmonton seem similar in size. Since the two are studying in this city, they like Edmonton better. "It's a dream here in the summer. If only it wasn't so cold on the streets in the winter," says the Canadian. He's heard the same thing in Minneapolis, he explains. "Minneapolis is on the prairie, too, and it's cold. We're further north, but it's not colder here."

Unfortunately, he doesn't get anywhere with his suggestion to get another round of drinks from the bar. Erik thinks we're not in Reno because many people go there to have fun. We're in a busy big city, and the two tell me they have a chemistry lecture coming up the next day. They've also chosen a complicated field of study, Erik thinks, where they obviously don't spend long nights in a bar during the first half of the week. At least he and they had a friendly chat. But whether he was hanging on their lips or not, they disappeared that night. Erik can only, lonely as he is, go back to his hotel.

The next day, he is standing in what used to be the largest shopping mall in the world, the "West Edmonton Mall". On the one hand, he wanted to look at it after visiting the giant mall in Minneapolis. On the other hand, a shuttle to Jasper in the Rocky Mountains leaves here at a small bus station. The train was fully booked.

There is a streetcar in Edmonton, but it only crosses the city from north to south and does not go to the mall to the west. That's why he spent 50 minutes on two city buses. Erik finds the mall attractive: while in Minneapolis, the stores were arranged in a large circle, in Edmonton, they are long, straight aisles. He enters a bookstore, a nice, big store that seems well-stocked. This time, he skips the fiction, where he usually likes to browse. Instead, he heads for a corner with railroad books. "My goodness, what a selection," Erik mutters to himself. There's everything: travelogues from trips through the US and Canada, illustrated books, guidebooks, and maps with route networks. He thinks he would stock up now if he were a real railfan. Then he would have to leave the store with his travel bag, which would be many pounds heavier. But as it is, he only buys a small volume with the history of the "Canadian.

Erik notes that the mall is getting a bit long in the tooth. The white steel struts on which the glass roofs rest already have flaking paint, partly blind mirrors are attached to the struts, and the light marble floor may also have seen better days. From 1981 to 2004, it is said to have been the largest shopping center in the world – before larger ones were built in Asia. It was created by a wealthy Persian immigrant family in the 1970s. It has other superlatives: Erik walked through the "world's largest parking lot" into the mall, where the "world's largest indoor amusement park" awaited him. It has the "largest roller coaster in the world, with a triple loop and located in an indoor space," as it is somewhat convolutedly called. When it gets cold on the prairie, "Edmontonians" can enjoy the "world's second-largest wave pool.

His mouth remains open when he stands before a glass pane and looks at the wave pool. The bath is indeed huge. His gaze goes from left to right, and the pool seems never-ending. In addition, dozens of water slides look ominously steep. If he hadn't brought all his luggage and the ticket for the shuttle to Denver, he probably would have gone swimming. He notes from the description that the waves are supposed to be 1.5 meters high. They were limited for safety reasons, and the facility could make even higher ones. "Now that's what I call an engineering gem," Erik says.

After a stop at the food court though, and a lunch, Erik looks for the bus to Jasper. Seated in rows of three, the few passengers who have climbed into the vehicle and let the gigantic mall take them to the Rocky Mountains. The beautiful road stretches long, sweeping curves through the prairie until the mountains appear on the horizon. The "skyline" of the Rocky Mountains comes closer, rising from the flat land like a barrier. The mountain peaks are still white.

Further down, the ground is brown and gray. It looks excellent from aboard the little bus. It reminds Erik of how his train once headed toward Denver and the "Rockies," rising like a wall on the horizon at the end of the flat prairie. In Jasper, he wants to stay in a hotel for a few days until the next train with free seats can take him on.

❋

AMELIA FROM EDMONTON

She desperately needed a vacation in the mountains. Amelia felt how worn out she was. Another week or two at her job, and she probably would have collapsed. With her professor, she completed a new study on wildlife in the Rocky Mountains as a biologist. Proofreading alone had consumed days. Amelia was good at what she did, she knew. Compiling the research, writing it out, and putting it into the context of a study suited her. Her professor also knew what he had in her. If only there weren't the jealous colleagues: Amelia felt she had risen much too quickly for them. That's why they were now putting obstacles in her way. One of them, Mark, had been less than subtle about it: When he got to read the study draft, he unerringly brushed against Amelia's findings and doubted their value. Amelia knew Mark would have been too happy to work on this study himself. However, in lengthy discussions with her professor, she convinced him that Mark was wrong and that her research findings were essential to the whole program.

She sighs and leans back. Amelia has boarded a bus to take her to Jasper. The resort in the mountains was just the proper destination for her, where the Athabasca River and the Miette River meet. She had booked a lovely room with a balcony in a nice hotel for a few days and wanted to relax there. She carries her new Nikon with her in her bag, with which she wants to take photos. For this, she plans some hikes through the mountains and intends to visit lakes and gorges. She also has a photo book in her bag. She wants to delve into it to finally hone her technique. Because even though Amelia had a good feel for motifs and image composition, she knew nowhere near enough about apertures, depth of field, and ISO values, she realized. She takes the book and flips through it. As she does so, her thoughts drift. Fortunately, she felt healthy at the moment. Otherwise, the stress of her work as a biologist would have taken a lot more out of her. Amelia has been sick for a long time, suffering from severe diabetes. Her doctor at the Edmonton hospital had once considered an organ transplant. But fortunately, that was not current. The thought worried her, gnawed inside her that she could get a donor organ. But if it would help, maybe it would be worth the risk and effort?

Her illness was less of a problem in her everyday life. But it had become a heavy burden for her three years ago. At that time, she had to go to the hospital, and even worse, Jack, her fiancé at that time, had separated from her. He didn't stand by her under challenging hours but took off when he realized Amelia was chronically ill. Just like that, he had left. She had been very depressed for months and could hardly return to work after the hospitalization; so much had the separation from Jack burdened her. He had become part of her life a year earlier, and after his engagement proposal, Amelia thought she was now steering into a pure love. But what was safe? She sighs, barely able to concentrate on the book. After this depressing experience, Amelia had become very cautious about making new acquaintances. She didn't want to be hurt again in such a way so soon.

She looks around. Amelia thinks the man who has taken the seat next to her looks like a nice person. He seems pretty quaint with his flannel shirt, beard, and wispy hair. Friendly and sincere, that would be what she is looking for. Then she looks at her book again.

Just as her thoughts drift, not to camera tips, but back to her failed engagement, the man approaches her. Amelia is annoyed by his clumsy inquiries about photography. She answers in monosyllables. That she likes to take pictures when she's sitting on a bus with a camera book going out into nature is evident, she says. Extremely taciturn, she brushes off the conversation. "I guess you can see that. Yes, I'm going to

Jasper," she returns to him. Her dismissive manner probably doesn't sit well with him, Amelia sees. The man makes a disappointed face and looks demonstratively out of the other side of the window.

Now, she has a guilty conscience. Was she too monosyllabic, she wonders? Was she being mean to him now? But she actually likes him. I hope I haven't scared him off, she thinks. She has always reacted very reservedly when men approach her since the engagement. For now, this man with the beard seems to have had enough of her. But if they both go to Jasper, he'll stay there, too. And maybe she'll have a chance to see him again? As she looks out the other side of the windows, she muses that she would be glad to.

ERIK GOES TO JASPER

Erik is looking forward to coming to Jasper now. After his drive through cold big cities, he wants to visit a vacation spot. On the shuttle, a woman across from him catches Erik's eye. She is engrossed in a book about photography, he realizes. He puts on a smile. She looks nice: She may be in her mid-30s and has brown, long hair. She wears reading glasses, which give her an intellectual look. At first, she doesn't pay attention to him, then she looks back. She seems slightly puzzled, grins briefly, and then delves back into her book. Erik tries to pull himself together and speaks to her.

"You're probably going to the mountains to take pictures, right?"

She doesn't look up. "Yeah, I guess that's the way it is. I'm taking pictures and going to Jasper."

"Are you from Edmonton?"

"Yes, yes. Just like the bus from Edmonton." She continues to read the book, turning a page, wholly engrossed in the text.

"I'm sure there are beautiful motifs in the mountains," says Erik - well aware that these are pretty lame sayings he puts on. Accordingly, they don't have any results. But that's also difficult, he thinks.

"We'll see," it comes back monosyllabically.

He capitulates. This woman clearly doesn't want to talk to him, even though they're both on the same bus going to Jasper. Erik thinks she's plenty buttoned up. No, actually, he thinks she's arrogant when she won't even look up to exchange a few words with him. Or does he make such a dull impression on her? Erik sighs. She isn't as lovely as she seemed to him at first glance.

He thinks to himself, what the heck, and looks out the window on the other side at the mountain world. Then he leafs through the brochures that are on display on the bus. At last, he feels like a "harmless tourist," not just passing through. There is, for example, an offer from the bus operator: A brochure advertises a cable car and a shuttle there. But it only runs in the summer season, not in March. So he has to skip the pleasure of going up the 2263-meter-high mountain "The Whistlers." There are other attractions. Among other things, an indoor swimming pool, which is supposed to have a thermal pool. Such a pool with hot water would be something for him. Among other things, there's "Maligne Lake", where you can take boat trips. Every attraction that is open now is really an attraction. Those that are only open at the height of summer have to rely on streams of visitors - and could be a "tourist trap".

MALIGNE CANYON

"Do you want to share a cab?" the young woman asks him the following day as he stands outside the hotel, perusing a board advertising attraction.

Erik is surprised: Isn't that the brown-haired woman who sat next to him on the bus yesterday? The one who seemed so arrogant that she didn't give him a glance? And she's talking to him now?

"Share a cab? Do we both have the same destination?"

"Well, maybe." She smiles at him. Suddenly, she seems pretty sympathetic. "I've been looking at what there is to do in Jasper. Since the gondola up the mountain is closed, you and I might want to go to the gorge."

Erik has to grin. "That's perceptive of you. Do you want to take pictures there?"

"Ah yes, you were asking about that yesterday," she says, looking at Erik's first attempt to strike up a conversation with her.

"Your book was not to be missed."

"Yes, I actually want to take pictures there. That's my hobby," she says, holding up her valuable camera, which is housed in a leather case.

"We could both go to the gorge together, of course," Erik suggests. "All right, I was really aiming for the same goal."

"And if we ride together, not only do we save something, but we don't run the risk of getting lost."

"How are we supposed to get lost here?"

"Not if we take care of each other," she adds - and has to laugh.

"It's a deal. We'll share a cab, drive to the gorge together, and make sure we don't get lost."

"There's one more thing: You now have the responsibility of negotiating a good price."

That's fun, Erik thinks. But he doesn't want to let her off the hook that quickly. "The price is our joint business, after all. As good as you talk, don't you think it would be better if you negotiated?"

"Oh no, negotiating prices, that's a typical guy thing. That's not my part of our trip together. I care for the sights and ensure we don't get lost. And you take care of business."

That was snappy. She just made up the division of labor like that. "Wait a minute, who says I don't want to pick out the sights, too?"

"I can say that for sure: Because you're obviously not from Canada. I can already hear that in your accent. So you're a tourist. Maybe from overseas?"

"Hit. I'm from Germany, and I'm traveling through Canada."

"So you need someone to show you the sights. I could possibly take care of that. You just have to take care of business."

"I don't really want to be a typical tourist. But our deal is good. You've set that up beautifully."

Now, a light red shadow runs across her face. They both quickly bump into a funny conversation, and now they're goading each other. She slips out an "I can thread a lot of other things," then bursts out laughing. "I'm sure you can," is his lame response to her remark. Erik smiles, thinking that she seems likable after all. "I like the way you take things head-on."

"Well, you're no slouch yourself."

There is a cab behind the two of them. He negotiates a price with the driver to take them to the gorge. If he were honest, the driver could actually have named any price he would be willing to pay. The main thing is that he looks smart in front of the nice

Canadian woman, Erik thinks. Now, just keep the thrifty tourist from hanging out.

They both sit down in the back seat. Erik thinks it's nicer that way than if one of them rides in the front and they can't talk at all. Actually, Erik believes that when two people get into a cab, they should always sit in the back.

"But now you have to tell me what you're doing here," says the Canadian.

"Right now, I'm doing the same thing you're doing: taking a cab to the gorge ..."

"... which is supposed to be one of the great sights here ..."

"... At least when the cable car is closed."

"And what else do you do?"

"I'm going across North America by rail."

"Really? Do you have too much time on your hands?" She has to laugh.

"It's more cumbersome to vacation like this than I had previously thought. But it's fun. You get to meet interesting people ..."

"... with whom you can then share a cab. Even if this is involuntary."

"Exactly. Involuntary, that is. Of course," says Erik. Was that another little backpedal now? He continues the conversation and reports that his trip was enjoyable: from Seattle to Minneapolis and now on the way back.

So he heads for the canyon with Amelia from Edmonton. After they get out, they start walking into the canyon. The paths there lead along between steep rocks, and even some bridges lead over the deep crevasses. During the hike, they share stories of their lives and travels. Amelia works as a biologist in Edmonton. She spends most of her time in her office at the university, sometimes in the lab. But rarely enough, she goes on field trips, such as to the Canadian mountains. She also once took a trip on a research vessel out of Vancouver, where they studied marine fauna. "I wish that was a bigger part of my job," she notes with a sigh.

The passion with which she talks about her job at the university is something you don't often find in scientists, Erik thinks. But then she's a bit more buttoned-up and monosyllabic again – and seems almost as arrogant as she did on the bus. Yet, the atmosphere is cheerful, and they are surrounded by cool, fresh mountain air, Erik thinks. They enjoy the view through the forest of the canyon and the surrounding peaks.

After the tour, they head for the nearby restaurant, the Wilderness Kitchen, at the entrance to the gorge. "We deserve a reward, don't we?" says Amelia. Oops, thinks Erik, now we're going to have another meal? A nice opportunity. The "Kitchen" serves hearty dishes which suit the surroundings. Amelia orders the crispy chicken, and Erik goes for the smoked pulled pork.

"Sounds like a good choice. I could have bet you'd order the burger," she laughs. "Preferably with fries as a side order and ketchup."

"What makes you think that?" he asks.

"You're big and strong, so you could use a burger."

"I confess: I was wondering if you'd order the veggie roast, the veggie".

"Oh yeah? Well, just because I'm a biologist doesn't mean we're all vegetarians. Besides, our food does fit in with a Wilderness Kitchen. You with the pulled pork and me with the chicken."

The food is indeed good. Amelia cuts off a piece of chicken and hands it to him. "You must try this." Indeed, he is not a poultry fan, but this one tastes good. He gives her some of his pulled pork on her plate. "The sauce is wonderful."

Amelia's gaze goes through the window to the vast mountain world. "As a biologist, I always find it very calming to look out into the world around us," she says. "Funny, I just remembered a trip we took when we were kids." She's thawed out a bit now, Erik thinks.

"My dad was always an explorer on vacation. One day, we got on a train in Edmonton and went to Vancouver." She reports that her father is kind-hearted, perhaps too kind-hearted at times, as he can't hurt anyone. That he had a love of nature. He taught me a sense of fascination with the world around us. He often spoke of the most intricate details of plants and animals and how there is hidden beauty in every nook and cranny."

Sometimes, she can't get enough of the picturesque landscapes of the Rocky Mountains. That's why she has her camera with her to capture the moments. "My father told me stories of his adventures back in the day. I think that must have been the moment I thought about becoming a biologist. I wanted to spend my life unlocking mysteries of the natural world." One evening, he said, they both went for a hike on the Pacific Ocean beach in Vancouver, and the sun was just setting on the horizon. "That's when he said to me that I needed to embrace my emotional side as well as my scientific side."

"That was very profound." Amelia seems to know a lot about herself, he thinks.

"Well, I think I developed a certain passion for nature." That's why, she says, she studied biology, took a job at the university, and, bit by bit, built up a reputation in her field. "Sitting here like this, I must think about that again, too. Why I became what I am." A smile creeps onto her face as Amelia sits by the window, lost in her memories.

As a biologist, climate change is one of the issues Amelia considers essential. She tries to do a few things for climate protection in her everyday life, including using public transport more than her car and coming to Jasper by bus. On the other hand, Erik is a bit cooler on the subject. Although, yes, he does like to take the train. But so far, he's told himself: so many people are concerned with climate change. He doesn't want to "get attached" to it but rather devote himself to issues that shouldn't be allowed to fall by the wayside. For example, he considers social justice to be more critical than detached debates.

"How can we be sure that climate change is not simply a natural cycle? Is it really as urgent as everyone says it is?"

Amelia leans back in her chair and thinks about Erik's argument. "You know, Erik, it's true that the Earth has experienced natural cycles throughout its existence. But what we're experiencing now is something unprecedented. The pace of change far exceeds what nature has prepared for, and it's happening because of human activity. We are responsible for doing something about it for the environment and future generations that will inherit this planet."

Erik sighs because he has often heard such general arguments. But his skepticism subsides a bit when this Canadian woman here in the mountains tells him. "It's easy to dismiss climate change when it doesn't directly affect our lives. I'll admit that. But there are just a lot of other pressing issues. Sometimes it's social justice versus climate change."

"These are both important issues that should not be pitted against each other," Amelia says.

"Yes, it sounds easy. Example: If people are to install expensive, new heating systems in their homes to reduce CO_2 emissions, it costs so much that many can't afford it."

"Then you have to help them. But you can't slacken your efforts because of that."

"No, you can't. You're right about that. I have to admit, you got me thinking."

"That's all I'm asking, Erik. It's not about winning debates; it's about creating dialogue and inspiring change. And if I look at how you travel, at least with the trains, you're already doing that."

Erik thinks she seems to have passion and suspects their opinions differ.

After dinner, they drink another glass and discuss further the view of the mountains. Then they have a cab called, drive back to Jasper, and move back into their hotel rooms.

Erik sits in the room with the sloping roof and the mullioned window in the armchair. The clouds are very high in the evening sky. What was that about the trip to the gorge? He thinks that he didn't really like sharing the cab in the first place. With the woman from the bus, to boot. Would he instead have done the hike through the gorge alone? No, that's not true. He wanted to travel, not to hike alone, but to meet interesting people. Amelia seems like an exciting person, after all. He thinks about how they sat in the pub: Her long hair fell to her shoulders, and her gray-blue eyes looked at him vividly. The long brown hair, Erik remembers, didn't he already find that attractive in Candice?

But Amelia is different. He listens to her spellbound as she talks about her work and life in Canada. Hasn't she chosen the same destination as him, Jasper? For her, it may be a short trip out of her city, while for him, it's to a stop on a journey through a whole other world. Is there more at play than an afternoon hike together? No, or maybe there is? After all, they were both having a great time. They have the same sense of humor. She had a nice laugh. Even when Erik had to search a little for the right words in English. But then, she was a bit monosyllabic at times. Erik believes that Amelia needs to trust when she meets someone. He hasn't entirely managed that yet.

He realizes that he is thinking a lot about what Amelia is thinking. Even though the afternoon in the gorge was beautiful, she made no effort to continue the meeting. She said goodbye formally, almost a little coolly again, and disappeared.

Pancakes pile up on his plate the next morning, maple syrup flowing over them. Erik did as the other guests in the breakfast room and piled some scrambled eggs and bacon next to them. Then he sits by the window and looks out onto the street. There is no sign of Amelia. So he eats his breakfast alone, reading a newspaper for a while. These pancakes taste delicious, he thinks, and he tries to ignore the calories that come with such a pancake.

Thereafter, he walks through the town. The large "Jasper Station" is right under his nose. You can get on two trains: The Canadian, which goes to Toronto or Vancouver. Or one goes to Prince Rupert in the north of British Columbia. The train also has beautiful silver steel carriages with blue ribbons under the windows. It would be 720 miles to the northwest of Jasper. But like the train to Vancouver, this one only runs three times a week – so today, nothing is going on at the beautiful station, with its gray stones and its roof of green-painted wood. Freight trains roll through the place. Some passenger cars are behind the station, but they are not running. The platform is deserted.

There is no sign of Amelia in town either. In the afternoon, he sets off for the "Aquatic Center," the swimming pool located a few streets behind the hotel. He walks past well-kept front gardens and villas that fit perfectly into the Canadian mountain world: Some are made of dark wood, others of stone. All have roofs of shingles. This is a pleasant town to live in, he thinks. Since Edmonton, he has come to like Canada. A visit to the swimming pool also lifts his spirits: There, he can swim decent laps in the hall and visit a vast "hot tub," that is, a hot pool.

You're not allowed to submerge your head in it, by the way, for whatever reason. When Erik does it briefly, the lifeguard nastily admonishes him. So be it. He returns to the hotel, then goes out again in the evening to eat, yet remains alone all day. He notices this when he sits in a lonely way at a table in a restaurant. When he finally goes to sleep, he wonders what has become of Amelia from Edmonton: he has not discovered any trace of her all day.

"Oops, so many pancakes on the plate? You'd better think about the carbohydrates," a voice says to him the following day as he pours the maple syrup over the batter.

Amelia stands in front of his table and smiles. Erik is happy to see her again. Then she wasn't a figment of some lonely traveler's imagination in the Rocky Mountains, he says to himself.

"Well, your plate doesn't look bad either," he replies. "I see sausage, bacon, and more meat. And a grilled tomato."

"Yes, there you see it: plenty of proteins. That's kind of the diet I'm on, too," Amelia replies. "May I join you, pancake lover?"

"I'd love to. I wondered if you were still here after not seeing you all day."

"I was up early and went into the forest on a photo safari. But I didn't see you either."

Could it be that they missed each other? "Now, don't tell me you missed me?" asks Amelia.

"Well, maybe just a little? Perhaps not," he replies. "Although, hadn't we decided to look out for each other before we visited the gorge?"

She seems to like that. A happy smile forms on her face. "That would be great. No, that didn't just slip out."

He makes a small advance. "I'll be happy to take care of you today, even if you don't do it with me."

"That's not true at all. I'll take care of you. Oh, I'll get right on that. Better put those pancakes away."

"Wouldn't you like to try one?" He holds out the plate of pancakes, dripping with syrup, to her.

"No, don't do that. I ... I can't eat something like that."

"Okay, I'll put them away. And if it's better ... I'll get some egg now, too."

"Erik, I'd better tell you right now so you won't be surprised. I have diabetes, and I take insulin with every meal."

"Oh, Amelia. But that...", Erik doesn't even know what to say. "Many people have that these days, don't they?"

"Yes, that's right. I just have it a little harder and have to inject more. But that doesn't mean anything. Just that I prefer to leave pancakes like that."

An hour later, they are both walking through the town. Erik doesn't want to make a trip to an attraction at all. After just one day, he realizes that he has missed Amelia's company. She is gaining more confidence. She has just told him to his face that she is diabetic. That was pretty frank. He thinks nothing more of her illness; he has also experienced colleagues in the newsroom who suffer from diabetes.

They take a long walk through the town and the neighboring woods. "Sometimes I get lonely, too," she confesses. "It's not that great to go on a photo safari alone in the forest." To this, she smiles.

Later, Amelia talks about her family. Her father works for a public utility company in Edmonton. The company's headquarters are located in the city. "I know train travel in Canada relatively well, by the way," she tells Erik. When she was a student, her father was able to arrange a job through an acquaintance in Toronto. For that, she was grateful to him. "I would rather not stand at a cash register or serve in a café. Although I did actually end up doing something similar."

Amelia worked as an "On Train Service Attendant" for VIA Rail in the sleeping cars. She rode the trains between Edmonton and Toronto, serving passengers and caring for them in the sleeping cars. "That was billed at $24 Canadian an hour, which was pretty good pay," Amelia said. He wonders if she liked it. "You were constantly on the move. You traveled. And you did it in pleasant company: the travelers were actually all sophisticated. Many older Canadians were among them, but also younger people from all over the world. The colleagues were quite nice. Oh, and there was accommodation in a small train compartment on the long journeys and meals included."

Did the job have special requirements? "They wanted you to be friendly all the time, of course. You actually had to smile all the time." Amelia's face turns into a broad grin, which Erik thinks looks a bit fake, especially since he had seen her genuine smile a few times before. But you would surely be satisfied with the grimace if you didn't know it. "You had to be able to get this, lift loads up to 23 kilos." Maintaining the spirit of officially bilingual Canada, she also had to prove that she spoke good French in addition to English.

If she hadn't wanted to be a biologist, she thinks back, she might have even gotten stuck with the railroad. "That would have been quite fun." But that's just how it stayed, with a student job she did during semester breaks when summer crowds on the trains were hefty. "Besides, the way up was blocked: Once you're in as a service attendant, you tend to stick with it. He's unlikely to move up to administration in Toronto." Erik can imagine: There appears to be an invisible barrier separating service personnel on the trains from the administration and the railroad's technical staff. The way it is with any large organization, really. Even the ship's personnel rarely move up into administration in a shipping company. But it would not be out of the question. For Amelia, however, "VIA Rail Canada" was just a student job, but now she knew what it was like behind the scenes.

When they arrive at the hotel in the afternoon, Erik wants to spend more time with her. He asks her if she would like to have a drink with him in the evening – and she says yes. He realizes that the meeting makes him nervous when he gets to his room. Furthermore, he says to himself, "It seems obvious to go out for a drink when you're staying at the same hotel and have spent the afternoon together – right?" Then Erik picks out a passable shirt at length from his rumpled Minneapolis travel wardrobe. He opens the door to the small bathroom. He then tries to smooth the shirt: First, he dampens it, then blow-dries it. This has worked every time so far, and this time, the trick doesn't let him down either.

The hotel bar looks like an exclusively furnished, rustic club. When Amelia comes down the stairs, he is amazed: she is wearing a dark evening dress. It's not exclusive, but it's still very stylish. My goodness, he thinks, she looks great. It's good he has a pressed shirt. They sit in the bar in two wing chairs and order long drinks. They're well-poured, and Erik quickly realizes it's going to his head. Not only that, but they talk even more than they did in the afternoon. Jazz music plays softly in the bar. Erik feels that she literally attracts him. He can't take his eyes off her, and her voice sounds wonderful in his ears. Suddenly, she puts her hand on his and looks him in the eyes. "I feel something," she says softly. Wow, Erik thinks, now she's told it. "Me too, I find you attractive," he still brings out. They hold hands, but then a force pulls them both forward like a magnet - and they kiss long.

They stand up. Erik touches her hand. Then they walk up the stairs and come to his tiny hotel room. He closes the door.

Amelia is waiting in the dark room in front of the bed - and they are already falling over each other. It happens quickly: Erik doesn't think about what he's doing for a second. She seems to feel the same way. There is a heat between them that seems to literally glow. Their lips find each other, and their hands explore each other's bodies. Before they know it, they end up on the bed. He feels her growing lustful with each breath, and he, too, can barely contain his excitement. Amelia moans loudly.

Erik kisses her neck. She squirms as he gently touches her and runs his hands over her body. He feels her hands on his back and enjoys her touch. That's when their bodies melt into each other. He realizes they will both soon reach ecstasy, but he can't grasp many thoughts. Finally, the climax is a wild rush of pleasure. They sink back, exhausted, between the ransacked sheets on the bed. Deep inside, they feel a deep peace.

Amelia and Erik sit on the bed half the night. She has opened the transom window, and although they are naked on the mattress, they feel hot. Moonlight shines in from outside. The pale pane is above the high mountains, shining on the tracks and the train station his window looks out on. Quietly, they talk to each other, funny things, and then they laugh again. Finally, Amelia gets up, throws something over, and says, "I'll be right back." She sneaks out of the room. A minute later, she's back in the doorway, holding a bottle of wine. "It's cold. I stored it on the balcony," she says. They open the white wine, pour themselves two glasses, and toast. "Me, I'm not usually so quick," she says, a little embarrassed.

"Believe me, neither do I." Erik realizes that Amelia and he share the same feelings. He feels enchanted. Amelia touches him deeply at night, in the Canadian Rockies, in this small hotel room, with the open window letting in the cool mountain air. He lies with her in a rumpled bed, the empty bottle of wine beside it.

The first thought in his room the next morning doesn't please him: Is the train supposed to take him away from here this time, too? Should a timetable, as it were, decide his fate? He turns on his side and looks into Amelia's beautiful, sleepy face. She opens her eyes and smiles. "Where did I end up here? In the room of a visitor from overseas? What am I doing here?"

"Let's say: You liked it so much here in my room that you didn't want to return to your own. I admit: I also really wanted you to stay here."

She smiles again. No trace of thoughts like "the morning after" is unspoken in the room. There is a loving togetherness.

But the following "Canadian" to Vancouver is waiting for Erik. Amelia must also return to Edmonton because her short mountain vacation is over. At 9:30 a.m., the train is ready to leave in front of the station, and Amelia and Erik must say good-bye. They do so warmly and lovingly. For a brief second, Erik thinks back to the farewell in Montana, but then he and Amelia kiss each other long and passionately.

"Take care. I hope to see you again," Erik says.

"We will. I think we will," Amelia replies.

He climbs up the steps into the car as the train is almost leaving. The door closes, and he quickly goes to the next window. He looks out onto the platform, where Amelia is standing and waving. He throws her a kiss - which she returns. Then, the "Canadian" rolls out of the Jasper station.

THE TRAIN TO VANCOUVER

Erik looks for his seat in the coach car because there is no comfortable compartment with a bed in this section. But he doesn't care after his time with Amelia. He can also stretch out like this and wander through the train. The ride with the "Canadian" is one of the most spectacular train rides in North America and leads through breathtaking scenery. Erik thinks the route from Jasper to Kamloops is awe-inspiring because the track runs right through the Rocky Mountains. Shortly after Jasper, the stunning landscape begins, with high peaks, deep valleys, and views of glittering rivers and lakes. The ride to Kamloops takes eight hours and offers a wealth of views - scenically, Erik won't be able to forget the trip.

He looks pensively out of the window. "Was it a mistake to travel on to Vancouver?" he thinks. Well, he had already asked himself that question in Montana. But something had happened meanwhile. The attraction that was building between Amelia and him had led them to each other. Wouldn't there be many more important reasons to still stay in Jasper?

On the other hand, Amelia wanted to go back to her hometown. But couldn't he have thrown his plans out the window? Railroad through the Rocky Mountains, an expensive ticket to Vancouver - he could have easily gone the other way and flown to Vancouver later. However, he didn't change his plans. Would Amelia even have liked him to follow her? Sure, this kind of thing does well in a Hollywood movie, but real life is just more complicated, Erik notes. It's sometimes very complex, and the script isn't written. Were he and Amelia just experiencing a vacation acquaintance, already forgotten the moment she boarded the shuttle bus back to Edmonton? But she didn't give the impression of taking acquaintances fleetingly and casually. Not at all. She might be like him in that respect, Erik thinks. What was that sentence: "We'll see each other again, we will." She seemed very sure of that. Does she have clairvoyant abilities? Or does she see something he hasn't seen yet? In any case, she appears to be an extraordinary person. Possibly because they are both from the north. He doesn't know, he thinks, sighing slightly. But he will find out.

While Erik is indulging his thoughts, the person sitting next to him, a young student, starts chatting. He's getting chattier and chattier, Erik realizes after a few minutes. He discusses his school, Canada, university, sports clubs, family, and siblings. His stories degenerate into monologues. He didn't know there were such talkative Canadians. But let him, he shuts down. The student is on his way from Edmonton to Kamloops, where he gets off the train at about 6:30 p.m.

Now Erik is happy to take his rest, especially since the seat remains empty. A last night on board in North America follows. The sun sinks behind the mountains, and the train picks up speed again, while he puts the chair back and makes himself comfortable as best he can. Erik notes that the "coach" class works once you're satisfied with pillows and blankets. He chews on a sandwich from the cafeteria, which has to serve as dinner instead of a sumptuous meal in the dining car. The train moves slowly through the canyons, but this has the advantage of quiet travel. The wild night in Jasper that he spent with Amelia, now take their toll: Erik falls quickly asleep.

He wakes up early in the morning as the train has left the mountains and is rolling through the flat land near the coast. The train has become noticeably faster and louder. Outside, you no longer see lonely valleys, but houses, towns, roads, and railroad crossings pass by. Erik thinks the "Canadian" wants to really step on the gas again. At nine o'clock, with an hour delay, the train arrives at the "Pacific Central Station". This large station has long-covered platforms south of the city center. Not only does the "Canadian" depart, but trains to the USA also leave from here. This brings life into the station concourse, through which a long stream of travelers pass who have left the long-distance train.

Many visitors rave about Vancouver, Erik thinks. They are right to do so. After the drive through the prairies, through places like Winnipeg, he is happy to be back in a fascinating big city. Especially since he has again treated himself to a feudal hotel for the last two nights before the return flight. That was a tip: The receptionist in Jasper asked him about his travel plans. She had called a friend who worked at the "Hyatt" in Vancouver to reserve a nice room.

That was hospitable of her. So, Canada can be very welcoming. He is amazed when he opens the door to his room on one of the highest floors, looks out onto a glass front, and sees a panoramic view of the city. This feels very different from Winnipeg, Erik notes. No, loneliness isn't gnawing at him here.

Erik lets himself drift through Vancouver, again without a guidebook. Following a tip from the receptionist, he heads for the "Gastown" neighborhood, which is quite touristy in the front part but has fascinating streets and stores further east. But he is even more taken with Granville Island, an island in False Creek, in a bay south of the city. A large bridge leads there. There, Erik walks past galleries through a market hall, the "Granville Public Market," with many merchants and displays: fruits and vegetables in all shapes, varieties, and colors. Erik likes the fresh mood this spreads on this somewhat gray March day. There are also beautiful marinas. What he likes about the island is that it's not quite as made up as other neighborhoods in Vancouver. The houses are partly renovated, partly brightly painted, and partly need some repair.

He doesn't have much time to marvel at Vancouver's sights. But his stay was enough to get a feel for the city. The place is cosmopolitan, Erik finds, and also very lively. It would certainly be worth coming back. Although, actually, he'd rather travel to Edmonton.

Then, he has to hit the road. Since his work now calls him

back to Germany, he has to take the plane. He rides the subway from the center to the airport with its new "Canada Line". After he can finally board, he finds that the flight promises to be quite pleasant: the plane is hardly booked, and there is room everywhere in the rows of seats. He stretches out. Erik dreams of the Rocky Mountains, the prairies, the trains, and especially of Amelia from Edmonton. What are her plans? She seemed to have some. Because as she had said: We will meet again.

CHAPTER 4

The Coast Starlight and the Pacific Surfliner

Edmonton, This year, in September

"I think I'm in love," Amelia says.

I was not prepared at all for this opening of my sister. Amelia surprised me. On the other hand, when she said something so seriously, she was firmly convinced of it.

"Well, that's great. Who is it?"

"His name is Erik, and he's from Germany, from a city called Hamburg."

"Oh, that's a long way."

"Well, if it was easy, maybe I wouldn't have fallen in love."

"That can be. Amelia, you were always so picky," I tell my sister. "You're a real biologist. You like to get to the bottom of things, don't you?"

"Yes, but even though I was picky, this bust happened to me three years ago. My engagement fell apart. After that, I was really fed up with all the love stories. I thought before that, soon I'll be like you and your wife and have a family."

"You couldn't help it. What was that guy thinking, proposing to you first, then changing his mind, and then moving away? Nobody treats my sister like that! But let's not talk about the past. How did you meet this Erik?"

"I was in Jasper two weeks ago, remember? He was on the same bus as me. At first, I thought he was a blowhard. He asked me about my camera."

"Does that already mark a blowhard?", I ask her, thinking about how cautious and reserved Amelia has become around men since their broken engagement.

"No, and he wasn't one. We shared a cab and went to a gorge. Then we walked all day. Finally, we, well, spent the night together. He seems to be very deep and serious."

That Amelia told me this was not so unusual. We discuss many details of our lives, including tonight, when I visit her in her Strathcona apartment. Amelia likes living here, and I also like this neighborhood near the University of Edmonton. "I wish you very much that he is serious. Otherwise, he will have to deal with me."

"You should have seen his face. When I said goodbye, I told him, 'We'll see each other again. The sun literally rose in his eyes. That's when I thought, too: I think I love him."

"But tell me, don't you think he's very far away?"

"Yes, I guess you're right, that's him. He took a vacation in North America and traveled across the country on trains. All by himself. I think he's looking. I think I might be just the one he's looking for, though."

"How are things between you now?"

"Imagine we talk on the phone every other night. It's harder for him than for me. Because of the time difference, he usually calls when it's the middle of the night in Europe. But we also write emails and send each other photos. There must be a way for both of us."

"I wish you that." I couldn't help but think that Amelia, unlike me, had been unlucky with love so far. I was living with my childhood sweetheart, now my wife, whom I had met in high school. We are happy, as are our parents. They must have done a lot right, too. Yet our father has more time on his hands since his retirement, while our mother still works as an art historian. But they manage. They seem to love each other very much.

"But don't tell our parents yet. I want to see what can develop from it first," says Amelia.

"Of course not." I mean, thinking that I haven't seen her so content in a long time. Amelia also felt constricted in our family. There were reasons for that. My parents, and I probably too, tended to want to protect her. We didn't realize until late that this had become too much for her. That's why she sometimes holds back now, at least towards our parents.

I notice that there is something very fulfilled about her. "In any case, you should see each other again, right?"

"Yes, we have to. And as soon as possible. But until then, all we have is the phone and video chat."

ERIK IN HAMBURG

This year, in September

Thoughts of Canada and Amelia have helped Erik get over the worst in Germany. But he finds his professional situation particularly hard to bear. The magazine's situation is terrible: The large advertising sections continue to melt away, and the situation is becoming more critical. He thinks: Isn't it strange how his gaze turns to another country, continent, and person when things are going downhill at home? As if one suspects that disaster is coming and tries to turn the wheel and take a different course to escape the catastrophe.

Fears of job cuts are rife at the publishing house. Erik and his colleagues hardly know how to plan the significant editions anyway. The editor-in-chief tries almost heroically to fight for every story and every picture that has to be purchased. He struggles for every job that the publisher wants to cut. But publishing director "Cookie Monster" only has the online edition in mind, the fast and colorful news. He's all about selling online subscriptions. The magazine, actually the brand's drawing card, seems indifferent to him and on the hit list. "If you don't do a better job as editors soon, we can close the store down altogether," he throws at the editor-in-chief. Erik notices something else: It's strange when hardship doesn't weld people together, as it used to in the editorial department, but when this hardship drives a wedge between them all - which is precisely what the publishing director is after.

He actually likes to start at work. But after just a few days, Erik already feels like a foreign body in this environment that is poised for doom. Initially, he still made the mistake of telling about the adventures of his train journey in North America.

Most importantly, he told Andrea he took an extensive trip through the U.S. and Canada and fell in love with a Canadian woman. Why does he do this? Because he wants to share. Because he thinks she might be interested in how he fared. But she listens to his story, nodding as they sit together in the newsroom lounge, but doesn't say much. What does he expect? After all, she doesn't tell him anything about her love affairs, which still seem to exist.

Erik feels pretty stupid later on. Without any need, he gave a colleague and one with whom he was in a relationship an insight into his life. He hadn't considered that Andrea didn't see him as a friend at all but as a competitor. One can say, from the outside, that Erik is gullible. He himself was to realize this only much later.

His other colleagues are unhappy about his stories, even though they work at a travel magazine. Nor does it occur to anyone that Erik could make a report out of his experiences. They now buy them cheaply from freelance writers. As a "desk editor," it's not his job to write anything himself. Moreover, such personal stories don't fit with the job's overworked, overwrought doom and gloom. Colleagues who used to work together hand in hand are no longer as friendly in their dealings. There is no collegial climate because they are all under intense pressure.

Here, twelve-hour days in the office have now become the rule. The editor-in-chief may love nothing more than the magazine, the staff, and the editorial team. Still, he can't show this love because the "Cookie Monster" doesn't give him a chance. The austerity drive continues. The core of the problem remains: Subscribers are canceling faster than new ones can be won for the online edition, while advertising pages are declining.

Erik realizes that he wants to return to North America. He may even have to. He may be able to arrange it to get the next vacation in September.

Meanwhile, he has decided not to tell anyone what he is up to. He doesn't want them to know. Because the most important reason for him to return as quickly as possible is, of course, Amelia. He really wants to see her again. Above all, he doesn't want to make the mistake of waiting too long again. After all, there was one thing in favor of his plan: If it was possible to extend the working hours endlessly and also to attempt to save personnel, it was not possible to reduce the vacation days - as much as the "Cookie Monster" would like to do that. Even if the number of his days melts, he still has something saved. Because

Erik has had little opportunity to spend money during his dreary, hard-working life, his coffers are relatively well-filled.

With slightly shaky fingers, he redialed her long phone number late in the evening. He longed for the sound of her voice and wanted to plan his next trip. They talked a lot on the phone, wrote emails and even letters. So it's about time. When the ringing doesn't stop, his heart pounds excitedly. Finally, she picks up.

"Hey, Amelia. It's me," Erik says, and his voice probably betrays the hint of excitement.

"I was hoping you would call today. I've missed you like crazy."

"I missed you, too," Erik replies, a smile spreading across his face. "I can't wait to see you again."

"Neither do I," she says in faraway Canada. Her voice softens. "As I've come to know you, could it be that you already have a plan for this?"

"Yes, you've combined that clearly again. Look, we'll meet at your place in Canada. How about we take a little vacation?"

"I think it's great," she says, now her excitement is evident. "When did you think of this?"

"Well, I've been tinkering with the idea for a while. Then, I looked at the possibilities. I might get a vacation soon. What do you think, maybe we'd like to take a trip together, say to the West Coast?"

"That sounds perfect," she replies. "I'll get it done, I think. I'm going to make this work. Because you know, we're going to see each other again. I can't wait for that."

They spend the next hour on the phone, discussing their memories of Jasper and honing their plans.

"You know climate change is an important issue for me," Amelia says. "I also checked in a CO_2 calculator once: Your trip from Hamburg to Vancouver will consume 1.3 tons of CO_2."

"Yes, these transcontinental flights produce significant carbon dioxide," Erik acknowledges. "But what other way would there be for us to see each other again? We'd both have to be able to sail across the ocean."

"Not a chance. I admit sometimes it's not easy to be a staunch climate change activist, even as a biologist. You just have to come here."

After they say goodbye, Erik hangs up the phone with a smile. The thought of seeing Amelia again fills him with a feeling of happiness.

REUNION IN VANCOUVER

Erik is standing at the airport in Vancouver, in front of the reception building with its steel and glass construction. Near him are three artfully crafted Native American totem poles, carved from wood and colorfully painted, surrounded by a flower bed and lawn. This is part of the small airport park just outside the arrivals terminal. Fortunately, he has just completed a Canadian immigration, which was decidedly friendly - unlike back before in Winnipeg.

Erik remembers how the great travel writer Paul Theroux criticized in his book "The Deep South," which he had read on the flight, that many works of travel literature begin in the middle, on the spot. "I opened the windows of my room, took a deep breath, and enjoyed the view of the sea and the little fishing boats bobbing on it," something like that. That's undoubtedly true. Except, Erik thinks, as he looks at the totem pole: What to write about a transcontinental flight from Europe to North America?

Perhaps the journey by bus to the airport in Hamburg? But what about the twelve to fourteen-hour stay in a pressurized cabin at an altitude of ten thousand meters? Is that such an experience that it would be worth writing a chapter about it? The flight via Frankfurt was one hour longer than via Amsterdam. The further West you go, the shorter the distance across the North Atlantic. One hour can make much difference on such a long-haul flight in economy class. London is actually the suitable transfer airport from Hamburg to North America. But this time, he had a Lufthansa ticket. It didn't mean well for him. Neither his seat neighbor, a student who proudly showed him her new iPhone the whole time, could make it more bearable for him, nor the middle seat in a row.

Well, Erik is just not Paul Theroux. If he were the travel writer, he would have taken four months for his train journeys through North America and would have traveled through this country full of freedom. But anyone trapped in a "daytime" job and has to pursue "dependent employment," has to stick to his vacation times.

During the somewhat sad time in Hamburg, however, Erik stayed connected with more people in North America: There were Eline and Drake from Aspen, Colorado. They sent each other some emails with photos, and he told them about his experiences in Jasper. But there was also Candice, of course. How the relationship with her had evolved into a "long-distance friendship" that wasn't planned; that was the way of things. Must that make him sad, he wondered? It did indeed make him a little bittersweet. But it remained the way they had probably wanted it. And there was one thing he couldn't forget: If he had stayed in Montana, he wouldn't have traveled to Minneapolis and later to Jasper. Then, he would not have met Amelia.

Amelia and Candice are two entirely different souls who have attracted his attention in their own way. Amelia is the woman he fell deeply in love with. Her presence alone could ignite a fire in him. Her passion for nature fascinated him, and they could discuss the wonders of life. Furthermore, her seriousness and dedication made her even more fascinating to Erik. Her brown hair and striking blue-gray eyes added to her appeal and made her undeniably attractive.

Candice, on the other hand, is a friend. A woman Erik enjoyed spending time with, but that's all she was. She had a certain charm and liveliness that made every encounter with her exciting. Erik couldn't deny the thrill he felt when he was around her. As the saying goes, Candice was a woman you could steal horses with. But deep down, he knew that his heart now belonged to someone else.

As Erik pondered the contrasting qualities of these two remarkable women, he wondered what it was about Amelia that had so captivated him. She dressed very differently: while Amelia preferred long, colorful dresses and wore jewelry, Candice was reasonably practical: she felt most comfortable in jeans and bright shirts, preferably made of flannel so that she would look almost like a "cowgirl", Erik thinks.

Is he drawn to Amelia's intellect? Her dedication to her work as a biologist? Or is it perhaps the depth of her feelings that touch him to a degree he has never experienced before? But as much as Erik longs for Amelia - he feels a little guilty. Candice has been there for him, providing companionship and support. He values her friendship, even if it doesn't compare to his deep love for Amelia. In the end, Erik knows he must follow his heart. After all, he can't deny the depth of his feelings for Amelia, regardless of the consequences.

But what about Candice? Erik can't help but think about the impact his love for Amelia would have on their friendship.

Would they be able to maintain the bond, or would it crumble under the weight of the newfound love? As Erik ponders the unknown future, he is confident that his love for Amelia burns brighter than ever. It's a love that has power, that could ignite his soul and propel him to new heights. It is a love that is to shape his destiny.

Erik drives from the airport to the city, where he wants to recover in a hotel from the "long haul" above the clouds. In the city, not the "Hyatt" awaits him. It is a slightly run-down hotel but conveniently located near "Gastown" with its historic streets and brick houses. "My, this place doesn't look good," Erik mutters as he enters the hotel's first-floor hallway. A man greets him somewhat taciturnly at the simple reception desk. With his room key in his hand, he climbs up another floor, still wondering whether he should subject Amelia to this hotel tomorrow. But when he unlocks the room, he finds it clean, and it has a large bed.

Erik sleeps as if on clouds, of which he also dreams. Then he wakes up. It's the middle of the night. Of course, he thinks, it's the time difference. But he can make his way to the airport in time. Amelia is flying from Edmonton over the Rocky Mountains. "After all, it's one thing to get on a train with you, which I look forward to. But if I'm traveling myself, I want to take the plane. Besides, I'll get to you faster that way," she said on the phone.

There he is again in the terminal, watching the arrivals area. Two large carved totem poles look down on the travelers here as well. They seem to want to keep track of things, just as he does. Time passes, and Erik realizes how nervous he is. But here comes Amelia from the security area, shouldering her travel bag. Her brown hair blows from her quick stride. She sees him and smiles. Then she walks faster, reaching him, and they embrace - kissing long and intimately. It feels familiar to Erik but also a little unfamiliar. First and foremost, though, it feels good. The magic he had sensed in Jasper is back.

"It's so great to see you here again," Erik says.

Amelia smiles at him, "Yes, I feel the same way. Oh, we are in my home country. So I say to you: welcome to Canada."

The chemistry between the two is immediately apparent. "What an experience. I meet you here in Vancouver," she says. "I have to tell you about my work as a biologist. You wouldn't believe the things I've seen," she says, her eyes sparkling with excitement. "Last week, I studied the mating habits of squid, and let me tell you, they're pretty perverse creatures." Erik laughs at her description and imagines squid doing wild things.

"You experience some crazy stuff," he says.

"No, the craziest thing is yet to come with you," Amelia says. "So, where are you taking me? Off to the Hyatt?"

"Well, not quite. But it's comfortable," he says, and they make their way to the hotel in the Gastown Quarter, where they spend the next night together - endlessly happy about their reunion.

"You'll have to come visit me in Edmonton sometime, though, and meet everyone," Amelia says late that evening as they leave the bed one more time.

"Oh, yes, I would love to do that. I had thought we would meet again on neutral ground first."

Amelia points to the rumpled bed: "Yes, that's a very neutral floor you've chosen here. We did maintain neutrality for, what, five minutes? And the hotel is like the Ritz, I would say."

"You won't even notice," Erik tells her, "when we're under the covers."

"I'd better take a look there," Amelia says, and she's already disappeared underneath.

Erik senses the spark that had ignited their souls in Jasper had only grown more intense during their months apart. Now they are together again. In the heart of the city, Erik and Amelia are in each other's arms. Their love has weathered the storm of their long separation. With a gentle touch, Erik's hand caresses Amelia's face, his fingertips tracing the contours of her skin. Amelia closes her eyes and surrenders to the feeling. The room seems to melt away as they lie there.

Amelia's fingers stroke the sheets, her senses tingling with anticipation. Without saying a word, Erik and Amelia allow their souls to intertwine in love and passion. In this Vancouver sanctuary, the outside world ceases to exist. Time stands still as Erik and Amelia's bodies move in rhythm. Their love fills the air, blending with the gentle sounds of their bodies in harmony.

Erik wakes up long before dawn in the morning while Amelia sleeps peacefully. Since he has no newspaper, he quietly turns on the T.V. for his first coffee. A presenter babbles, and pictures of a storm in the Cascades are shown. That looks exciting, Erik thinks, hopefully, they won't have to drive through it later. He drinks powdered coffee, which he always has with him. Because when there's no hotel breakfast, it helps to start the day while traveling. Outside, it is still dark. Very carefully, he wakes Amelia, who opens her eyes and immediately knows who he is.

"Hello, you German lover. You're up early this morning."

"Hello, my Canadian love. Did you sleep well?"

"Yes, after last night, I really did. With you."

"Could you also imagine getting up? Then I could take you to the station, and we could get on the train that takes us on vacation."

"If this one brings us both happiness, then for once, I'll get up really early."

They take a bus, full of tired-looking employees, from "Waterfront Station" to "Pacific Central," where the long-distance trains leave. Amelia looks tired while he is awake - that's what the time difference does. They walk through the station. On the left are the large cars of the "Canadian" with their stainless steel outer skin and blue stripes.

"Look, I arrived here with this in the spring when I drove from Jasper to Vancouver," he says.

"Those are the trains I know," she counters. "Oh, how I wish I could have been on that one. It was a mistake for us to split up in Jasper."

Erik is almost speechless. Amelia has said precisely what he had been thinking: they shouldn't have broken up. In doing so, she showed him how serious she was. "I've sat in a car like that by the window and thought exactly the same thing."

On the right is a border fence and a platform behind it. One must pass the exit, already in the station of Vancouver. The border official asks why Erik wants to leave Canada again when he only entered the day before, as the stamp on his passport shows. "I wish to take the train to Seattle with my girlfriend here, a Canadian," he says in the friendliest, almost slimy tone. The official suddenly nods in understanding and lets them pass onto the platform.

South with the Cascades

There is now a very different train than on the tracks of "VIA Rail Canada": They are modern, Spanish cars from Talgo, low and angular. One could think of being in Madrid or Barcelona if it weren't for the dark green and dark red color scheme, with a beige tint, which looks very North American, Erik thinks, and the colossal diesel locomotive. It is again a train of the U.S. company Amtrak, more precisely, of the state of Washington. Here, again, a service attendant greets them friendly.

"Oh, you booked business class," Amelia notes. "How does that fit the budget hotel you bought us last night?"

"Quite simply, that's the excuse to make the trip palatable to you." They sit down in the cushions. "I think you've succeeded. Very nice to ride the train with you."

They like the route: The railroad runs along the Pacific Ocean in large parts. After a long journey, the deep tooting of the horn sounds like music to Erik's ears as the train pulls away. On the "Cascades Corridor," the line between Vancouver, Seattle, Portland, and as far south as Eugene, trains travel up to 80 miles per hour. The train's appearance underscores its claim to be a modern connection: The "Cascades" is the only Talgo train in North America.

The recent history of this connection is tragic. When there were regular services to the East Coast after 1890, the rail network also grew on the Pacific Coast to connect Vancouver and Portland. In the early 1970s, Amtrak took over the line. But it wasn't until 1994 that the Cascades Corridor's heyday would begin when Amtrak delivered the first set of Talgo cars from Spain. They became popular. But the sixth generation has been retired because of a tragic event. By the time replacements are finally ready in 2024, only a few "Talgos" will still be in service. Otherwise, regular Horizon cars from Amtrak stock will be running.

In 2017, a new section south of Seattle was scheduled to open, considerably speeding up traffic to Portland. The "Talgos" were made for it, after all. But a train derailed behind Tacoma in December, entering a curve at 75 and traveling 50 miles per hour too fast. The cars were hurled through the air and down the embankment. Sixty-five people were injured, three killed in the "Washington Train Derailment." The National Transportation Safety Board demanded that the older Talgo trains be taken out of service as quickly as possible because they did not offer sufficient protection. "This is tragic. I remember the accident and the reports," Amelia says.

Outside the window, the suburbs of Vancouver pass by, looking well-kept. The many single-family homes with green lawns and tall trees look very inviting. On the wall, a monitor shows the route, blinking in a strangely rhythmic manner. A red line stretches from Canada down into the USA. The stations are red dots on the line.

As the train roars along the sea, the neighbor leans over from Erik's seat opposite. "I hardly know a railroad as beautiful as this one," he says. Bill is traveling with his wife, Lucy. They both like railroads, probably as much as Erik does by now.

"It's real travel, isn't it? You can see the landscape, you still know where you are, and you meet nice people," he says. Erik can agree. Bill reports that he sold his company a few years ago and went into a self-made early retirement. This gives him the time to travel across America by train. Others seek hobbies like boating, but for Bill, it's the railroad, of which he also has a miniature version in the basement, his wife notes with a grin. "You don't have a model train in the basement, do you?" asks Amelia Erik.

"Oh, if you only knew what a huge train set I have at home to play with all night."

The train stops on the other side of the border in Bellingham, Washington state. It brakes squeakily before coming to a halt. Outside, passengers are waiting on the platform, surprisingly many backpackers.

"They're probably coming off the ferry," Bill notes. "You can transfer to the Alaska Marine Highway here".

Erik wonders about the phrase "marine highway"?

"Yes, the ferry goes past Canada and then down the coast of Alaska. That way, you can get north without having to enter at the Canucks."

Erik didn't know the word "Canuck." Still, he realizes the context: it seems to be a derogatory term for Canadians in the United States. He looks at Amelia shocked. Lucy pushes her husband.

"Oh, we like to call you Squatch, too," Amelia says to the American's face. "That means big and unkempt. Or maybe bushed, which means uncivilized." She has several typical Canadian swear words ready. Bill laughs out loud. "I deserved that. I'm sorry I used that ugly word. It just slipped out."

"Apology accepted, Yankee," Amelia says, grinning.

Lucy tries to deflect. "The ferry is great. You guys should ride it sometime." Erik thinks he'd get on it immediately, but they plan to go south now. "Well, she's getting on a bit," Bill says, "but you can get to Alaska in three days."

The idea of the "Alaska Marine Highway" was the brainchild of two businessmen, Steve Homer and Ray Gelotte, according to Bill, who purchased a landing craft from Navy stocks in 1948. The sturdy vessel was well suited for the waters to the north. They later sold their company to the "Alaska Territorial Government" - it was not until 1959 that Alaska became a separate state of the USA. Then, the "Alaska Marine Highway System" was born.

"With cruise ships, you can do the route dozens of times every summer," he explains. "But with a small, older ferry, it's different. It's more individual." That's when you forget about on-board catering, he adds. "Backpackers" could set up their tents on the ship and spend the night. "Setting up a tent on deck? That sounds quite romantic," Amelia says. Lucy enthuses, "The route is great: in Canada, it follows the 'Inside Passage,' which passes sheltered between the mainland and the forested islands in the Pacific."

In Mount Vernon, the "Cascades" stops again. Amelia and Erik walk up and down in front of the station building. The train has only a few minutes to stop. Actually, Vancouver and Seattle almost form one metropolitan area, with the difference that a border runs through it. But the cities in between, Bellingham as well as Burlington, almost merge into each other. At least compared to driving through the Rocky Mountains or the Midwest. The Pacific Coast is densely populated here.

The rail line runs south of Bellingham, close to the Pacific Ocean, following the bays and ridges that drop steeply from the mountains into the sea. At Mt. Vernon, the line disappears inland and runs dead straight south next to the Interstate. Here we are back in America from the train perspective, Erik thinks: streets, railroad crossings, stores, warehouses, and logistics centers. It looks busy and exciting, but it's not as pretty as it was at the Pacific. Instead, the "Cascades" roars along. The red dots flash on the monitor in front of them, showing that Seattle is getting closer. Before they reach the metropolis, the train heads west to the water. Once again, it travels along the beaches of Puget Sound.

Many boats are out there. Seattle and its surroundings must be a true mecca for boaters, Erik surmises. The coast is large and wide, yet protected. The many marinas that the train passes are evidence that water sports are very popular. The small towns with names like Mukilteo and Edmonds are connected to the islands by ferries. There are picturesque settlements there - as far as they can tell from the train window. Shortly before Seattle, the train crosses a bridge that is an "old acquaintance" for Erik: It races across the "Lake Washington Ship Canal," the waterway he had traveled along with the excursion boat. He remembers wondering about the somewhat rusty railroad bridge from the deck. Now, he rides across the water on it. It goes into the denser development of Seattle, then into the tunnel in the city's center, and already the "Cascades" stops at the "King Street Station".

"Mm, I haven't even been to Seattle yet," Amelia says.

"Yes, it's a beautiful city. But our next stop is supposed to be Portland," Erik replies. "That's where I've reserved a fine hotel for us to relax in."

Erik thinks having two nights in Portland is better than one in Seattle and another in Oregon. "Recover? From what?" she asks. "I think we'll do more like the squids."

The train has a half-hour layover in Seattle, enough to stretch their legs. The pretty station building still has no opportunity to shop, as Erik notes. But they can get their coffee on the train. Erik and Amelia return to their seats. She takes out her backpack and rummages through it. Then she whips out home-made muffins. "These even have extra low carbs. That's my special recipe. We don't need a kiosk for our in-flight food," she says, handing Erik a moist cake. "These are really excellent. I didn't know you could bake so well."

"Yeah, and I know how to gear up for long train rides, too." They put the seat back and cuddle as best they can. Erik looks into Amelia's gray-blue eyes, and she into his. They have three and a half hours ahead of them before they are due to arrive in Portland.

The train passes the gigantic Boeing factory south of the airport. They are made there, just as they are in Hamburg and Toulouse: the airplanes that have made travel much faster, especially since the advent of jets in the 1950s. Erik thinks that's what made some journeys possible in the first place, mainly on routes that cross the North Atlantic. At the same time, in America, less so in Europe, they have relegated the railroad to one of the very back seats of transportation. At least, it seems to be experiencing a kind of renaissance in the Pacific Northwest.

PORTLAND AND MT. HOOD

Erik and Amelia are cheerful when the train arrives in Portland around 3 p.m. The large Union Station welcomes them with its gray-brown cement facade, interrupted by red-painted cross-beams and a tiled roof. But above all, Union Station is busy. The "Cascades" as well as the "Coast Starlight" pass through several times a day. The southern leg of the "Empire Builder" starts here, joining the train from Seattle in Spokane. The concourse in the station is just as impressive as in Seattle, with its marble-clad walls, art deco chandeliers, and fans.

Above the station rises a tower with an old-fashioned illuminated advertisement: "Go by train" is written there in neon letters. Amtrak's predecessor companies snuffed out this light when they ceased passenger service in 1971. It took 15 years for members of two clubs to raise enough money to renovate the neon sign in the mid-1980s. Since then, it has been back in operation, and the words "Go by train" even light up one after the other.

The sun is shining, and they take the footpath into the center instead of getting on the "Lightrail". Portland has had a light rail network since the 1980s, and the white-painted trains also stop at Union Station. But the walk through "Old Town" is delightful. Erik rolls his travel bag over the cobblestones and carries Amelia's bag a bit. Erik thinks it could be even nicer if there weren't many empty stores with taped-up windows on either side of the street. "Old Town has a silly history", Erik reads up later. It's where the roots of historic Portland lie, and later it became "Chinatown," the area of Chinese immigrants. The city government had the clever idea of turning Chinatown into a tourist attraction in the 1980s. San Francisco may have been the inspiration. So, much money was spent renovating the streets, and private financiers invested in the buildings. Only the immigrants of Chinese origin didn't like it: they moved away when land prices and rents began to rise.

Downtown is livelier, though, Erik notes. Here, the sidewalks are full of people, and the traffic is heavier. They turn a street corner and stand in front of their hotel - and he is impressed. The former "Multnomah" hotel from 1912 has been fabulously renovated. The building, with its eight massive floors and three wings, must once have been one of the top addresses on the Pacific Coast. In 1963, the old-fashioned hotel closed. Then offices of the administration were housed there. In 1995, renovation work began: Only 276 suites were made from the 700 rooms, but the hall, the social rooms, everything was faithfully restored. Since 1995, the "Multnomah" has opened as the "Embassy Suites." Erik and Amelia enter the reception area in the marble-lined hall. Upstairs, in their room, they marvel at the suite they will now occupy for two nights. "Lest you think I've become a megalomaniac," Erik tells Amelia, "I booked the hotel with a travel website that lets you reserve accommodations in a city whose name and location you don't get until you pay." He says he's had good experiences with this system. "I'll take your word for that. Especially after the accommodation last night," Amelia returns.

The "Multnomah" breathes the spirit of optimism of the West after the turn of the century in 1900 - and is now on the list of historic places. "The grand dame on Pine Street" the hotel is called in a brochure. Before turning to downtown Portland for a drink, they make a detour to the hotel's basement. That's where a spa has been set up, in a high basement hall with thick, ornate columns. There is a huge, very hot swimming pool in it. Amelia is as enthusiastic as he is; she also likes "hot tubs". Here they can relax. "I've never experienced a swimming pool this big that was as hot as a hot tub," she says. "There's no tension left behind."

A little later, they sit at the counter in a bar in modern curved leather chairs. The place looks "trendy" and is crowded. Pioneer Courthouse Square, the heart of downtown, is just a few blocks from Multnomah. Over their second drink, they strike up a conversation with neighbors. Scott and Shawn are native Portlanders, which is not common in a country where people move an average of twelve times in a lifetime. But they like it here, and neither would want to leave their city for anything like a slightly better job.

"We've both been there," Scott says. "The long discussions, the prospect of more income, but what's the point of all that effort?"

"Yeah, we've discussed it before and always stuck around," Shawn adds.

What makes Portland so unique, Erik asks them.

"Look at the beautiful downtown," Scott counters. "There are many nice neighborhoods here. Housing isn't as expensive as in Seattle or San Francisco. At the same time, the city isn't as overrun with tourists - no offense," he adds.

That's true, Erik thinks, in the other metropolises on the West Coast, especially San Francisco, as a resident, he would also be a bit annoyed by the tourist crowds.

"Most importantly, we don't have as many techies making everything unaffordable with their income. That's the main problem with San Francisco and its Silicon Valley," Shawn says.

He doesn't ask them in tourist fashion what they should definitely see in Portland. They tell him that all by themselves. "I don't think you'd want to visit the rose gardens or the Japanese gardens, but if you were a flower lover, that would be great for you; those are the number one attractions here," Shawn says. "But I think your girlfriend would like the flower gardens, so you should take her there."

Does it show on Erik's face that he's not a flower lover? "Yes, you lack a certain interest in flora," Shawn laughs.

"But we have something for you: Powell's City of Books, you should go there," his friend advises. "It's a used bookstore. There are over a million titles there. It's downtown, that way." He points his arm toward the bar counter, which makes Erik laugh.

"Right behind the bottles that are on the wall, right?"

Both nod. "Are you museum guys?" asks Shawn. Sometimes, in bad weather, Erik counters. "Portland Art Museum and Museum of Science and Industry, both good. Those would be your addresses."

Most importantly, the "counter acquaintances" think the Portland area is great. The fact that they believe he's an "outdoor" fan, if he's not supposed to be a flower lover, is something Erik also likes.

"You could visit Mt. Hood. Then you can forget about the gardens in town." The mountain is the great volcano that visibly towers over the city. "It's worth it. Do some hiking and then go to Timberline Lodge for coffee."

"I have a great idea," Amelia says later at the hotel. "I'll take you to Mt. Hood and skip the flower gardens, don't worry. But then we'll do something nice in San Francisco, too."

"That's great. Do you have any ideas yet?"

"I'd like to go to Sausalito."

"Deal, we'll take a boat tour to Sausalito to the houseboats."

They wake up in the morning with a little hangover in the pompous "Embassy Suite". In the "Multnomah" basement is a large, brightly lit breakfast room with a sumptuous "Breakfast Buffet". Amelia loads eggs and bacon onto her plate. Erik can't help but eat some pancakes again. Then, they're on the road with a small backpack, ready for an outdoor adventure. It takes three hours to get there. Looking at the map, Erik sees that Portland is beautifully situated on the Willamette River. West of the city, it merges into the even larger Columbia River, which can also be navigated by ocean-going vessels. This makes the geography seem a bit confusing at first glance. At least the suburbs are served by public transportation, so you can get to "Mt. Hood".

"I can imagine that such a trip in the Midwest would not have been possible at all without a car," he says on the light rail train. "Yes, you just would have had to rent a car," Amelia says. "Although it's very nice that way, too." With stops in the suburbs of Gresham and Sandy, they get closer to the massive volcanic mountain. The bus is a shuttle, the "Mt. Hood Express," specifically designed to take visitors "Car-free" to the volcanic mountain. Through the village of Goverment Camp, the bus winds up the small road to the famous "Timberline Lodge".

Both are overwhelmed as they arrive at the top: The lodge nestles on the mountainside below the summit of the 11,250-feet-high volcano, which still has a few white spots on the glacier at the top in late summer. The view of the surrounding mountains is broad. They can see the next volcano at the back of the horizon. Amelia and he stand in front of the lodge and marvel.

"It's almost as beautiful here as it is in Canada," Amelia says.

"Yes, tell me, now your tour guide has also taken you to a beautiful place for once."

"But my tour guide also got a good tip from our two counter friends. Admit it, you wouldn't have found this up here alone."

"Oh yes, I do because I can read the brochures in our hotel."

"I see, so you prefer to get your travel knowledge from brochures rather than guidebooks, huh?"

"Well, I could have asked the receptionist."

"Of course, she would have shown you the way to the rose gardens straight away. Then again, I would have liked that."

"Then I guess we wouldn't have come to Sausalito," he teases her, adding, "Amelia, isn't it beautiful here?"

"Yes, seriously, it's nice up here."

The mountains that are part of the "Cascade Range" and the "Pacific Ring of Fire" are lined up like a chain: To the north, Mount St. Helens, which gained notoriety for its eruption in 1980; to the far north, Mt. Baker near Bellingham. To the south, they see Mt. Jefferson and the "Three Sisters," three volcanic peaks close together. The land in between looks flat from above, but it didn't appear that way in the valley. An impressive picture: The valleys with their green forests, the stony mountains, and some white peaks in the haze on the horizon. Back there is California, the destination of the trip.

They stand in front of the portal of the old Timberline Lodge. A tunnel leads into the building to keep the entrance clear of snow in winter. The lodge is an idea that originated at the time of the Great Depression and was part of a job creation program. The building is a kind of enormous mountain hotel. The exterior walls on the first floor are made of solid stonework. From the second floor on, heavy wood was used for the construction. The heart is the main hall, which is hexagonal. A history plaque indicates that Oregon timbers were used throughout the building, including cedar, Douglas fir, hemlock, western juniper, and ponderosa pine. "Well, there you go, a nice listing of all the types of wood that can be used for building here," Amelia says.

"Oh, what the heck," Erik says, "We'll go get a coffee first, right?"

"You're the man with the time difference, aren't you? As early as you got up, you could do with that coffee."

So they walk into the impressive hexagonal hall. Erik takes a black coffee, and for Amelia, he orders a latte - with cinnamon on the milk foam. The view goes to the mountainside outside. The interior of the hall is also very ornate. "Some movies have been filmed here, not the least of which was Steven King's The Shining," Amelia says. No wonder the fictional "Overlook" hotel from the book fits well with the character of this wooden hotel, and thus, with a horror movie set in a remote mountain lodge.

The center of the room is a large fireplace framed by stone slabs. Around it are the seating areas with red upholstery and lots of wood. There is even a balustrade with more seats in case it should get packed here in winter. Amelia takes some photos with her camera. Purely taking pictures with her smartphone, she doesn't think much of that. "I prefer to do it with my Nikon," she says. Meanwhile, Erik has seen some photos of Amelia that surprised him. In any case, they weren't amateur shots. He's not a professional photographer, but he deals with pictures daily in his job, and often enough, he's picked out images for his magazine. Amelia has an eye for photography.

Now, they scramble off from Timberline Lodge across the slope. Not to the top, that seemed too strenuous for them. Also, not with the chairlift, that would be banal. No, they hike down, in the direction of the small village "Government Camp". They are always accompanied by a great view of the surrounding peaks and the rutted valleys. The trail is a good six miles long, quite a walk for an inexperienced city dweller like him, perhaps a bit less for Amelia. About two hours should be expected, as they said at the lodge. All right, they can accept the challenge. In between, they walk past the steel structures of the ski lifts. A long, straight aisle leads toward "Government Camp", but nothing can be seen there.

Erik later learns that the world's first "ski bus" ran here just for a few years. It was a resourceful entrepreneur who wanted to make it easier for skiers to get to the "Timberline Lodge" in the late 1940s. However, the lift he had built was something special: on wire ropes, a line bus with a diesel engine could wind its way up the mountain, suspended in mid-air. The ropes ran over pulleys from the bus roof, over the wheels without tires, and back up again. The whole thing sounds absurd, Erik thinks, but it apparently worked. But the bus is said to have been terribly noisy and swayed. It only lasted a few years. As someone in Government Camp is said to have once said, "Just because an idea can work doesn't mean it's a good idea."

Erik is still looking down to the valley when Amelia falls. She has tripped over a rock onto the meadow. Nevertheless, she cries out in pain. Erik is immediately on the spot. Amelia tries to sit. Erik gently grabs her by the shoulders and helps her sit up. "My leg, it hurts so damn much," Amelia whimpers. Erik is startled. He carefully takes her leg in his hands and stretches it out. Then, he supports Amelia with his backpack, so she can lean against it.

Her eyes are full of tears, and her face is distorted with pain. She looks into the trees for a while, down the slope. Then, she slowly relaxes. "Amelia, are you feeling better?" asks Erik, concerned.

"Yes, slowly, the pain is subsiding a bit. I wasn't paying attention on this hiking trail. And then I tripped over this stupid rock."

"But this is also a beast, this stone. It lies in the middle of the path. It's a wonder it didn't get me."

"Then we'd both be lying here whimpering right now," Amelia says. Erik has to smile a little. She tries to stand up. She succeeds on her right leg, but immediately flinches when she tries to step on the left.

"It still hurts like hell."

"Where exactly does it hurt?"

"It's definitely on the ankle," she moans. Erik looks at her with concern. "Should I call for help?" he says, pulling out his smartphone.

"Hold off on that. I don't think it's broken. I hope it's just sprained. Then we'll make it to the valley."

That was brave and also somewhat optimistic of Amelia. They made it down to the village of Government Camp. But he continuously supported Amelia, sometimes even carrying her a bit. He did manage to lift her up. But he couldn't have brought her the whole way. And if he had, he would have had to shoulder her. It must have been two hours before they finally arrive at the settlement between the mountain houses. However, the place does not mean well for them: they ask for a doctor in the next open pub. There isn't one here in the summer, says the innkeeper. In winter, it would be different. He then leafs through a directory of the region. "The closest orthopedist is in Gresham near Portland. Or on the other side in Hood River."

"We're not here by car," Erik points out. But Amelia has sat down and is already searching for a route on her smartphone. "We can take our shuttle bus there, that should work. If necessary, we can take a cab for the last few meters," she says.

The innkeeper brings her some towels to put a bandage around her ankle. "I would drive you if I didn't have the place open," he says. But Amelia is brave: "I'll manage. We'll get on the bus, probably leaving in three-quarters of an hour."

While they wait and drink coffee in the pub, Amelia tells Erik that it happened to her once before while skiing in Canada. Back then, it was just a sprained ankle.

"Do you actually go skiing in Europe?" she asks.

"You won't believe it: there are plenty of skiers in Hamburg, even though the city is far away from the Alps. But every spring, quite a few people head south to the Alps, and some north, to Norway, for example, and go skiing. Yes, that's what we do."

"Are we going skiing sometime, too? I'd like to see if you can."

"Sure thing, Amelia. We're going skiing." As a Canadian who hails from Edmonton, Amelia apparently is excellent at skiing, as she told Erik.

The innkeeper brings her a glass of water with painkillers. "With that, you should at least make it to Gresham," he tells her.

Finally, her mood brightens. "My dear Mr. Guide, that was a magical trip up a volcanic mountain," Amelia says. "With a painful ending for me. But I tell you: I am so grateful to you for carrying me halfway down the mountain."

"Amelia, I would have carried you all the way to Portland to help you."

"Really? You couldn't have done that. But the main thing is to get to the doctor now."

The two later board the shuttle and arrive at an orthopedic office in Gresham, which is not far from a bus stop. Amelia's foot is x-rayed there. It's not a fracture, the doctor tells her a little later. It is a sprain that has swollen. He believes that with plenty of rest, it will be fine. Amelia has talked to the doctor for a long time, Erik later notes. But now she makes a reasonably composed impression. The only thing she shouldn't do anymore is take the bus. Of course, the two of them ride a cab to the hotel. There, Erik prepares the pillows for her on the suite's sofa. "You're going to lie here until noon tomorrow. No, stop. In the meantime, I'll put you to bed. And then you lie here again, and I'll have breakfast served to you."

He goes with a bucket to get some ice from the machine

next to the elevator. He then makes her a cold bandage, which he puts around Amelia's ankle.

"Phew, that's cold. But Erik, now I love you even more than before," she replies, "and I can still kiss you."

THE "COAST STARLIGHT" - FIRST PART

At just after 2 p.m., the long-distance train is scheduled to leave Portland, taking them to San Francisco in one "big jump." Erik asks at the reception desk, so Amelia can stay at the hotel until shortly before departure. Then, he makes a brief trip to the bookstore before hailing a cab to the train station. Amelia insists that they continue the journey. Erik finds a copy of Paul Theroux's "The Great Railway Bazaar" in the bookstore, and it appears to him to be the original 1975 edition with its colorful cover. It fits, he thinks. Theroux describes trains as a world unto themselves, where anything goes, where people eat, sleep, and drink. A "bazaar," he writes. And even though his enviable journey is to take him from London to Tokyo, he immediately boards a long-distance train with Amelia as well, which could be a bazaar: It's the big, two-story "Superliner" coach again, rolling into the Portland station. First, the two locomotives pull in, the "Genesis" models Erik is now familiar with from long-distance trains out west. Each of them has over 4200 horsepower. Then, the baggage car and the "sleepers" follow so that they can board.

Further back, there are the dining cars, observation cars, and the "Coach" cars. It's a world of its own on rails. South of Eugene in Oregon, there is currently no passenger train except the "Coast Starlight", which runs overnight. It is only before Sacramento that the California rail network begins its connections.

The little "roomette" has not changed, even though they are not booked in the "Empire Builder" but in the "Coast Starlight". He helps Amelia, whom he has already carried to the second floor of the car, from the aisle to the seat by the window, where she can rest her foot quietly. Then Erik sets off again to find ice in the dining car for a new bandage. Later, he uses it to make a new wrap for her ankle. He then sits down in the seat opposite. "They're so wide, there's room for me and your ankle," Erik says, and Amelia has to laugh.

Erik thinks everything has its place in the compartment, making it charming. There is a shelf for the bag, and the blue curtains facing the aisle and the window are back. The reading lamp on the seat's headrest, which looks a bit strange, is also still there, as are the controls for the temperature. Amelia says, "Well, the gentleman has come up with something. This is a funny compartment here. I've never seen anything like it in Canada." Erik is pleased that she likes the little compartment.

He opens two bottles of mineral water and hands one to Amelia while the Portland suburbs pass by outside. Salem, Albany, Eugene is the triad of stops the train makes before it leaves Eugene shortly after 5 p.m. and "disappears" into the mountains toward Klamath Falls. The area is noticeably more sparsely populated. The forests are more expansive, and the hills, valleys, and mountains are a bit steeper. Erik looks out of the compartment through the window at the dark woods, deep in thought.

"You look so serious," Amelia notes.

"I was just thinking how beautiful it is here. How little I still like my life in Germany. Work drives me crazy, even though I once liked it a lot. But it made me lonely."

"My dear friend from Germany, a frank word. Shall I tell you how I see the situation? You are on the lookout. You are running away."

Now Erik is baffled.

"What do you mean I'm running away?"

"You are looking for something new. Your old life doesn't seem to offer you that much anymore. So you get on a train and travel across the U.S. and Canada, all by yourself."

"What's wrong with riding a train?"

"Well, you might as well be sitting by a swimming pool in the Caribbean looking at the girls."

Erik grins. This remark is typical of Amelia again.

"So that's what you would recommend?"

"No, of course not. Because if you hadn't gone to Jasper, then we wouldn't have met at all. You have so many choices, but you chose this one. There's more to it than that."

"And what could be behind that?"

"You're going away. You want to leave. You're taking the train because you would like to escape your life."

She seems to have seen right through him, Erik thinks. He feels caught and looks at her.

"Oh, now come on, don't look like that. I want to break out myself. I'm not happy. I'm sitting alone in this cold city in Canada. I like my job, but don't like the conditions I have to work under. Then I'm driving to Jasper, and you're standing before me. Now you and I are on this train together. You're searching, just like I am."

"You know all that about me?"

"But of course, it's as clear as day. I have fallen in love with you. Because you are the person you are. And because you are searching. And because I want to be part of it. We can search together and find something new for us that will make us both happy."

Erik doesn't know what to say, but again, he feels the force pulling him forward. Without thinking, he kisses Amelia. Going on a search together sounds great to Erik.

. . .

The train rumbles over the "Penga Pass" route. This line was built to provide a faster connection for trains traveling between Eugene and California than the old route over Siskiyou Pass. Beyond the town of Chemult in Oregon, it is getting dark in the "Cascades". Amelia and Erik return to the dining car, which is not far from their sleeper compartment. Three times, Erik has made sure whether she really wants to go there for dinner. But Amelia thinks she can manage since the swelling has decreased a bit. And so they are back at a table in the dining car, chatting with a couple from Los Angeles. Erik wonders how the dining car attendant puts the passengers together; is it coincidence, or does he make an effort to put people who have something to say at the same table? It can't be a number because they come from another car.

The couple returns from a visit to Vancouver. The way there by plane, quite pragmatically, but on the way back, they wanted to "treat" themselves to the train. They also spent a day in Seattle: The "Coast Starlight" leaves there earlier than the "Cascades" arrives, as they report. They don't really mind: "If I want to go fast, I can fly. If you're going by train, you can be ready for something. It's nice, but definitely not fast," says the man. He then wants to know if the trains are similar in Europe.

" The trains are fast but uncomfortable compared to these," Erik says.

"Our network in the U.S. is great, but there aren't enough passenger trains," his wife says matter-of-factly.

"In Europe, with you, it must be fun to ride the train," the man says. "We're from Los Angeles, which is the capital of car travel. So maybe trains are more exotic for us," the woman thinks.

Amelia stands up and disappears briefly with her handbag.

Erik suspects why he has noticed it more often: she determines her blood sugar and the insulin dose she has to take, i.e., inject, for the upcoming meal. He thinks she's courageous. She doesn't make a big fuss about it but is able to "manage" her disease herself as best she can. Will it stay that way, he wonders? In any case, he would be there for her.

Then she comes back, and the main course is served. It's the "Amtrak" steak again, the one Erik already liked at the Empire Builder, with the baked potato and green beans. "I think the food on your U.S. trains is pretty good," Amelia says. "We've had excellent food at VIA, too, but this is somehow better. Which could just be my company," she adds, looking at Erik. The two sigh. "How beautifully you do it," the woman notes.

"We sometimes have a dining car in Germany that runs between Hamburg and Berlin. It's a Czech train," he explains to diners. "They're excellent at cooking. But it's not so much food on our trains anymore. They put bags in the microwave."

The man had heard that there is no alcohol on German trains. "Is that true? Do you have Prohibition?" he asks.

"No, only on local trains, the commuter trains. On the long-distance trains, of course, there's beer."

"In the U.S., drinking is actually everywhere," his wife finds. "Smoking is almost non-existent now, but drinking is. Take a look at the bar menu here." That's right, Erik had already noticed that at the California Zephyr: At happy hour, there were cocktails at knockdown prices. Here, too, one glass after another is drunk in the dining car.

"Do you like our beer?" the man asks somewhat incredulously as Erik orders another. "Yes, you can get used to it, even as a German," he grins. They both drink wine, and the steward brings them more glasses. "Careful with the dessert," the woman advises them. Thick pieces of cake are placed on the table in front of them, juicy but also immensely rich. "Again, Americans are good at making these fat cakes, served even on the trains," Amelia notes. "And they like to drink coffee after dinner, even late at night," Erik adds. Accordingly, the small group orders coffee while he tells you about their plans for San Francisco. Amelia, of course, has given up alcohol because she takes painkillers.

Emeryville, the transfer station to the bus to San Francisco, is reached by the "Coast Starlight" at 8:30 a.m., this time before Oakland because they are coming from the north. The night they slept deeply because the swaying here kept within limits, unlike in the Midwest. Erik slept on top of the cot while Amelia stretched out on the bed below, continuing to keep her ankle steady.

"Quite cozy, our little compartment. I could get used to that: Traveling across the continent with you in a compartment like this, with nothing to do but read and eat," says Amelia, while fetching the paper cups with the coffee. The "jump" from the Pacific Northwest to California was made overnight. They've driven through the dark mountains and the connecting plains above Sacramento. Now, the double-decker car squeaks to a stop at the modern platform Erik is familiar with. He knows where they can find the bus into town. Then, it's back over the Bay Bridge and down to the harbor, where the Amtrak bus stops.

IF YOU ARE COMING TO SAN FRANCISCO ...

Market Street is bustling with activity. Again, Erik has taken Amelia's travel bag, but this time, he has strapped it onto his roller bag. He can pull the bags along the smooth sidewalk. "How gallant of you to take my luggage," she says.

"How gallant of you not to pack so much," he says.

"Oh, I know there are women who need a huge selection of clothes for their excursions. But, hey, you're talking to a former sleeping car attendant. I know how to pack for trips like this."

"The main thing is that you manage to get to the hotel with your ankle."

"I can handle that. It's already back there."

When they enter the hall of the Palace Hotel, Erik is over-whelmed. It looks even more luxurious than the Multnomah. Does he have to be careful that Amelia doesn't think he's a snob? At the sight of a gigantic bouquet of flowers standing on a large, heavy table in a huge vase at the entrance to the hall, she says, "Hm, what was that about your thrift? Well, I'm not sure. I don't think you're a rich schnoz."

"No, Amelia, I am not. I booked the hotel again through this portal, and the price was cheap. I am innocent," he returns.

After checking in, they cross the magnificent marble hall. A mixture of tourists and business people are staying here. They look elegantly dressed, Amelia notices. She and Erik arrive at their room on the third floor. There, they lie down on the bed. "It's also nice when a bed doesn't sway," she notes. He makes her a poultice out of ice cubes. Then Erik tells her that the thought of making a book from his travels has crossed his mind. She's taken with the idea. "We can even plan through that together if you like," she says, asking an interesting question, "In German or in English?"

Erik hasn't even thought about that yet. For her, it goes without saying that the book has to be published in English because they speak English to each other. That's the only way she could understand it. Amelia also speaks French because she learned it in Canada as her first foreign language. "I think that if I don't write the book in French, which I can't do, I'll do both:

in English for the readers in Edmonton and in German for the audience in Hamburg," he replies.

"But you do leave out some details about us, don't you?" she tosses at him, "or do you want to write everything, like about the squids and what they're up to?"

"Don't worry. It's going to be a travel book, not an autobiography. It's about travel, trains, and a woman from Canada I love." Amelia beams, the compliment falling on fertile ground.

In San Francisco, they didn't leave the beaten tourist path. Not because they couldn't have. But because they want to immerse themselves in it. They take a cab to the "Old Fishermans Grotto" on Fishermans Wharf in the evening. But even if the place is a bit kitschy, very touristy, and perhaps a bit overpriced, Erik enjoys going there with Amelia for that very reason.

"Oh, I don't want those huge crabs, though. As a biologist, that's going a bit too far for me," she notes, looking at the food being served at neighboring tables. "I think it's going to be a sumptuous meal. I'd better take precautions," says Amelia, disappearing briefly with her handbag. Erik is impressed by how controlled she is with her diabetes.

They start with the "Monterey Clam Chowder", the thick fish soup. Then there is "Fried Calamari" for Erik and "Salmon" for her. They exchange pieces from plate to plate again. Dessert is the "Grotto Mud Pie," which the Italian-American waiter warmly recommends to them. "Of course, we do what the waiter says," Erik says. They both swiftly empty the bottle of wine. Outside, the yellow sign glows with a red crab held by a steering wheel.

"I like it here. Who said this was supposed to be a tourist trap anyway?" asks Amelia.

"I don't know exactly, either. But you could get the impression."

"All right, my German tourist. You took your Canadian out to the first tourist trap in the place."

He looks into her bright gray-blue eyes and feels a tingling and familiar feeling. Two worlds meet here and find their common ground. Erik only looks forward to the next few days even more. The room at the Palace Hotel is not a suite like the one in Portland, but it's pretty close. In the evening, with a view of the comfortable bed, they both feel like doing something other than examining the room's furnishings. Because now Amelia's ankles need to rest again. But that doesn't stop them from a few heartfelt kisses.

They visit all the sights between Market Street, Coit Tower, and Fishermans Wharf again. Behind the former "Ghiradelli" chocolate factory, they walk along Marina Boulevard on the edge of San Francisco Bay. Then they take a cab, which they use to cross the Golden Gate Bridge. The way would have been too far for Amelia to walk. They drop off at a park on the other side. It is a slightly foggy day and relatively cool - just as the weather in San Francisco can be worse than in the rest of California. Next to them, sailboats glide across the blue-green waters of the Pacific.

Amelia looks around briefly, then bends down and pulls two flowers off a plant. She puts one of them in her long brown hair. Then she turns to Erik and puts a blossom in his hair as well. "Well, you know, we're in San Francisco. If you are going to San Francisco, be sure to wear flowers in your hair," she quotes the song by Scott McKenzie that was once the anthem of the hippies. Erik also finds that very romantic.

They board a bus that takes them to Sausalito. Erik says he doesn't find traveling alone tragic, except for the Winnipeg stop, where he felt really abandoned. "Well, and then I came into your life as the main prize," she adds. "Well, sure, no doubt about it. By the way, there are travel writers like Theroux who think that if you're going to write about a trip, you have to do it alone so that the impressions aren't distorted."

"Then let me see if I can falsify your impressions. I'll make every effort to do so," Amelia promises. "It's true that if he's traveling as a writer, he doesn't need the entertainment of a fellow traveler. Although that might have done him some good." Amelia finds Theroux a bit grumpy. But she now thinks it's time for a meal together in Sausalito rather than "unadulterated travel impressions."

Later, they stroll through Sausalito. You could spend a lot of time in this place. Everything seems to be set up for it: The waterfront paths, the green trees, the eateries, the small stores, and, of course, the houseboat settlement a bit further north. He understands why Amelia wanted to come here; he finds it charming, too. The settlement is at least as beautiful as the one in Seattle that Erik had passed by on the steamer. "I guess these aren't hippie boats moored here anymore," he notes. "but dressed-up, floating houses." Still, there's something "cool" about Sausalito, Amelia adds, a getaway town at the bay's northern end.

It is already late in the evening when they return by ferry. The ferry leaves the gloomy "Alcatraz" with its former prison, now a museum on a small island in the middle of the bay, on the left. During the day, visitors crowd the gloomy walls. But the two skip Alcatraz: Their mood is too sunny for such attractions. Erik's heart warms as the ferry sets course for San Francisco, and they stand at the stern looking out over the bay. He grabs Amelia by the hand and kisses her.

THE "COAST STARLIGHT", THE SECOND PART

Erik and Amelia left San Francisco South by train. Actually, they should retake the bus, cross the Bay Bridge, and board the Coast Starlight long-distance train in Oakland. But Erik would like to see "Silicon Valley," the center of global computer technology in which the region has developed since the late 1960s.

As a journalist, Erik had always been fascinated by computers. From the moment he got his hands on his first Commodore computer as a child, he had become almost a little addicted to the devices. What fascinated him even more were the seemingly endless possibilities they offered. He was animated by discovering the applications and the impact of the technology on the real world - not so much the technology that went into the devices or the programming possibilities. Erik had learned that in his school days but had not used it much and had forgotten it quickly. He remembered what Frank once said: "The critical ones are those who can sell inventions. Now, Erik has not become a salesman, but he is fascinated by the effects of technology. He wants to feel a little of the vibrant atmosphere in Silicon Valley, the tech giants, startups, and research centers.

It is clear to him that "Silicon Valley" is not a place you can walk through, but a region that stretches south of the bay from "Redwood City" to "Saratoga" and "San José" in the southeast. In between are well-known cities like "Palo Alto", "Mountain View" and "Sunnyvale" and, of course, "Cupertino". At least Erik's laptop was designed there, but it was probably manufactured in China. Almost all the big tech companies are based here, from Alphabet, Google's holding company, to Hewlett-Packard, Adobe, and Apple. And even though the "high-tech" industry is hard to grasp as he drives past the big company headquarters, he gets a feel for it.

That's why they don't travel via Oakland but go to the train station in the middle of the city, the "San Francisco Station". Currently, only Caltrain, a commuter train that crosses Silicon Valley, departs from there. But later, the "California High-Speed Train" is scheduled to arrive here, the planned high-speed train between San Francisco and Los Angeles. Because San Francisco is located on a peninsula, the tracks can only go south from the city. The corridor that "Caltrain" travels is narrow and very busy. That's why the line has to be upgraded for "High-Speed Rail".

With loud roars, the diesel locomotive pulls the double-decker cars out of the station. Erik finds the wagons a bit strange: Below, the passengers sit in rows of four; above, there are individual seats on a kind of balustrade. But this is also due to the roaring diesel locomotive, which pulls the queue of cars from station to station with quite a noise.

The train with the funny name "Baby Bullet" winds through the densely populated area. They pass "South San Francisco" and then the "SFO" airport. In the suburban station of "Millbrae" they could change to the subway, to the "bart", that sixties futuristic subway, which not only passes under San Francisco but goes under the bay on its "Transbay Tube" and opens up the eastern towns of the Bay Area. Erik thinks "bart" is pretty fancy: the stainless-steel trains are fast, up to 60 miles per hour, and look different from ordinary mass transit systems with brown carpeting and aluminum walls. But they stay in the "baby bullet." The ride takes a good hour and a quarter. Commuters sit on the train, carrying backpacks and drinking cups, some with bicycles, for which there are extra "bike racks." It all makes an extraordinary impression with the many "tech hipsters" out and about here in Silicon Valley. Outside, the stations alternate with family homes, office buildings, and small shopping centers.

Finally, they can get off at the San José train station. They step through the station concourse onto the forecourt. Neither Amelia nor Erik know a lot about San José. They are traveling here without a guidebook. But there must be something to see in a big city with a population of half a million, especially in the middle of prosperous Silicon Valley and south of San Francisco. An American at the airport had once told Erik that the region was only "enjoyable" around the Bay Area. Just beyond Fremont or Walnut Creek, it would be barren. A woman who had joined him while waiting for the flight to be called was more radical: There was nothing to see outside San Francisco.

The two are lucky because they discover a motel that is close to the center and not far from the train station. In the area, there are some renovated former warehouses with pubs. The city center itself is very proper and tidy. The few historical buildings seem to have been renovated from the ground up. You walk between the palm trees on clean sidewalks through the center. There is little to see: few stores, a square with a cinema, and coffee shops. A light rail system runs through San José, connecting the center with the suburbs. But wait, there's a technology museum on Market Street called "The Tech". Aren't they in Silicon Valley? "We can take a look at that," Erik suggests, and Amelia nods.

The history of computer technology is on the agenda here. Frowning, Amelia stands in front of the exhibits, such as a long row of hard drives; the only exciting thing is that there were once hard drives as large as they had ever seen. "Aha, so that's what they put in computers in the seventies," she notes. "You might want to keep in mind: Most of the exhibits that the Computer Museum has on hand were developed here on site and were also produced in the past," Erik says. The exhibition runs the gamut of multimedia museum didactics; there are films, audio and video exhibits, and whatever else you have to make an exhibition attractive. This should promote interest in the natural sciences, which is why a visit should be a must for many school classes in the region. It could also be the ancestor of numerous "science centers" that now exist in many European cities. To ensure things don't get too dry, superhero movies from the Marvel studios are also shown in the attached IMAX cinema.

After a while, they leave the building with its large dome again, walk through the sparkling clean downtown, and look for an Italian restaurant where they have dinner. Amelia thinks San José would probably like to be an enjoyable, big city; you can probably tell. San José isn't necessarily that, though. Even if the vast, beautiful streets with palm trees and proper facades spread a pleasant atmosphere, the city seems a little artificial. They agree: they don't need to spend more than one night here.

Behind San José, the Caltrain, the commuter railroad, still goes a little south. After that, however, they would have to take the bus. So, for the two of them, there is only the long-distance train, the "Coast Starlight", with which they can travel in the direction of Los Angeles. They board the train at the "San José" station, which has come from Oakland on the bay's eastern side. On board, there would have been the whole selection of compartments, from the luxurious sleeping car with its own toilet and shower to the roomette, which Erik is familiar with, to the coach chair. As much as he would have liked to book a compartment, it was out of the question.

For one thing because the train runs during the day. It arrives in Santa Barbara shortly after 6 p.m. Then there's the price. The seats are available for $112, while the extra charge for a compartment would have been $380. He would rather spend the money on a fancy hotel in Santa Barbara. At "boarding," he was already entirely professional, able to help other travelers, greeted the service attendant, took the luggage to the upper deck of the car, and looked for the seats. They hear an "All Aboard" call, slamming the doors, then the train jerks and heads south.

Amelia thinks it's a shame they don't stop in Monterey, that historic town south of San José on the coast where John Steinbeck's "Strait of the Oil Sardines" is set. The aquarium there is also said to be worth a visit. Steinbeck himself had been born in Salinas. In this town, one could change from the train to the bus and make a detour to the former fishing village. But they have taken a seat and want to save the visit to Monterey for another time. Now, they want to ride the train all day at the Pacific.

Erik thinks the landscape is different compared to northern California: While there were still many trees on the mountains and hills between Portland and Oakland, they are rather bare here. Brown grass grows everywhere. It almost looks a bit like the desert. It is about 125 miles, about 200 kilometers, from Salinas to San Louis Obispo, where it goes back to the coast. The route is the primary connection from northern to southern California if one disregards the railroad line to Bakersfield and the Interstate, which runs much further inland. Only the "PCH", the "Pacific Coast Highway", runs directly along the coast. Erik knows it because he drove along it in a rental car many years ago. He tells Amelia that that was a spectacular drive because the highway runs in large, sweeping curves past rugged mountain slopes far above the Pacific, and the area is sparsely populated.

"There's a fantasy castle, Hearst Castle, on a hillside above the sea. The newspaper publisher William Randolph Hearst had the castle built for his great love, the film star Marion Davis," reports Erik Amelia.

"That sounds very romantic," she says.

"Yes, the fantasy castle is very opulent. It's on a lonely stretch of highway, where it winds along the coast past coves and ridges."

"The location also sounds impressive."

"Yes, but the romantic one has been a little motel I stopped at that time. It's on a rocky outcrop, high above the cliffs and surf. The rooms were in little cabins, and the whole place was lit up by colorful strings of incandescent lights. I drove the car straight toward it, and the points of light came closer and closer on this lonely highway when it was already getting a little dark. I pulled over, walked around the motel, and thought, This has to be one of the most romantic places on earth. This is where I want to go one day with someone special."

"Which didn't exist back then?" asks Amelia.

"No, there wasn't. I photographed the motel and wanted to write something about it once, but I did not. But now I'd love to go there with you, I was just thinking. Except we can't because it's too far from our train trip."

"But you seem to know what I would like. That sounds good with you in a romantic hotel, lonely on the cliffs. Let's just see if we can find a similar motel down south."

"That's what we'll do, Amelia. A little hotel, a cottage for the two of us, somewhere by the sea."

Erik does not know if they will succeed in finding such a hotel in Santa Monica or San Diego: somewhat enchanted but very romantic. But he decides that one day he will go with Amelia to the place near the "Hearst Castle".

"So, where are you going to?" asks the man across the aisle. He smiles friendly and interested, may be around 50 years old. As many Americans like to do, he starts a conversation with the question. Erik reports that they are on their way to Santa Barbara, where they want to take a break on their way to San Diego. A German and a Canadian are going by train through the USA. "An unusual undertaking, but not so crazy that it can't be done," he thinks, "but it's certainly not easy." He's traveling from San Francisco to Los Angeles, "nothing special," he says. He doesn't like the Interstate anymore and doesn't feel like flying. "Although, there's not much to see here either," the American thinks, pointing to the hills. "I had imagined this would be a little nicer. Oh well, I guess the best part of the trip is yet to come at the Pacific Ocean."

Erik thinks that a "Greyhound" or even a "Flixbus USA" ticket is probably out of the question for him. He seems to be part of the upper U.S. middle class, judging from his high-end casual clothes. In most parts of the country, where few passenger trains run, he would most likely be found in his car. He explains that the fastest connection from San Francisco to Los Angeles is via Bakersfield. One could take the "San Joaquins" from Oakland to Bakersfield, which takes six and a half hours to cover the distance. But then one must get on a bus that takes the last two hours to Los Angeles. That would be due to the "Passenger Rail Gap," the gap in passenger service between the two stations. The culprit, he said, is "Tehachapi Pass," which would be heavily used. Hence, the railroad company no longer allows passenger trains there. The new high-speed line is expected to take that route, finally eliminating the "gap." "But it looks the same on the whole trip," assures the American. "This time, I'm spending the extra time and want to see the Pacific."

There is no Pacific Ocean, only hills and occasionally the road of Highway 101, which follows the railroad track. That's why Amelia and Erik can make themselves home in the observation car, where seats are accessible. He fetches sandwiches, complete with Coke, from the lower deck. "I have to tell you that there are travelers who now pull a bottle out of their pocket and fortify the Coke with vodka," Erik says. "Who does that?" answers Amelia, her face contorting, "unless you're an alcoholic?" Erik has to laugh. "We've been there, done that, at the California Zephyr."

The click-clack of their train echoes through the car. Amelia leans back in her seat and lets out a soft sigh. This train ride is also a chance for her to escape the hustle and bustle of the university, where she spends most of her day. "You know, Erik," she says, a mixture of frustration and resignation resonating in her voice, "I really like my work at the university. The research, the lectures, it all fascinates me. But sometimes my colleagues really get on my nerves."

Erik nods in understanding because he knows this feeling too well. "Oh, Amelia, I can relate to that. I've heard many stories about the cutthroat environment in science, and it doesn't seem much different here."

Amelia's eyes widen. "It's discouraging, isn't it? Like a constant struggle for recognition, as if everyone is trying to outshine the next colleague."

Erik leans in closer. "What do you think is the cause of this behavior? Could it be a weakness in academic teaching?" Amelia pauses for a moment. She has thought about this question many times but has never found a clear answer.

"I'm not sure. Maybe it's the intense pressure of constantly proving yourself to stand out from a sea of talent. But whatever it is, it's affecting the atmosphere in our department."

As the train moves on, Amelia and Erik delve into this topic. They share their experiences. The more they talk about it, the more they realize how widespread this is, not only at Amelia's university but at many others as well. She feels a mixture of relief and longing. She is relieved because she can leave the toxic environment behind, if only temporarily. And also, of course, she is traveling with Erik. Longing, because she knows she will be confronted with all this again when she returns. Would there ever be a time when science would value collaboration over competition? Or would competition forever leave its mark on academia, robbing people like Amelia of their joy and enthusiasm?

"Maybe I should do something entirely different," Amelia finally sighs. As she does so, she looks at Erik with promise. "Yes, that would be something," Erik says, "whatever comes of it." Meeting Amelia has opened up a whole new, big world for him, too, one he's only gotten a whiff of so far.

Finally, the train arrives in San Louis Obispo, a town that already belongs more to the southern part of California - just as Salinas and Monterey belong to northern California. After a short stop, the "Coast Starlight" sets course for the Pacific. Then it's finally time to see the blue of the sea, which will now pass by for hours after it once appeared behind the windows of the panorama car. The train moves between the hills and then heads for the coast at Pismo Beach. On no other section does the "Coast Starlight" have such dense contact with the shore, except perhaps for the stretch beyond Seattle. Behind "Vandenberg Air Force Base", the rail line was built directly on the shore, and the Pacific moves very close to the tracks.

This goes on until Santa Barbara and beyond, all the way to Oxnard. The train runs about 150 miles, about 241 kilometers, directly on the Pacific Ocean, while the road has to make do with the interior. It's a relatively lonely place for the rail line so close to the ocean. But now they see the breakers rolling up to the beach. Sometimes, a spot for surfers appears on the shore. The panorama car is packed - understandably so, the view is spectacular. They stretch out on the seats. Erik does not want to return to the "coach" seats, which are also on the "wrong" side of the train, facing the land. Mile after mile, the spectacular scenery continues: Some grass right next to the tracks, then dunes, and then the beach with the waves of the Pacific breaking in the sunlight. He is convinced this section must be one of the world's most beautiful railroad lines. But just before 6 p.m., Erik sees the next stop approaching. "Well, we can spend another 20 minutes in our reserved seats," he says, and they walk back through the long train. "It's spectacular," agrees his seatmate from earlier. "It's worth it." He is now also lucky enough to sit on the "right side" of the train.

Santa Barbara is a small, big city on the Pacific Ocean that comes across as classy. Erik had written the city off as an exclusive "retiree's domicile". It may be worth a visit after all. He had heard that Santa Barbara should also have a university and a surfing scene. But when they walk from the train station across the main street with their luggage, there is no trace of students or surfers. After all, the author Tom Coraghessan Boyle is supposed to live here, and he will know where it's nice, Erik thinks. But downtown there are only expensive stores with exclusive fashion and big cars parked in front of them. Erik suspects that to feel at home here, you must be of advanced age and have a lot of money in your bank account - along with the necessary credit cards to get this money into circulation quickly.

He looks up the statistics on his smartphone: The median income in Santa Barbara is a staggering $89,000 - far higher than in many other U.S. cities. "Now you know where we've landed," he says to Amelia. According to the statistics, there are almost only white and Latino residents there, but virtually no people of color.

Accordingly, the hotel he had reserved is also exclusive. It is built in the "Spanish mission style" typical of Southern California, with white plastered walls, dark wooden beams, and tiled roofs. A funny expression, Erik thinks, because in the U.S., you can immediately imagine something about it. But do people in Spain know what the Mission style is supposed to be? The house is surrounded by a hedge and a large garden of vibrant green. Their room is vast with a sofa, has a large bathroom with a bathtub embedded in the floor, and a terrace overlooking the Pacific Ocean, or more precisely, overlooking the thoroughfare that runs along the Pacific. Every dollar they had saved on the train seems well spent here. "Now we're really letting ourselves go again. We can feel like two rich Americans of advanced age in Santa Barbara."

This starts with a visit to the hot tub outside in the hotel's garden, which is again very hot and continues with a drink on the garden terrace and then dinner in the hotel's restaurant. They still want to walk through the town, but the chic hotel captivates them. They do not leave it at all that evening but retire to the vast room - only to try the bathtub embedded in the floor, a kind of whirlpool in a marble wonderland. Did they pay too much for the room, Erik wonders? Yes, they definitely did. Is it worth it? They may not quite fit in here, but they're comfortable on the massive bed while crickets chirp outside.

"I'm not used to luxuries like this," Amelia notes. "Of course, we've done some traveling. We used to travel with the whole family, and later, I also traveled alone. We didn't live badly on our trips, either. But not in such luxury when I think of this bathroom."

"Well, neither do I," Erik replies. "The quaintest trip I remember was an Interrail tour during college."

"What's that?" she asks, "Sounds like rail."

"You buy one of those Interrail in Europe tickets, which are cheaper for students. By the way, for adults, too, we can get that sometimes."

"And then?"

"Then you can spend two weeks or even several months crisscrossing Europe. You have a flat rate for trains, so to speak."

"So railroading to the hilt? After all, that's what my job was at the Canadian."

"Yes, except that you can try out all kinds of routes. And

because the trains are virtually all already included in the price, as an interrailer, you usually sleep right on the train. Not in the sleeping car, that's not included. But in the seat or aisle, with your sleeping bag and backpack with you."

"Did that intrigue you?"

"Yes, it did. Most of our student group in Hamburg went to Italy and then south to stay a few days in Sicily. Some moved on to Greece. We went from Italy to Spain and then straight on to Portugal. That was great. But I don't remember the nights in the train seat so fondly."

"Well, and now look what's come of it. You're an established journalist, and you can put your Canadian girlfriend up in such a posh hotel where the bathroom has a marble floor," Amelia laughs.

"All the time, I couldn't do that. When my savings run out, we have to sleep on the seats on the train."

"Well, I would still love you then, of course. Maybe especially then," says Amelia.

However, after the stopover in exclusive Santa Barbara, the two are now tempted to head to the big city. Amelia doesn't know Los Angeles yet. Erik knows it from previous trips. Meanwhile, they no longer have to rely on the long-distance train, the "Coast Starlight," because from Santa Barbara, they can already take a commuter train, the "Pacific Surfliner," to Los Angeles. A fine move of the state of California to subsidize this connection. The cars look familiar, made of the same aluminum used in long-distance trains. Only the interiors are less designed for long travel. They are the somewhat narrower "surfliners," not the roomy "superliners".

For the first 30 miles, they can still enjoy the view of the Pacific. The train lives up to its name, "Surfliner," as it continues directly along the beach. On the eastern side runs Highway 101, and on the western side, there are mainly beaches and waves to see, and occasionally, surfers at some "spots". The train is almost empty in the morning, and they can spread out on the rows of seats. Every few rows, there is a table with four seats. It reminds Erik of a German intercity. They have room to set up their food the gigantic-sized paper cups of coffee, and group some cookies around them. Erik especially likes that there's a regular connection. They could catch the next train later if they were to get off in places like Oxnard or Ventura to check out the pier. Erik thinks that's quite a difference compared to a train that runs only once a day or three times a week. California is different from many states. There is simply more passenger rail traffic here.

He leafs through an Amtrak annual report that is lying in the car. Incredible, he thinks, what the public company discloses there. Anyone who wonders what the state pays in subsidies, where the trains run, what they devour in funds, and even what the sale of snacks in the cafeteria brings in will find all the answers in these reports. Also, where investments are pending, and that the "Los Angeles Union Station" they serve is in the top five of all stations in the USA.

Erik notices something: He no longer feels the need to get off the train, as he often did last year. He wants to be where Amelia is - and if that's on a train, he wants to stay with her. They have left the picturesque Pacific coast behind Ventura and are now rolling through the "Santa Rosa Valley", the "Simi Valley" and finally, the endless mush of the "San Fernando Valley". To the left and right, factories and industrial plants pass by, attractive and many not-so-beautiful houses, but always surrounded by palm trees and the one or other shopping center. Straight as a die runs the railroad line. This may sound a bit boring, and Erik thinks that the "Valley" is not exactly considered one of the exciting places on the West Coast. But he thinks it's interesting to "observe" the suburbs through the train window: You get a sense of the city that awaits you when you drive through its suburbs for a long time. How can little wooden houses look so proper? Are there people lying by the swimming pool in the midday sun? This area, with its wire fences, might it be safe at all if one were to walk the streets here now? Why are there now houses with piles of bulky waste in their gardens, close to the tracks? Who commutes by train from this platform that just flies past the window, but where the "Surfliner" does not stop? Who is commuting across the five lanes of the "freeway" in both directions, under which the train is speeding through?

"Tell me, what about train travel fascinates you?" asks Amelia. "I mean, I have fond memories of my trips as a student. There seems to be more to it with you?"

Erik considers for a moment. "There's something nostalgic about it. But for that, you might as well be on a museum train and limit your trip to a few hours."

She nods. "Then, of course, there's the comfort, and I admit, I already like these wide, comfortable seats better than the ones on European trains."

"They can't be that uncomfortable. I'd like to meet them sometime."

"We'll definitely get that done," Erik says.

"But what really fascinates you?" she asks.

"Well, the comfort comes at a considerable cost in terms of time. With a plane, distances that take a day by rail could be covered in a few hours, including getting to and from the airport and going through security, even if they are extremely inconvenient."

He explains to Amelia what attracts him to train travel is the "social component". The train is a microcosm of cars with seats, beds, compartments, a cafeteria, and a restaurant that rolls through the landscape. A wide variety of people now board this microcosm of steel and take their seats. "Most of the passengers are open-minded and talk about their journey and their destination. Some go above and beyond and tell about their lives." One advantage for him is that many North Americans are more talkative than passengers in Europe. Erik understands them. If he were traveling by train in Spain or Argentina, he knows it wouldn't work without the language. It would probably be the same in France.

Erik continues: "The atmosphere is safe." He tells Amelia about the episode with the belligerent men in Salt Lake City. "That didn't escalate, but that was also due to the attentive fellow passenger who intervened at the right moment because she sensed the explosive atmosphere. But you could still have called the conductor in a worst-case scenario."

"Oh," says Amelia, "you have to watch where you're going with you."

"If you have a place to retreat, like the Coach Class seat among other people, it's not really a problem," he says. "But having a compartment like we had is even better." That's what makes a train ride like this such an experience, he thinks: One can step into the public areas of the train, the restaurant, or the observation car, where one can learn more about fellow passengers in conversation. But one can also pull the door shut if it feels like it. After experiencing train travel for several days, Erik explains that he clearly leans toward a compartment if it's affordable. After all, he says, it's no small feat to sit in a coach seat for 36 hours.

"Especially when you don't really have anything to do, and you just stay in your seat," Amelia says. "That's what we liked back when we were students: We rode the train all day, but we had the time to work on something. That kept us moving all the time. Otherwise, I think I would have gotten bored."

"Look, if we were to drive around the U.S. by car now,"

Erik continues. "Certainly, there are few more convenient options than traveling in a car in the U.S. because the infrastructure in the whole country is designed for that. From the wide interstates, it's never far to a restaurant, a café or a motel."

"The sights in the cities and towns we pass can be approached without a timetable," Amelia adds.

"Yes, but it's not a social way to travel because, at the end of the day, you're traveling the world in a tin box by yourself or in a small group."

Not only car drivers travel like this, he continues in his reflections, sometimes it is the same with boaters. As Erik has observed, many sailors travel the sea alone in their little plastic boats. When surrounded by water, they often have little contact with the land or the population.

"What about ships? Wouldn't you like that too?" asks Amelia.

"That could be. But look: ship voyages for passengers really only take place as cruises. And the exuberant luxury, the gigantic size of such a ship with its thousands of passengers, is also a difficult way to explore the world, for me anyway."

Erik thinks back to how he once stood in the harbor of Nassau in the Bahamas in the morning, and several giant ships arrived from Florida. Suddenly, masses of travelers poured over the city, which made a considerable turnover in its stores and eateries with the "Cruise Ship Passengers". It is not because of them that Nassau suddenly becomes very uncomfortable, but because of the large crowd they appear in.

"Ha, I know what you mean. I've read David Foster Wallace, and he's right." Amelia means the book "A Supposedly Fun Thing I'll Never Do Again", in which Foster-Wallace "settles accounts" with cruise ships.

"But he's also a little mean sometimes because you wonder

why he's going at all," he says. "A lot of what he writes is true. Although sometimes I wondered why he was going at all."

"But isn't that the way it is in every serious travel book," Amelia counters. "The author describes not only the beautiful parts but also the ugly, unpleasant parts of a trip, and already you're wondering why it's going? Life isn't all sunshine any more than a trip is. I don't think you'll do it any differently."

Erik has to agree with her.

"There's one thing that bothers me about this: it's the huge amounts of pollutants that cruise ships like this blow out on the seas," Amelia adds.

"I disagree: The shipping companies have recognized this and are installing filters in the new ships. In doing so, they are reassuring passengers who might have a guilty conscience about it," Erik says. "But for me, the problem that should be investigated first is the crew's working conditions on these luxury ships."

"There again, I hear completely the socially critical journalist, for whom climate change is only a side effect," says Amelia.

"Climate change is not a byproduct. But working conditions are a problem that is often overlooked. Ships like this need an insane amount of staff. So how can the voyages be offered so cheaply? But only by paying the crew meager wages. The Filipinos on board accept this because it is still more money than they would earn in their home country. But the passengers pay low prices for long journeys, which is the real problem. The exhaust filters for CO_2 emissions could be installed for relatively little money."

"But until that happens, cruises aren't a very environmentally friendly way to travel," Amelia says.

"Well, at least our train rides are halfway climate-friendly, don't you think?"

"Yes, they are, as long as we don't occupy one of the giant

compartments on the train by ourselves. But they're also reasonably socially acceptable, as far as Amtrak and VIA employee pay is concerned."

"Then we've found our way of traveling," says Erik. They both look out the window at the scenery outside. Los Angeles is getting closer, and the train is slowing down.

"Tell me, is there anything you like about riding the train? I mean, you actually know a lot more about it than I do."

"Oh no, you're our walking encyclopedia when it comes to trains," she says teasingly. "I actually like everything." Amelia smiles. "There's something magical about it, don't you think? I mean, sure, the views are incredible, and it's nice not to have to drive yourself. But it's more than that. It's environmentally friendly and climate-friendly. And it's like being transported to another world or maybe another time."

The train ride, she says, has something adventurous about it that can't be compared to any other mode of transportation. "Then it's like you say: it's the people. Everyone on this train has a story, and some of them tell us."

LOS ANGELES AND SANTA MONICA

The Surfliner enters the tangle of tracks outside the Los Angeles train station. In the 1930s, "L.A." got its big Union Station, as Erik knows, which came into being shortly before the car and the airplane started their triumphant march over the railroad. Los Angeles had already been planned as a sprawling city with various centers, but there was to be a central train station at its heart. Union Station opened in 1939 and is considered a "masterpiece" of so-called Spanish Colonial architecture. "So, the Spanish mission style?", Amelia asks him. "Exactly." The magnificent facade, impressive entrance hall, and courtyards make the station an "architectural jewel."

Well, "jewels" exist in the Midwest, too, at extinct railroad stations. What makes this station special, Erik wonders? At least there's life there again. Union Station serves as a hub for many modes of transportation. Various rail lines, including Amtrak and Metrolink, meet here with regional connections. In addition, Union Station offers connections to buses and the Los Angeles subway, called Metro.

But Union Station is also known because it has been featured in many movies and television series. It may be because of its architecture and atmosphere. Still, he has the impression that it is because of its proximity to the studios in Hollywood. If you're looking for a cheap station for your production, there's one right on your doorstep and a very impressive one. In general, Los Angeles is probably over-represented in film productions. In any case, this station has served as a backdrop for films like "Blade Runner," "The Client" and "Chinatown." What also makes the station pleasantly different from other stations is that there are stores, cafés, and restaurants that travelers and commuters frequent.

"Los Angeles is a city that seems to be returning to its urbanity," Amelia says as they walk downtown. New apartment buildings and a subway add urbanity to the place used only as an office location for decades, shunned after dark for many years. "After all, it's quite interesting to stroll downtown from Union Station," Erik says. Pershing Square, the heart of downtown, is a good walk from the station.

"Over there is the posh Biltmore Hotel," Amelia notes. From the Beatles to John F. Kennedy, numerous celebrities have been guests there. When "downtown L.A." had reached its low point and was visibly deteriorating, reopening this hotel in the 1980s was a highlight. The park feels the same way. "At one time in the 1920s, this must have been a great place, with tall trees, palm trees, and tropical plants," Amelia says. Then, the "suburbanization" of the city set in, and the park fell into disrepair. "Did you know that they seriously sold the remaining palm trees to Disneyland, where they served as a backdrop for an attraction called the Jungle Ride?" asks Amelia. After that, an underground parking garage was built there. For many years, the park remained little more than a barren concrete wasteland. It wasn't until 1994 that it was closed and completely renovated so that today it's actually quite an attractive center again.

But despite the tall buildings, most of which have been carefully restored - it's not a downtown as attractive as San Francisco, Seattle, or Chicago. Perhaps it's the lack of stores or the few restaurants. They head west and take the Metro one stop to "Mc Arthur Park.

"I want to see that one," Amelia says.

"Why Mc Arthur Park, of all places?" he asks.

She rummages in her purse, pulls out her iPhone, and hands him the headphones. "Wait, that's why I want to visit the park."

He hears "Ding, Ding, Dada" and recognizes the song. However, it is not Donna Summer singing. Her version is the best known, but a man. It seems to be older. "It's the park that songwriter Jimmy Webb named one of his compositions after, which was then sung by Richard Harris. You're listening to that right now. But Tony Benett also recorded the song, as did the Four Tops." But the "Mc Arthur Park Suite" didn't really become successful until the disco version that Donna Summer released in 1979.

Amelia knows more: Jimmy Webb was inspired to write the song by his relationship and breakup with his girlfriend, Susie Horton. It was in this park that Jimmy and Susie met and spent their best time together. Sometime in 1965, she worked for a company at the park. Webb once explained in an interview that

"Mc Arthur Park" was symbolic - a sign of a love affair coming to an end.

"But that's sad," Erik slips out.

"That doesn't mean you. It's not you and me. But he's singing about the love of his life," says Amelia. By the way, the song has already landed on the list of the worst pop songs of all time, probably due to the lyrics. Harris sings:

Someone left the cake out in the rain,

I don't think I can take it,

because it took so long to bake it,

and I no longer have the recipe.

So the lyrics may be a bit simple, maybe funny, but the melody is very complex at the same time. The piece is considered one of the most complicated and challenging to play pop compositions.

The two enter the park from the subway station and walk through the lively green space. A few years ago, it came into disrepute due to growing crime. Still, now it is more heavily patrolled, as Amelia has read. The park now also provides shelter for the homeless, as do many places in Los Angeles. They are drawn to California because of the warm weather. Many people walk through the greenery, families picnic on the lawn or use the barbecue areas, and lie on the shore of the lake. When you see the water against the backdrop of the skyscrapers of downtown "L.A.", you can feel something like an urban heart beating here. Erik doesn't feel melancholy, like Jimmy Webb, as he walks through the park with Amelia - more like the happy days Jimmy and Susie are said to have spent together here.

The next stop is Santa Monica because they want to visit Los Angeles' neighboring city on the Pacific Ocean and settle in there. A few years ago, that would have meant a long bus ride for them, as Erik knows. But in the meantime, the "metro" has been extended: A light rail goes all the way west. It's one-stop back by train, and then from the "Metro Center" it's a good hour through the city. The train is sparkling clean and runs briskly. "It's a good way to get to the sea through the 'settlement mush,'" he thinks.

In Santa Monica, however, they are in for a disappointment: the motel they enter not far from the beach looks nowhere near as nice as the advertising photos on the web. Clearly worse, however, is the bored and super-cool man at the front desk, who only yawns wearily when Erik addresses him. "I don't have a room available, nothing to do," he says unkindly. "But we have a reservation on the net. There's the confirmation," Erik says, holding out his smartphone. The man doesn't even look at the display. "I'm not interested. We're full and out of here now." Erik's breath catches. "Did he just say 'get out of here' to me?" he asks, turning to Amelia. "Yes, you heard me right," the man behind the reception desk says. Amelia is de-escalating. She tugs Erik's shirt and pulls him out of the reception area. "There's no point, I don't want you at each other's throats right away. And actually, I don't want to stay here in this dump," she adds aloud. They stand outside.

Erik finally manages to use his smartphone to book another hotel, which is a bit cheaper but much further inland. That's how it is in Santa Monica: The city has its high point on the water, at the "Pacific Palisades" park, and in the center with its beautiful pedestrian zone, the "5th Street Promenade". This is where everything strives to go, and that's why prices also strive to go up here. Everything further east slowly becomes cheaper - be it restaurants, stores, or even motel rooms.

The ride on the city bus becomes a bit annoying. The two have to wait a long time. He can see it on Amelia's face, even if she doesn't say it. Getting around by public transportation in this car city doesn't seem to excite her. It wouldn't have been impossible to switch to a rental car. But they want to get a room, and in the end, it was quicker to take the "Big Blue Bus," as it's called in Santa Monica, to the motel than to organize another rental car, say at the airport. In the hotel in the "hinterland", the receptionist is friendly and seems happy about new guests. The room, however, is set back behind a concrete superstructure and has virtually no daylight. The furnishings have clearly seen better days, even though they shine in a lovely retro orange-brown. Well, they had a fancy room in Santa Barbara, Erik thinks. Here, at least, they are still part of Santa Monica life, which they enjoy extensively in the evening - first by bus to downtown, then through the 5th Street Promenade. The street, a pedestrian zone since the 1970s, has become more chic and trendy with each renovation. Today, there are many restaurants, bars, and high-priced stores. From there, it's not far to the pier, which juts out into the Pacific from the beach here.

There, they are approached by a man who seems to carry an entire jewelry store in the lapel of his jacket. "Wouldn't you like to buy something," he asks. Amelia looks at the gold chains with a grin, laughs, and thinks it would make a nice souvenir.

"I know the phrase: never buy jewelry from a street vendor, no matter how cheap it's supposed to be," Amelia says. "But I like this one."

"Is that really made of gold?" asks Erik.

"But of course, real gold for only ten dollars," says the flying merchant. "I hope it's not hot stuff," Erik answers.

"No, not a hot commodity," he says.

"Actually, it doesn't matter if it's gold," Amelia says. "We need a souvenir to remind us of our visit to Santa Monica."

What they want with the jewelry is not entirely clear to Erik. But he understands Amelia's wish for a souvenir. So they buy two bangles from the flying merchant, who seems happy, for

$20. "We know it's not gold, but we need a souvenir," he tells him. So they can put on each other's bangles, which shine in two shades of gold and brass, twisted into each other. Both look nice. Whatever they're made of doesn't matter. Amelia seems happy about her new souvenir.

On the pier, there are not only merry-go-rounds, a parking lot, and a roller coaster racing above the wooden planks and the sea. They like the atmosphere here: It's chic in Santa Monica, it's not cheap, but it just doesn't have that wealthy-set atmosphere of Santa Barbara.

A new sunny day on the edge of the Pacific Ocean city greets them the next morning. After breakfast outside their room, on a concrete outdoor seating area, they walk to "Venice Beach." The long boardwalk that starts at the Pacific Palisades in Santa Monica leads to this place. They spend a good hour and a half walking from the Santa Monica Pier to Venice in the morning sun. The location is something like the incarnation of Southern California life: a wide sandy beach, behind it the boardwalk, with cafés, somewhat overpriced ice cream parlors, bric-a-brac stores offering masses of cell phone cases in pop colors, and open-air training studios. This is the "Original Muscle Beach," the beach where the strength-training craze is said to have originated back in the 1930s. Here, many Southern Californians still rollerblade or inline skate on the concrete slabs of the boardwalk. But the majority are bicyclists and pedestrians. Some street artists paint their works on concrete barriers: They are the "Venice Boardwalk Murals" who, for example, are currently painting an image of Arnold Schwarzenegger as a bodybuilder. Or there are street artists offering portraits with easels. Amelia hesitates for a moment and looks at the portraits. She grins but then says, "We can always have that painted by us" - and they continue walking. "We still have our jewelry from last night, after all." The parking lots behind the boardwalk always have "vans" with surfboards on the roofs. In the "Ocean Park" neighborhood, they walk under an avenue of green trees that somewhat keep out the burning sun.

On the promenade they finally reach Venice. Amelia has made herself wise in a travel guide she took with her. "This place is part of Los Angeles, unlike Santa Monica. Venice was founded as a seaside resort in 1905," Amelia reports as they sit down on a bench along the boardwalk. "To drain the marshland, real estate developer Abbot Kinney had miles of canals laid out where waterfront property could be purchased. This is said to be the connection to the city of 'Venice' in Italy." Amelia describes that at one time, there were gondola rides, a miniature railroad, and even a long pier similar to the one in Santa Monica in Venice.

Initially, the Los Angeles City Council had the seaside resort on its radar. Among the few investments that came was to fill in the lagoon and convert it into a large traffic circle. By the 1950s, many canals had been built over, and Venice must have hit rock bottom, earning the nickname "Slum by the Sea." "That led to two developments," Amelia says: first, crime grew through gangs. It wasn't until the 1990s that the police managed to get a handle on it. Second, the low rents and its location attracted many artists, poets, writers, European immigrants, and the "Beat Generation." Venice became hip - which at the same time laid the foundation for gentrification in the decades to come.

Yes, Erik understands that. First, the area fell into disrepair, then it became "hip," and thanks to that, it has been "gentrified". The shallow marshy canals you can cross on bridges a few hundred meters behind the beach smell a bit boggy. Perhaps they had chosen a bad day for the visit, or there is just not enough water flowing through the narrow sluice to the Pacific Ocean in the south - they walk quickly along the shore. Only a little further, at the vast "Caroll Canal", the air becomes fresher. There are also many small rowboats on the shore, along which there is a walking path.

"So this is where I could already imagine a cottage," Amelia says.

"Yes, but do you want to live in this giant juggernaut that is Los Angeles?" he asks.

"No, I'd rather do it in Sausalito on San Francisco Bay, that is, if money is no object. You know what? This cold Edmonton may be pretty nice. But I'd much rather live in that kind of environment in Southern California."

"I understand that well. When I think of rainy northern Germany, I feel the same way."

They stroll back to the beach and walk along the 400-meter "Venice Fishing Pier," which stretches far into the Pacific but is little more than a long concrete pier.

"How about one of those beach houses back there?" asks Amelia.

"Oh yes, if you could live with the little house I can offer you," Erik replies.

"I can contribute from my job as a biologist, too," she counters. Actually, he wouldn't care if he had to cut back, Erik thinks. If he could live with Amelia in sunny Southern California, he would also live in one of the run-down apartments a few blocks inland.

"The main thing is that we have a little space. Then we can set up: I'll open a small laboratory, and you'll have an office. Then you can set up a research institute for railroad history," says Amelia, teasing Erik.

"Well, sure, you have squid in glass cases to study, and I spend all day leafing through dusty archives about railroads," Erik replies.

In any case, the real estate makes a difference to the expensive Santa Monica: Here, chic apartment buildings can be found close to the beach, while a few blocks to the east, houses stand empty, and building plots eke out a desolate existence. Further south is the entrance to one of the largest marinas in the world, the "Marina del Rey", a gigantic development project, but too far to walk. The rest of the day is spent on the beach and on the "Boardwalk" in Venice Beach.

The following day, they have breakfast again in the sun outside the hotel room on one of the concrete tables. Again, Amelia and Erik smile at each other as he pours coffee into two mugs. "This could go on," Amelia says. "Is it going to go on like this? What do you mean? That we sit in the sun every morning and drink coffee together."

"I'm all for it, Amelia. I bring you coffee in a paper cup every morning in the sun. You know what? We'll find a motel just like this in San Diego, and then we'll just keep doing this."

After all, they want to go to the southernmost major city in California. To do that, they have to catch the train again, the "Pacific Surfliner," which leaves downtown at Union Station. That means first taking a bus, then an hour of light rail. The distances in Los Angeles are gigantic, Erik realizes, not only when you're stuck in a traffic jam on one of the freeways by car, but also when you're traveling by train.

"Come on, let's take a detour to Hollywood," Amelia suggests. Again, a bus takes them from Santa Monica through the Westwood neighborhood to Hollywood Boulevard.

They get off at the intersection of Vine Street and Hollywood Boulevard. This is the epicenter of the area, the Hollywood Walk of Fame, which is visited by over ten million tourists a year. "There are now 2752 stars embedded in the sidewalks," Amelia recites the guidebook. They are reminiscent of actors, and someone came up with an old-fashioned movie camera as a symbol. Likewise, there's the symbol for a television, a record, a microphone, and two masks meant to represent theater. But of course, the Walk of Fame is a movie boulevard. Accordingly, 47 percent of the stars are dedicated to movie actors, while just two percent go to theaters. Some celebrities also have multiple plaques: Frank Sinatra, for instance, is honored for cinema, music, and T.V. But Erik also knows another side of the story: he didn't get a star for being a casino owner. The idea for the stars dates back to the 1950s, and the local chamber of commerce wanted to use them to promote tourism.

Erik can still remember earlier visits to Hollywood Boulevard: the area was a bit run-down, even though tourists still flocked there. But the cheap souvenir stores, bars, and takeaways gave the boulevard something cheap. That has changed, as one can see. Hollywood is once again a hip destination, almost a must-see for any tourist visiting Los Angeles. Big brands like Disney have opened stores. The famous cinema "Chinese Theater" has been built into a shopping center, the "Ovation Hollywood", just like the "Dolby Theatre". Although the "Academy Awards" are presented here every year, the mall has only the usual stores found in U.S. malls and a large tourist offer for Hollywood visitors. There are pictures, T-shirts, coffee mugs, sun hats - in fact, anything you can put the words Hollywood on.

No, Amelia also does not want to acquire such a souvenir. The machine is running again, and money can be earned with the "Hollywood" myth. Behind this is also the "Heart of Hollywood Master Plan" that the city of Los Angeles has adopted: The sidewalks will be widened, there will be outdoor restaurants, bicycle lanes, and less traffic. The revitalization of the boulevard, which already looks quite vital again, is to be completed by 2026.

"Look, there's the Metro, we can take it now," Erik says. "That's wonderful: just take the red line to Union Station," agrees Amelia.

By the Pacific to San Diego

Amelia and Erik hurry through the art-deco station concourse to the ticket counter. They get lost in the maze of travelers. Erik stops and looks around. But he can't spot Amelia anywhere. He feels himself getting slightly nervous. Where is his traveling companion? Oh no, traveling companion, where is the beloved Amelia? After five minutes, someone approaches him from behind. "Peekaboo, there you are," says Amelia. "I missed you already." Fortunately, they have found each other again.

Outside on the platform, the train waits for them and they make themselves comfortable. It's a fabulous 55 miles, about 89 kilometers, through the jungle of houses in Los Angeles, through the suburbs. It takes them three-quarters of an hour to get to Anaheim alone. Amelia smiles at him as they sit in their seats and roll through the city.

Amelia talks about her parents, uncles, and aunts who live in Canada - and are spread across the country between Edmonton and Toronto. Most of all, she talks about her brother. "He's only a year older than me. We're pretty close. I've told him about you, too," she says with a smile. "He has his family and a cottage in a suburb of Edmonton. He's really chatty like that. In contrast, I, actually a sensible biologist, am a true hippie, wandering around here with a traveler from Europe," she says with a laugh.

Erik talks about his family in Germany, his uncle, and aunt, with whom he grew up. He also tells Amelia about the rebellious part of his youth. This affects her more than Candice, who thought the whole thing was a funny episode in his life. "Well, I'm glad you got your act together," Amelia says. "Then I hope you don't rebel right back."

"Right away again? What do you mean?"

"Erik, I don't think you ever got over the loss of your parents."

"It felt that way to me, too."

"You carried this loss around with you as a child. And when you became a young man, the frustration made its way out. You must have rebelled because you sought a way to express your feelings. You could not blame your aunt and uncle directly. So you rebelled. That should affect them, too."

"Now that's some real analysis on your part."

"Well, I'm just a biologist, not a psychologist. And my kitchen table psychology should also be taken with a grain of salt." Amelia smiles at him. "But better some kitchen table psychology than none at all. And that's what your story sounds like to me. But because you're a reasonable person, you stopped your rebellion again when you realized you would pay for it. And I don't think you really wanted to hurt your uncle."

"No. I think he knows that, too."

"But now you're in danger of rebelling again."

"You think?"

"Well, you've got a lot piled up. From what I know about you, your situation at work is crying out for rebellion: You've put an insane amount of work into this magazine. But no one will thank you for it, I'm afraid. The readers won't because they won't buy the magazine anymore. Your publisher won't because they don't appreciate how hard you work. Especially not because they don't look for new ways they could survive as a magazine. What you told me about the online forums your publisher is relying on, they can't be serious."

"Yes, that's precisely how it feels: They're not making a

serious effort to get out of it. They're not thinking in new categories; they've locked into a model, which doesn't work. Selling online subscriptions for shallow news, that's not the core of our magazine at all."

"And that's where the problem for you comes in. Your frustration will find its way sooner or later. You have too much pent-up inside you for that."

"You really think so?"

"Oh yes, I hear that clearly. But if you react again as you did before, it will result in rebellion."

"I promise you that I will not join a motorcycle gang."

"Oh, we also have some great motorcycle gangs here in Canada. At least, I think so. I don't know for sure. I wouldn't mind if you got yourself a motorcycle. But there's one thing you absolutely must not do."

"And what might that be?"

"To put it in your words, you're going off the rails."

"I couldn't do that."

"Erik, I think your feelings are pretty strong, and something like that can develop a power you are not even aware of yet. You have harmed people who have nothing to do with your situation. Just think about the shops you 'facilitated'."

"Yes, that was lousy of us. The small shop owners didn't have much themselves and had to fight for survival," Erik admits. "Today, I realize that, too. At the time, I didn't see it."

"I think you did, or you wouldn't have stopped being a gang."

"Yeah, maybe."

"In any case, today, you have to find a way to deal with the frustration that the situation has brought you. Somehow, your anger will find its way out, I'm sure of it. You just can't go on as before. Otherwise, it will end badly."

Again, Erik is completely taken aback by Amelia. He senses

that her analysis is correct. He can't just go on with his job in Germany like this. Because that could end badly for him.

"But those are also just the thoughts I have. I'm not saying that it all has to be true. But I feel there's something to it. I think you can take a lot off and still keep going. But the frustration will find its way. I feel the same way in my job."

"You were lucky, though, that you hadn't thought about joining a motorcycle gang, right?"

"Me? Oh no, I wouldn't have dreamed of that. I grew up totally sheltered. I think my problem is that I grew up much too sheltered. My parents and my brother always took care of me. There were reasons for that. However, it's become much too tight for me in the long run."

Amelia has to laugh as she pursues a thought.

"What are you laughing at?" Erik asks her.

"I thought maybe it's time for me to rebel. Yeah, perhaps I need a motorcycle myself. Or this little edition of it ..."

"A moped? No, Amelia, that would look pretty weird if you rode a moped. Either get yourself a real motorcycle or a particularly fancy bike that's more on trend."

"But that's not particularly rebellious."

"Then it would have to be a motorcycle for you."

Erik tells Amelia more about his family. Because there is another part, with which he is closely connected. He has an aunt and uncle who live in South America. "I really like those two. They sometimes come to visit us from Argentina. Then we tell each other everything. I would love to visit them one day."

"So you haven't made it to Argentina yet?"

"No, even though it would actually make sense. Who knows, Amelia, what do you think about going there?"

"What, to Argentina? Well, I'd want to come with you, of course."

"That would be the nicest thing. They are really likable. Maybe because they live on the other side of the world, I'm their connection to Europe."

"That sounds great," Amelia says. She looks Erik in the eye.

"Tell me, why is there actually no woman in your life in Germany? There isn't, is there?"

"No, there isn't," he says, looking a little sad. Amelia smiles at him encouragingly.

"But she does exist here, doesn't she?"

"I do hope so. I'm very much in favor of it."

"Oh, I can tell you firsthand, I'm very much in favor of it, too."

"Well, if you ask me, there was a woman. We liked each other, at least in the beginning. Andrea was a colleague of mine. I thought there could be more - she didn't think so. We broke up, and that's already ..." He thinks for a moment. "That's two years ago. Since then, I've been alone with my work."

Amelia looks out the window. Then she looks at Erik again. "Your story is similar to mine. We were even close to getting engaged. I really thought it would be soon now. But it wasn't. We, my fiancé at the time and I in Canada, also broke up," she says, and the tone of her voice is sad. "That was four years ago for me, and since then, I've also only known my work, just like you."

Then, her expression brightens. "Don't you think: What you and I are experiencing, how you and I are together, it's different. It feels right."

"Yes, it is different. I can feel that. It feels right and important. Can you put it that way? Right and important?"

"I know what you mean," Amelia replies, beaming.

Further on, the train rushes through the city, past streets, intersections, stores, and residential buildings. The "Surfliner" rolls into the Anaheim train station, which is partly covered by a freeway. The two of them, however, are now very cheerful. They can't see anything of Disneyland in Anaheim, though; it's hidden behind an industrial park. "So this is Mickey Mouse's home," Amelia notes. "Yes, Walt Disney planned Disneyland in Anaheim back in 1948. The amusement park was his dream. In 1955, the original Disneyland opened."

"Did he live here, too?" asks Amelia.

"Not quite. The house that Walt Disney moved into with his wife Lilian and their two daughters was in Holmby Hills, behind Beverly Hills. That's about three-quarters of an hour away."

Walt Disney not only had a knack for animated films but also a soft spot for trains: In Holmby Hills, he even had an elaborate garden railroad built in front of his house, which guests could then ride.

"He was also excited by visions of the future," Erik mentions. Disney, for example, was convinced that the monorail was the ideal mode of transportation for the future. The "Allwegbahn" he chose was even a German development. Today, monorail trains roll along their concrete tracks at the amusement park. Yet Los Angeles transportation planners, much like Seattle, had been working on a monorail concept for the entire city in the 1960s, in keeping with the zeitgeist for a futuristic mode of transportation. Science fiction writer Ray Bradbury praised the project this way: "Remember: subways are for cold climes, snow and sleet in wintry London, Moscow or Toronto. Monorails are for high, free, open spirits, for our always nice weather."

"Well, that's a nice phrase. So, the monorail wouldn't be for a city like Edmonton. So why hasn't the railroad been built?"

"They didn't get it right. Hundreds of thousands of man-hours went into designing the network, developing the stations, and animations to make the project palatable to citizens. Unfortunately, the Monorail Commission got bogged down, applying for more and more funding to rehash the ideas, until finally it was cut off and the project was killed."

"That's a pity. But I also like to ride this train with you," Amelia replies.

"It doesn't have much in common with an elegant monorail. But it actually runs, and not just in the plans of a few futurists."

The air conditioner hisses quietly again while it gets over 86 degrees Fahrenheit outside in sunny Anaheim. They've taken a seat on the right side, and there's a reason for that again. The endless suburbs don't stop yet; they still have to roll through Irvine, Santa Ana, and San Juan Capistrano. But then the "Pacific Surfliner" reaches the ocean from which it got its name. At St. Clemente, it again runs so close to the water and the narrow beach that you might think the blue waves are about to crash against the train. Interstate 5 runs parallel and is set back on the land side.

Amelia is thrilled, and Erik also finds this section of track more impressive than anything he has seen. In the small town of St. Clemente, the train stops briefly at a mini-station, then rolls south, continuing along the water. If the train were a boat, it would be listing: almost all the seats on the side facing the ocean are occupied. If you don't get sucked in by that, Amelia says you must be a commuter and use this train a lot. "You'll find plenty of seats on the left for that," Erik notes.

Small coastal towns follow, and the view of the long, beautiful sandy beach in the sun. Only before La Jolla, in Sorrento Valley, does the "Surfliner" make a turn inland and exit the valley behind the University of San Diego. The "Scripps Coastal Reserve" marshland was apparently not intended to be lined with rails by the line's builders. After that, the picturesque scenery comes to an end. From there to San Diego, the train covers the last twelve miles of its route directly near Interstate 5. The lagoon of Mission Bay and Lindbergh Field, San Diego's airport, whiz by before downtown comes into view. The central station here is the Santa Fe Depot, which, like many in the U.S., was threatened with demolition but saved in the 1970s due to many citizen protests. The trip from Los Angeles to San Diego took them under three hours.

Amelia and Erik don't want to stay downtown, but want to live right by the ocean. The two attractive neighborhoods for them are "Pacific Beach" and "Ocean Beach," both located directly near the ocean, separated by Mission Bay Lagoon and Fiesta Island Park. Both would have to be accessed by bus, as the light rail does not stop there. Pacific Beach is a very hip but expensive neighborhood. It has a spectacular coastline, as promised by a travel website that seems to advertise the area. Likewise, it refers to the "vibrant nightlife" along Garnet Avenue. This is also where a real attraction is located on the beach: it is the "Crystal Pier Hotel", which consists of 1930s bungalows built directly on the pier. It looks very original: You would have as a room a small hut standing on a dock made of wood over the sea. It must be a fantastic place. However, so are the prices that are called per night there. That's why Amelia and Erik chose a motel in Ocean Beach, the neighborhood closer to the center.

They drove there by bus in just under half an hour. In between, Amelia reads that San Diego is considered one of the safest big cities in the U.S. and grins, "We don't have to worry about that if we want to do something at night." He thinks back to when they were in Santa Monica and thought about going to Hollywood Boulevard at night to stroll around - and then decided against it.

Ocean Beach was once known as the "Haight-Ashbury" of San Diego, after its "great model," the alternative neighborhood in San Francisco. The community became a magnet for hippies. But it took time for residents to accept the new visitors who flocked here - which they eventually did. Today, the "Ocean Beach People's Organic Food Market" is a testament to that. Of course, this isn't a "hippie neighborhood" - but the slightly gentrified edition of one that used to be.

"Beach casual" is the name given to the style of the locals here, a term Erik likes very much. "We're so beach casual, too," he says to Amelia, who actually doesn't look "casual" at all in the summer dress and with her travel bags. But still more "casual" than in "Coronado," the exclusive neighborhood in the south with the widely known beach hotel. That would be simply "Upscale." Of course, Ocean Beach has a history of massive new construction plans to redevelop the somewhat run-down neighborhood that attracted the hippies: Real estate developers wanted to build resorts, hotels, and a marina. But opposition from local residents stood in the way. With the help of a 1972 height restriction, larger apartment buildings were not allowed. Ocean Beach has remained a community of tiny homes to this day, including commercial streets with stores and many bars and restaurants.

The motel Erik and Amelia have chosen is really to their taste. At first glance, it may have seen better days, and the paint is peeling in places. On the other hand, it's not as overpriced as some other oceanfront hotels in San Diego. It is a two-story building with a courtyard from the sixties. But it has been colorfully decorated. On the walls hang surfboards, flags, and all sorts of nautical paraphernalia, as Erik calls it: There are glass balls in fishing nets, old anchors, and a large sail is stretched over the patio. The lady at the reception is amiable. Erik and Amelia get a nice big room on the second floor. Their balcony is just the balustrade leading to the rooms, but there, they can sit on two comfortable wooden chairs. "I think this is cool. Is this our common taste?" Amelia asks him.

"Yeah, it's fancy. I think this is the place for us."

Well, they were both not quite right then. Many surfers stay in the motel. What seems quite "cool" at first glance is annoying at second. These surfers, all of them alternative-looking twenty-somethings, form a closed community that likes to party in the hotel's small courtyard but wants to keep to themselves. This is told to him by his room neighbor, who is enjoying a week's summer retreat here. He tried it, but the surfers didn't want him among them. Erik also notices that every attempt to converse with the surfer group ends rather monosyllabically. He finds this annoying because they start their barbecue event on the beach in the evening, right on time after returning from water sports, with pounding music.

Well, so be it. The sun is shining, and they rush to the beach - but certainly not to surf, even if boards that cost only 15 dollars a day are rented there. Instead, they swim in the clear, warm waters of the Pacific.

In the evening, all hell really breaks loose on the wide Newport Avenue leading away from the beach. The spectacle, with its bars and restaurants, is just a few blocks from their motel. Unlike there, the people here are cheerful and outgoing. They go to a "Shushi & Tapas" restaurant right on the main street.

"Do you actually like sushi?" asks Amelia.

"Yes, I like to eat that sometimes. But not all the time. It's not exactly my favorite dish."

"Ha, I should have guessed that. If you'd rather have a burger, there's one up the street."

"No, Amelia, it fits here. I'll have sushi, too. Or stop. I'll eat sushi if you take tapas, like in Spain."

"That suits me fine because I was looking forward to the squid."

"That's right, they come from the tapas part of the menu. But you examine the squid, and then you eat them too?"

"Yeah, why not?"

"Mm, I was just thinking. Then I'll eat the raw fish."

"We biologists are tough, you know," she says with a grin.

The food is good, Erik thinks: The sushi pieces are not drowning in a thick rice coating, but there is plenty of fish. The squid Amelia ordered comes with lots of garnishes and herbs. "But now I have to try some of your fish," she says. This time, Erik immediately gives her the fork, not carefully cutting off a piece to put on her plate. She also hands him the fork with a selection of squid.

After dinner, they move to a bar on Newport Avenue. It's a "cool" place; Erik is pleased to see modern jazz playing there. "I think the music is great," he says.

"Oh yeah, I could get used to that too. Otherwise, a lot of bars are always playing loud rock, or worse. But this is nice, and we can still talk at this volume."

They strike up a conversation with the guests at the neighboring table. The "students" have traveled from Los Angeles to celebrate a weekend in the summer. They surf at Ocean Beach. Erik is amazed: they are approachable and talk openly about the fascination of their sport and the waves. "Actually, the party in the evening is just as important to us as the surfing," one of them tells them. "So there are nice surfers, too," Amelia notes.

The atmosphere here is less refined than in San Francisco or Santa Monica, but that's precisely what they like. There's something in the air that could be described as an "easy vibe" - or is it more the smell of marijuana that's in the air? The food is good;

there are Italians, burger joints, Mexicans, and other places to eat. But since Erik followed his rule and didn't take a guidebook, he doesn't know if this would be a guidebook recommendation. Amelia looks it up because she's prepared: "Lo and behold, there's a big section devoted to "Ocean Beach," complete with restaurant and hotel recommendations." However, they don't follow those, but drift and see what they like and where they want to go. "Just don't wander around this neighborhood with an open guidebook," Amelia says. "That could end badly."

The next few days in San Diego, they don't miss a beat: They visit downtown with their bus walk through the historic "Gaslamp Quarter", which in this warmer climate is better suited for a stroll than its Vancouver counterpart. They browse the "Horton" shopping center, a thriving "open-air mall" downtown. They stroll along the harbor and drive up the peninsula to the Hotel Coronado, which Erik and Amelia visit but then disregard because of the prices. Because she would like to, they also go to the "San Diego Zoo", a great attraction of the Southern California city.

As Erik and Amelia stroll through the zoo entrance, both are curious. Amelia's excitement can be felt by Erik, as she had dreamed of visiting this famous zoo for some time. They go through the lush greenery and vibrant animal enclosures surrounded by visitors. Amelia's eyes sparkle as she looks at the surrounding animals. But one exhibit holds a unique attraction for her - the octopuses. Amelia's fascination with these intelligent creatures stems from her work. She knew about their remarkable abilities to solve puzzles and interact with their environment. Now, she's excited to observe many of these elusive creatures up close.

With anticipation, Erik and Amelia stand in front of the aquarium that houses the octopuses. The dimly lit room enhances the atmosphere and casts a mysterious glow on the aquatic inhabitants. Amelia's heart seems to beat faster when she catches sight of the fascinating creatures floating gracefully in the water, their tentacles moving delicately.

As they approach the glass enclosure, something unexpected happens. The octopuses, known for their affinity for light, seem inexplicably drawn to Amelia. At least, that's what Erik thinks. They glide toward her, their eyes locked on hers. It's as if they recognize her presence. "I almost think I have a connection with them," Amelia says.

"I'm sure you do," Erik answers. Amelia finds the connection almost a little creepy, but simultaneously, she's delighted by the poignant moment.

Meanwhile, Erik observes how great Amelia's enthusiasm for these animals is. Initially, he had only come along out of love and for support - but during their visit, the zoo captivated him as well. Amelia's enthusiasm seems to have infected him. The visit to the zoo has opened his eyes a little more to the wonders of nature.

As they sit in a pub in the Gaslamp Quarter again that evening, they agree that this is the city they like best so far. Their neighbors, a younger couple from San Diego, catch on. They comment: "Los Angeles is a juggernaut, even though there's more going on there, of course," says the American. "We have everything we need in San Diego, just like L.A., only much smaller, more manageable, and much more pleasant." He points his arm down the street, and the gesture is probably meant to emphasize how pleasant San Diego is. "Then, if you're lucky enough to have a good job, San Diego is a perfect place," his girl-friend adds. The two seem to be correct, after all: Here down-town, you can take a wonderful walk in the evenings when the weather is warm, and there are quite a few pubs, bars, and restaurants in the Gaslamp Quarter. Erik doesn't dare imagine whether that would be possible in downtown L.A. at this time of day.

Erik and Amelia now want to add a little adventure to their visit and plan a side trip to Mexico. The "San Diego Trolley" light rail goes directly to the border. Neither Amelia, with her Canadian passport nor he, with his German passport, have anything to fear there, they tell themselves. "This should all go quickly and smoothly," Erik says. With a stream of travelers, they push their way across the border. Behind the checkpoint, on the Mexican side, it already looks more or less European, Erik thinks. They walk along a long corridor and arrive at the Mexican entry point, which they can pass quickly.

Next to the border, Erik makes out a steel gate in the fence that runs continuously here all the way to the sea. It could be opened to let trains pass. A railroad runs from San Diego to Tijuana, then detours via Tecate and returns to the United States. Currently, however, there seems to be extremely little activity on the line. The company "Ferrocarril Tijuana y Tecate" has been tinkering for several years to reopen the line and use it for the well-known brewery "Cuauhtémoc Moctezuma Brewery" in Tecate, for which large quantities of grain and corn syrup could be imported.

They leave the border building and find themselves on a tourist mile that seems to be entirely geared to the tastes of U.S.-day visitors who cross the here on foot. Beer for 99 cents a bottle? No problem. All-day lavish desayuno, breakfast? There is that. Want a hotel or hostel room? That, too, is available there in the one-star variety. The opticians, the pharmacies with discount prices, and the dentists must not be missed.

Erik reminds this part of Tijuana of visiting a market

across the German-Polish border. There are many shrill advertised cheap offers, but it is also amusing. There's only one thing you shouldn't expect here, among the low concrete buildings like you might find in a tourist settlement on the Canary Islands: any flair or picturesque ambiance. He's already glad the place isn't overflowing with brothels, like Ciudad Juárez, across the river from El Paso in Mexico. Although he has no doubt that there are quite a few of them in the center of the town.

The well-informed Amelia brings up something else: "Tijuana has the highest murder rate - in the world - at 138 per 100,000 residents," she says. "I find that disturbing."

"But that's hardly going to affect us," he placates, "most of the crime happens within the drug cartels, not with day visitors." Still, they do feel a little queasy. They leave the border spectacle via a pedestrian bridge that crosses the "Rio Tijuana" and leads into the center. Four-lane streets crisscross "Downtown Tijuana," which they walk through on sidewalks that are sometimes wide and sometimes precariously narrow.

The walk takes them through neighborhoods that are neat for a few blocks and then again resemble a tourist district of a resort. Maybe a little more, nastier, Erik thinks. He wouldn't even know what to shop for there other than eyeglasses, medicine, dentures, cheap clothes, or maybe even drugs if they were looking for them. Amelia hadn't imagined Tijuana to be this "rough around the edges." "But that's just the way reality is, bursting all romantic clichés," Erik notes. One would be doing Mexico an injustice if one approached it with a trip to Tijuana and then left it at that. "Here, close to the border, they cash in big time on the gringo tourists from the north. Much further south in the country, it's by no means as touristy. But the border town isn't there for beauty. It's there to make money." But because the two look like gringos, which they ultimately are, they are approached every few meters, and people try to sell them all kinds of things.

The only place in the city that Erik can find something to like is the "Parque Teniente Guerrero" in the center. Here, they walk along quieter streets, enjoy the greenery of the park in the midday sun, which has pretty cafés, and relax a bit from the noise of the narrow streets of Tijuana. After that, however, little keeps them there. They make their way back and are pleased when, after an estimated one hundred inquiries about whether they want to buy souvenirs or drugs, they reach the border bazaar again and the checkpoint through which they are leaving. It is a different world when you leave the building on the U.S. side: Everything seems incredibly neat, tidy, and well-kept, Erik thinks. It's a shame that the light rail only goes to the border. No train could take them deeper into "Baja California," as the state is called, so they could dip into Mexico. They find Tijuana confusing, unpleasant, and almost a little dangerous. But they also master this excursion.

Their retreat is Ocean Beach, and their motel there. When they return here, the room is theirs alone. No other tourists bother them there. They have their well-stocked refrigerator with a few bottles of wine ready and waiting. The days in Ocean Beach are exciting and fulfilling at the same time. Their relationship comes alive: Amelia and he are very familiar with each other. They both get to know each other well. Erik notices this because they sometimes sense what the other wants to say when he starts a sentence. At least Amelia manages to do that regularly.

One afternoon, Amelia reads a funny article from "G.Q." magazine that she found online. Amelia is Canadian. But in U.S. English, there's a common word: the "imaginary friend from Canada" or the "imaginary boyfriend." Boys or even girls in high school invent this when they don't have a romantic relationship - but don't want to be ultimately "uncool." They can then say that they have a partnership, but that it is more complicated. It's very amusing what author Maggie Lange writes in "G.Q.". "Do you know why it actually has to be Canadians who stand in for the imaginary girlfriend?" asks Amelia.

"I can imagine it. It's just further away," he says.

But she cites, "Canada is both near and far, both remote and not." Besides, she says, Canada is a big country with plenty of room to hide secrets. It's just foreign enough to fib about, she says. "Your girlfriend can't visit you in the summer because there are no summer vacations in Canada. She can't text because it's an international communication thing. There's no prom there, so she doesn't really understand it and can't go out with you."

He says it also saves you from follow-up questions because Canada is not as exotic as Belgium or Belize. And: "After all, it's an American tradition to use Canada as a substitute. Many television shows supposedly set in New York are filmed in Toronto or similar cities. The Canadian setting is almost American, just like a fake girlfriend is almost a girlfriend." Erik has to laugh and thinks it's a clever insight.

"Therefore, I am your imaginary friend from Canada, and you are my imaginary friend from Germany," Amelia states, joyfully sliding back and forth on the bed. Erik gets a bottle of wine from the fridge and two glasses. "Let's be real friends instead," he says, "and toast to the fact that we really exist, my imaginary friend from Canada."

"I knew you would get wine and say that very thing right now."

THE DEPARTURE

The following day, something unexpected happens that should put them both to the test. It seems cloudy because the sun is not shining through the window of the motel room, Erik thinks as he wakes up. The bed next to him is empty. He turns back and forth, but Amelia is not in the room. "Good her things are still there," he mumbles, half asleep, already sensing something is wrong. Then he gets up and fires up the small machine in the room to perk up a bit with a black coffee. After the first coffee, he usually sees the world with somewhat clearer eyes. So they're in San Diego, in their motel, he's still thinking - then the door to the room flies open, and Amelia comes in. She is holding her smartphone in her hand.

"Hello, my friend from Canada," Erik says.

"Good morning," she replies, smiling. But she looks absent-minded, even a little confused. As if she has to think about something difficult. After a short pause, Amelia looks at him.

"I have to go home," she says, "I can't tell you any other way. I have to go home because ... I have to go home."

"What happened? Did something happen? Did you make a phone call?"

"Yes, I did. No, it's all right. No. I can't say it, not now."

"What can't you say?" Erik is taken aback and feels he's been thrown out of his depth. Amelia struggles for words.

"Please, don't ask me. Don't drill me. I have to go home."

"Amelia, why don't you tell me what's going on?"

"No, please. Don't pick up the phone. Let me, please."

She starts packing up her things. As she does so, she goes through the room, taking this and that and letting it disappear into her luggage. Erik sits transfixed and watches. Her face has taken on a severe expression. The cheerful, exuberant gaiety of the past few days has given way to a serious look. She is methodical and organized as she packs her things. One piece at a time while he still looks on, puzzled.

"I'll explain it to you," she says, "but not now. I can't do it." Whatever it is, it must be existential, Erik thinks. Because he doesn't know her like that. So severe and, at the same time, so determined.

"Amelia, weren't those days beautiful?"

"Oh, if you knew how great these days have been for me. If you really knew what you mean to me." She sobs a little and says in a low, serious voice, "I love you. If you love me too, don't pick on me now."

Erik is flabbergasted. "Amelia, where do you want to go?"

"To the airport," is her simple answer.

"Okay, I'll take you to the airport, of course. I'll see how we get there." Wasn't there something? It goes around in his head. Wasn't flying quite expensive if you booked it on the spur of the moment? "Do you have a flight?" he asks.

"Yes, I just turned that off. Don't let that be your worry. Just stay here and relax in this beautiful hotel for a while before you continue your journey. I have organized everything for myself. It's a pity that ... of all things." Amelia turns away and doesn't speak further. She packs her bags and goes to the door. "Stop. I'll take you, of course!" says Erik.

So he accompanies them to the bus stop. Then they ride the bus, change and take another bus to the airport. She looks sad but doesn't speak much during the ride. Quietly, Amelia hums, "I am leaving on a jet plane". Erik takes her to the counter at the airport, where Amelia checks in for Edmonton via Los Angeles. Then she walks through the tunnel to the gates, past the security checkpoint, in front of which he stops. Very briefly, she turns around as if considering something. Then she waves and continues walking - and has disappeared inside the terminal.

❋

Erik drives back alone to the motel, which seems empty to him. He sits down on the bed where he has just been drinking coffee. No, he is not dead sad or extremely sad. That should still come; the memories are too fresh for that. Somehow, Erik thinks that her departure must be related to her illness. It seems to be due to her diabetes. But she could have told him, couldn't she?

As if Amelia's hasty departure wasn't enough - once things start to go downhill, they seem to go right. In the afternoon, the classic misfortune of a traveler many thousands of miles from home should happen to Erik.

"A swim in the Pacific will distract you," he says to himself. So he grabs a bag, puts in his bathing suit and towel, as well as his sunscreen, and heads for the beach, which is a few blocks from the motel. Once there, he sees a little house with "restrooms" where he could probably change. He goes into the den on Abbott Street and changes into his swim shorts. Then, he packs his things and leaves the cottage with the bundle. Erik stands on the beach and wonders if he has everything with him. Then he notices that his wallet is missing. It is not in the bag. Then he remembers that it must be on the washstand. He thinks that wasn't five minutes ago, turns around, and returns to the cottage. Once there, he looks at the washstand and finds no trace. No wallet, just the sinks, the soap dispensers, and the paper towels.

It runs through him: Someone must have grabbed his purse when he left the cottage. "What was in there?" he wonders. Well, it will have been all his cash, probably eighty dollars. In addition, his I.D. card and credit cards were in the wallet. Cards are more important than cash in the USA. Fortunately, he left his passport in his travel bag at the motel. As quickly as he moved again, he could hardly think. Fortunately, he had the plastic card for the room lock with him and didn't put it in his wallet.

In the room, Erik opens the travel bag, removes the bottom, and looks into the small bag he had hidden there. A stone falls from his heart. He is not lost yet. On the way back to the hotel, he had already thought about how he could contact the German consulate or who could send him money from home. But the bag contains 500 euros in cash and his spare credit card. On a previous trip to the U.S., his credit card had stopped working. After long-distance calls to the bank in Germany, it turned out that not much could be done about it. From this, he had learned, here is now the reserve credit card. He spends the next time having the lost cards blocked.

Erik tries to settle in with the new situation. First, he buys a new nylon wallet at a store in Ocean Beach and stocks it with cash and his spare credit card. He sits down in a bar on Santa Monica Avenue. After the practical problem is solved, the emotional problem returns. What was going on? Why did Amelia leave, and then so suddenly? He briefly considers returning to Germany. But he has a fixed return flight and has no desire to show up at home now.

But Erik has no desire to stay in San Diego either. He certainly doesn't want to stay in the motel, which reminds him of Amelia. He can still travel with a spare credit card. He gets comfortable with the idea: he could continue the trip and not fly back yet. He goes back to the motel and checks out for the next morning. Fortunately, they don't charge him for another night there. Then he adjourns to the room and pulls open the curtains to let in some light. At least the bed was neatly made in the meantime.

Erik opens his laptop and uses video to call Drake and Eline in Aspen, Colorado. He needs to talk to someone, and it's already late at night in Germany. The two of them had heard how he was doing, and especially what Amelia meant to him. It is straightforward for the two of them: "Do not go after her. We can imagine that the temptation is great. But believe us: she must have a reason. She'll tell you why if she loves you the way you love her." It does Erik good that at least in this lonely hour, he can talk to two people on the screen.

While he's still thinking about it, his phone rings. Erik sees a US-number in the display.

He picks it up.

"Erik, it's Candice."

"Candice, I had been thinking about you. I'm in the U.S., after all."

"Yes, you told me that. You're out with that girl, Amelia, aren't you? But that's not why I'm calling you now."

"Actually, I'm not with Amelia. But what is it? You sound a little excited."

"So am I. Erik, my sister, has disappeared. I have no idea where Michelle could have gone."

"Oh, no, that sounds like trouble. What happened?" Candice calms down a bit and describes to Erik what happened. Her sister had been visiting Kalispell, staying with Candice and her father. After a few days, she wanted to "go again," as she had told Candice. With some guys, she had met in a bar in the town.

"That was four days ago now. We haven't heard from her since."

Erik tries to reassure her. "Can't it be that she just has a lot on her plate, wherever she is?"

"No, Erik. I had a funny feeling again when she went off with those guys. That's why I made her tell me she'd be in touch after two days at the latest. She hasn't done that. Not for four days. No short messages, no chat, no mail, and certainly no call."

"Candice, that doesn't sound good. But you can't report your sister missing yet, either. At least with us, that would not be possible yet. There would have to be a danger for that. Although: four days is already a certain time."

"I'm not quite sure if there isn't some danger. You know about her weakness for getting into trouble, especially regarding gambling. Add to that the guys she went off with."

"Maybe you should think about it after all if more time goes by. But with an ad like this, you haven't found it yet."

"You think so? All right, then I'll wait a day. But at some point, I have to do something. Tell me, Erik, what did you mean earlier by saying, actually, you're not out with Amelia?"

Erik tells her the story - just as he had told Drake moments before. Candice was surprisingly compassionate. Maybe it will distract her from thinking about her sister, Erik thinks. After a moment's thought, she says, "I can understand you. It's an idiotic situation. But I can also understand her. There is something. It's difficult for me to say this: I'm sure she loves you very much. And she wants to make it easier for you."

Candice seems to shake her head, even if he can't see it on the phone. "I can't believe something like this always has to be so complicated," she moans. Then she pauses again. "Candice, are you still there?"

"I have an idea. You're in San Diego, and you're on vacation. You don't want to go back to Germany, do you?"

"No, I really don't want to, not just yet."

"Why don't you just come to me in Kalispell? You liked it up here in Montana, didn't you? You help me with my sister and take a few days off, then you can fly back."

"Candice, that's a great idea," Erik says spontaneously.

"And if you don't get on one of your trains, you might as well get here fast. Come away from San Diego. I know our little airport. There's bound to be something going there. I'll probably get a few days off, too."

That moves him. A visit to Candice in Montana should also help him - and most likely her. She states: "I can tell you that I like you and that this story doesn't leave me cold. Life takes strange paths sometimes. That's why I can be there for you a little bit."

"Boom," Erik thought. He hadn't expected that - in every sense of the word, including Michelle's whereabouts. The following day, he finds himself at the bus stop in Ocean Beach, where he was with Amelia the day before. He takes the city bus to the "Old Town Transit Center". But he doesn't want to change trains. Instead, he takes the bus to the airport, to "Charles Lindbergh Field". He would prefer to check in for Edmonton. What did she say? "If you really love me, you don't question." That was hard for him to do. He needed company now, and it certainly couldn't be the surfers at the motel. He wanted to meet someone else. So Erik set off for Kalispell, Montana.

CHAPTER 5

The Olympian Hiawatha

September, this year

Erik is on a small plane taking him from Los Angeles, where he changed flights, to Montana. As his aircraft steers its way northeast, he thinks about how he had searched all the connections on his laptop in San Diego. Of course, Erik couldn't resist checking the train connections. But the Amtrak trip would have taken a whopping 47 hours from San Diego to Seattle to Whitefish. The flight, including the time to get to the airport and go through security, takes about five hours. And he was lucky with the ticket price. That's why he's now sitting in the small Canadair regional jet from Continental Airlines, which touches down at Glacier Park Airport shortly before one o'clock in the afternoon.

He enters the regional airport's handsome, two-story reception building to go to the rental car counter. Erik takes a deep breath. It feels good to be here. Northern Montana is the proper antidote to San Diego and the memory of Amelia's hasty departure. If you want to put it musically, he thinks, it's like turning off the "Beach Boys" and putting on a disc of John Denver. The music of the vast mountains has replaced the surfer sounds. He's managed to get back to Kalispell.

Erik turns the rental car, a small Ford, onto the street west of downtown Kalispell, where Candice lives. He met her there back in March. He parks in front of her house, and she comes out onto the porch. Candice is clearly happy to see him.

"There you are, you German," she greets him. "You poor, abandoned traveler." They sit down in her living room, and he tells her about the past weeks, this time in much more detail. Candice shakes her head. "I don't want to worry you. But there must be something big and important behind it. Otherwise, she wouldn't have left so quickly, and otherwise, she would have told you. I'm afraid the whole thing is worse than you think. You will have to put up with it. I don't know why that is, and I can't guess."

Erik looks at her. "It sounds quite logical the way you put it. I don't even know what to do, though."

"That makes two of us, right? I don't know what to do about Michelle either."

"Does your father actually know?"

"I have by now. I told him. He doesn't know the full extent of Michelle's 'gambling excursions,' but since he had to help her back in Las Vegas, he realizes there's a problem blazing."

"And what does he think?"

"He also wants to wait a bit before informing the authorities. But he's as concerned as I am."

"Okay, if we haven't heard anything by tomorrow, we should file a missing persons report or something like that."

"I have an idea. It might distract you, and it might distract me. You've liked railroads since you went to San Francisco then, right? Do you still like them?"

"Yes, I think so ..."

"We're going downtown now, and you'll meet Otis. He's a close friend of my father's. They're both at the saloon this afternoon. That's how it is in our small town: you always know what the retirees are up to in the afternoon. Otis was on the railroad and can tell you a lot."

In the saloon, Candice's father greets them. He is a tall man, around 65 years old, with white hair and a mustache. His face is tanned, and he looks quite fit for his age. Also, he had heard about Erik. "So you're the German who stopped by on the train? And you had taken the rental car from Gideon last year?"

"Help," Erik thinks. Everyone really does seem to know everyone in this place. What the father knows about the friendship between Erik and Candice, he doesn't know. But he doesn't mention it, either. Instead, he is the hospitable man from Montana.

"Come, sit with us. Our corner is free. Erik, may I introduce you to Otis, my old buddy from the railroad?"

A man in a plaid shirt, perhaps a few years older than Candice's father, stands up and extends his hand. He sees that they both have cowboy hats hanging on hooks on the wall above the table. "Nice to meet you, Erik," Otis greets him.

"Also, Erik helped my two daughters last year in Reno," Candice's father tells Otis. "Michelle has been gambling again with Erik's boyfriend. They were pulling money out of their pockets. I would have loved to have gone there and paid them back."

"What's stopping you?" asks Otis. "You're not usually so reticent, are you?"

"Look, if they're having trouble playing with Italian-Americans at Lake Tahoe, who do you think could be behind it?"

"Mobster?"

"Exactly. And probably not the Seattle outfit we know up here, but rather some of the big ones that are also in Las Vegas. I don't want to mess with them over $4,000," Candice's father says. So he knows the whole story, Erik thinks.

"But if Michelle doesn't show up soon, I will change my mind and talk to Dwayne."

Candice explains to Erik, "My dad knows Dwayne Watson. That's the sheriff for Flathead County, where we are." Erik nods. "I'd let him know sometime then, too."

"I really care about Michelle. It might be better to involve Dwayne."

"I hear you're crazy about Railroads?" asks Otis Erik, probably to steer the conversation in a different direction.

"Well, I wouldn't say crazy. I like traveling on the trains as a passenger."

"Aw shucks, we're all crazy about railroads here in Kalispell. We had a few of them, after all."

Erik tells the group that he knows the "California Zephyr", the "Empire Builder," the "Canadian", and the trains on the West Coast.

"That's good. You've really gotten around," Otis says. "More than a lot of us have managed. But the biggest of them all, the best move, you don't know it. You can't know that one, unfortunately."

"Is there a train I missed, then?"

"The biggest of them all was the "Olympian Hiawatha." It ran for the "Milwaukee Road," the company I worked for years. Whatever you experienced on today's Amtrak trains: Nothing comes close to the Hiawatha."

Otis says that there are the well-known transcontinental railroad lines across the USA, the "Northern Transcon", the "Central Corridor," and the "Southern Transcon". Passenger trains like the "California Zephyr" or the "Empire Builder" also run on them. But there was another line on which luxurious trains with the Indian name "Hiawatha" ran, with large, streamlined cars and observation pulpits with futuristic glass superstructures. They raced from Chicago to Seattle in the 1950s and passed nearby in Missoula.

"There we were even at the train station. That's when you got a ticket," Candice says. "Where does the name come from, anyway?"

Candice's father knows that. He tells of the epic "The Song of Hiawatha," which the American Henry Wadsworth Longfellow wrote about the Indian Hiawatha in 1855. It was so popular that the railroads named their trains after it even later. According to legend, the Indian Hiawatha could run faster than arrows could fly.

"What makes the trains so special," Otis continues, "is not just the "Hiawathas," but the entire railroad company with its line to the Pacific. Not only is the company gone today, but so is its most important rail line, the Pacific Extension. It's one of the longest abandoned lines in the world."

"How can that be, that an entire railroad just disappears?" asks Erik.

"Yeah, that's a story. But I was there, down here in Missoula. You'd better all get another beer, and I can tell it to you." Otis is pleased to be able to tell of an essential chapter in his life. Candice's father is glad that his friend has found an audience. Candice is happy to hear from Otis, and Erik looks forward to the story of the "Hiawathas."

The Milwaukee Road

"Like so many things, it started small; the rise was followed by bold expansion plans and then the multiple falls from which there was no escape after more bad decisions," Otis begins. When companies go bankrupt and disappear from the scene, it's tragic for employees, customers, and suppliers. But the consequences are catastrophic when a railroad company disappears that has left its mark across the country, to which localities owe their existence. "Take the little town of Avery, right here close to Montana, on the Saint Joe River." Not 50 residents still live there. It's isolated in a valley, with Interstate 90 more than an hour's drive through the mountains. But the old "Milwaukee Road" station building and an old passenger car still stand in Avery. That's because Avery used to be one of the operating centers for the company. From 1909 to 1980, that gave many of the 450 residents wages and bread. Even a large hotel stood there, just behind the station. But the rail line has long since disappeared.

"Didn't the Lawsons move to Kalispell from Avery back in the day?" asks Candice's father about their neighbors.

"Yeah, they came here, just like me," Otis says. "We were lucky because Burlington Northern in Kalispell wanted to hire us. The old job at Milwaukee Road paid better. But what were we left with? Missoula, where I had worked, has been a major base for the company. I went along with all that. When the Hiawathas were hired in 1961, I was just 13 years old. Nevertheless, I started working for the company because they were still big in the freight business. I was there, and 32 years old, when the line shut down," he gestures to the side, "after everything went down the drain."

They listen to Otis spellbound. The older man seems deep in thought, recounting how the company was founded in 1847 as the Milwaukee and Waukesha Railroad in Wisconsin. The people of the city of Milwaukee rejoiced over the railroad: farmers and factories gained access to much larger markets. The railroad brought immigrants who could settle the empty land. After 27 years, the company moved to Chicago, where it also moved its headquarters - to a newly built high-rise.

If the "Milwaukee Road" had been a medium-sized railroad until then, its directors now had big plans. "Just doing some operation in Milwaukee and Chicago? As Otis puts it, that's not enough to play with the really big railroads," the circle of directors must have said to themselves. "They were convinced, 'We've got to keep up.' After all, the huge business is in transcontinental connections! Why don't we build a new line to the Pacific?"

"That sounds like a good recipe for disaster," Candice notes. "Yeah, it's easy to imagine how that went down today," Erik adds.

"You can hardly describe it if you weren't there. But then, I wasn't there then either. It must have been the basis for all the later problems," says Otis.

Appraisals estimated the cost of building the line at $45 million - Otis knows that amount would be $1.58 billion today. The decision was made to build. By 1905, the cost had risen to $60 million. After all, the line was completed in just three years. But this prestigious undertaking cost the company dearly because the Milwaukee Road was hardly allocated any land by the government and had to buy most of the territory.

"Whether the route planning was particularly wise is still debated among historians today because it bypassed some major population centers," Otis adds. "But wait, the difficulties were even greater."

Especially in the Rocky Mountains and the Cascades, it could get freezing in the winter, and the locomotives could barely generate enough steam to pull their loads through the mountains. A solution presented itself: Electric locomotives, which were ready then. By 1916, the Milwaukee Road between Harlowton, Montana, and the Avery, as mentioned above, Idaho, a distance of 438 miles, was equipped with an overhead line.

This investment was crowned with success because the electric locomotives ran reliably from then on, and the new "smoke-free" trains were well received by the passengers. The Milwaukee Road had another section of the line electrified, from Othello in Washington to Tacoma, a distance of 206 miles. This was the largest project of its kind in the world to date. All that remained was a 216-miles flat gap between the sections, which continued to be served by steam. The railroad attracted celebrities: None other than Thomas A. Edison praised the smooth ride when he took the new train. Warring G. Harding, the 29th President of the USA, did not miss the opportunity to drive a train with an electric locomotive over the track himself.

But if you calculate the total cost of the Pacific route, it had swallowed up $257 million. This sent the company into a tailspin because the traffic volume could not keep up. It had to file for bankruptcy twice, in 1925 and 1935, but managed to reorganize. It was not until after the Second World War that the Milwaukee Road experienced a heyday. The legendary "Olympian Hiawatha" ran between Chicago and Seattle via the "Pacific Extension" from 1947. The railroad advertised itself as running entirely on electricity and diesel, the most modern energy sources available at the time.

By the late 1950s, the entire railroad industry in the United States was reeling from the first wave of decline as the interstate system for trucks and automobiles continued to grow. But the Milwaukee Road was particularly affected. There were many competing railroads in the Midwest. The "Olympian Hiawatha" was mothballed in 1961. Yet, the "Hiawatha" stream liners, with their prominent glass pulpits at the end of the train, are considered a landmark in industrial design. These cars have been sold to Canada. One returned to Minneapolis, was lovingly restored by a club, and is now on excursion trips between the Twin Cities and Chicago.

"What a story," Candice thinks, "the fate of this company must have been hard for you."

"Yes," Otis says, "for me, but also for hundreds of others in Montana." Things didn't get serious for freight until the 1970s, when a strong competitor emerged from the merger of several companies with the formation of "Burlington Northern." Unfortunately, the other mistakes began to take effect: The railroad had invested far too little in maintaining its lines, locomotives, and cars. One lousy idea was followed by another: for a while, the "Milwaukee Road" sold its own wagons to financial institutions to lease them back from them. On paper, this created new revenue in the short term, but it made rising costs in the long term. When it could barely pay the leasing rates, the company had no choice but to sell more cars. The side effect was that the fleet of cars was getting older and older. This eventually led to a shortage of wagons, which deterred customers.

"It was sad, but at that point, our company decided to dismantle the electrified line," Otis looks back. The electric locomotives were at the end of their useful life, and they wanted to switch entirely to diesel. By 1974, only diesel trains were still running. A momentous decision: The sale of the overhead lines had been firmly planned, but the world market price for copper was falling at the time. At the same time, the fuel cost rose dramatically due to the oil crisis - and the diesel locomotives were consuming a lot.

Between 1974 and 1977, the Milwaukee Road lost $100 million and was forced to file for bankruptcy for the third time. "Then Judge Thomas R. McMillen took over and presided over the proceedings. His ruling was going to be the end for all of us," Otis says, and you can still see his disappointment today after so many years. The judge ruled that the company's main problem was that it had decidedly too many fixed assets relative to its revenues. In 1977, the company had about 10000 miles of track. So, less profitable lines were to be closed. By 1984, the network had been trimmed down to 3020 miles.

The most momentous shutdown involved the Milwaukee Road transcontinental service to the West Coast. Service ended west of Miles City, Montana, in February 1980. "We were all furious because we were out of jobs," Otis says. "Just about everybody had to move away. But I was lucky enough to get a job with a competitor, Burlington Northern, here in Kalispell, of all places." The Milwaukee Road continued to exist as a smaller railroad in the Midwest until 1985 when the Soo Line took over its last lines and disappeared.

They all look at Otis sympathetically. He had lived with the company until its demise. The story of the railroad is also part of the story of his life. Fortunately, he was only 32 years old when it ended. It reminds Erik a little of his industry, of publishing in Hamburg: Isn't it similar to the railroad in North America in the 1970s? Will magazine print editions disappear just like the big passenger trains, the "Hiawathas"? Is he employed by some kind of "Milwaukee Road," Erik wonders? Above all, will there perhaps be a renaissance, as there is today with the railroads?

Candice breaks the clouded mood. "So, men, I've gotten thirsty. What about you guys? I'll get us another round."

Today, Otis reports that there are "trails" for hikers and cyclists on the route. "If I were you, I'd check it out," Candice's father says. He's opening up a new topic. Because despite Otis' story, the thoughts in the round are about Michelle.

"Look, what do you mean by that, Daddy?"

"You guys have a few days, right? And I still have a piece of complete camping equipment in the basement. You can take that. How about it?"

"The track is really great, quite spectacular in the mountains," Otis says.

"Candice, you can pick up the equipment tomorrow. Then, we'll check back to see if Michelle has checked in. And then I'll go straight to Dwayne Watson and fill him in. If it's mobsters - we handle that differently in Montana than we do in Southern Nevada or on the East Coast," the father adds grimly. "We do that with law and order and our sheriff."

"Well, what do you say, Erik?" asks Candice.

"I guess there's not much we can do here except wait and see. Might as well take a trip."

In the evening, Candice had invited friends to her place. They heard from Erik - the German who had traveled through the U.S. last year and met Candice. He is back. It's the weekend, and her cottage has a party atmosphere. She opens several bottles of champagne, and the group is happy to join in the drinking. To that end, Matt, one of her friends, around 40 years old, unwraps a bag of weed. "He's married," Candice whispers to Erik. "But when he's here, he lets the hippie hang out." Would he be interested in science fiction, too, Matt asks him? No one burns for it more than Candice, he says. He is, but he certainly can't hold a candle to her in that department, Erik admits with a wink.

But in truth, his thoughts are not on the funny little party but far away. He thinks about Amelia, how she might be doing, and where she has gone. Erik can't get that out of his head. He misses her so much. Matt must have sensed something gnawing at him because he simply held the joint out to him. "Here, have one; I promise it'll make you feel better."

The joint is already circling in the round in this little house in the north of Kalispell. Erik thinks this is quite a party community he's found himself in. He relaxes and exchanges a few words with the cheerful Talia, Candice's younger neighbor. Then there's John, the neighbor from the next house. He is 50 years old and newly divorced. But at the small party, he acts very casual. Erik talks about his trip through California to Los Angeles and San Diego. What impresses them most is that he loves to ride the train. The evening progresses, and they sit in Candice's spiffy living room, drinking and smoking weed. Now Erik, too, feels like the hippies he used to chase after in neighborhoods like Ocean Beach. It's a very relaxed evening, even if he often had to think about Amelia. But the beers with Otis in the saloon, the drinks at Candice's, and the grass have fogged his head.

The sun rises early the following day in Montana in the summer. He blinks and looks at the living room window. This time, he hasn't gone to a hotel. But at Candice's, of course, he spent the night on the sofa in the living room; anything else would have been absurd. Erik says to himself, "Just don't reflect, don't judge, don't plan and think." If only it weren't for the nagging thoughts of Amelia, which he can't suppress even in the morning. So he quietly crawls off the sofa and looks around the small kitchen. It's all full of groceries in their colorful packages, which he looks at curiously. He decides he could just make some pancakes, but then can't find the necessary ingredients in the cupboards. So he makes some coffee first.

Then Candice gets up. "After all, we're supposed to hit the

trail today", she greets Erik. All they have to do is pick up the camping gear at their father's house, then they can go on the trip. "You're a city girl. You need someone like me from Montana who knows her way around out there," Candice says, "although I don't really know my way around there either." Then she makes the pancakes for breakfast, whose ingredients she pulls out of more cupboards.

They pack, drive off, visit the father at his house, and load the old camping equipment into the trunk. They're heavy, Erik thinks, but everything seems to be there, from the stove to the tent. Then Candice pulls out her smartphone, and they go through all the possibilities with her father's phone. He's holding a heavy device with a thick protective case, Erik notices, which is quite fitting for the rustic guy from Montana. "Calls, missing. Likewise on WhatsApp, Telegram, chatting on Facebook, on her other social media accounts, and, of course, no mails," Candice notes. Her father nods. "Okay, that's enough. I'm going to the sheriff's office on Main Street, and you guys head for the hills. We'll talk later."

First, they drive along the western shore of Flathead Lake. They reach Interstate 90 at St. Regis, which winds westward from Missoula. The mountains, with their pine green all the way to the horizon, lend these valleys something enchanting. They follow the highway west.

During the ride, Candice talks about her school days, which she spent with Michelle in Kalispell. Erik hears some anecdotes from "junior high" and later "high school" about Michelle, what pranks they came up with, and how they met their first boys. Erik thinks they must have really been like peas and carrots together.

At Taft, they leave the trail right at the border between Montana and Idaho. 141 miles from Kalispell, they reach the first section they want to visit: the "Route of the Hiawatha

Historic Trail". The trip begins here with the long "St. Paul Pass Tunnel," also known as the "Taft Tunnel." It is a highlight of the trail, which follows the crest of the Bitterroot Mountains near the "Lookout Pass" ski area. Seven miles from the start of the track, in the ski area, there is the bike rental shop, where they can also buy the "tickets" for the trail. This is because there is a fee to use the path. The ski area operators seem to have taken over the track right away. Neither Candice nor he are particularly athletic. Erik is a desk jockey, and although she's from Montana and is up for outdoor adventures, she's not much of a bike rider either. The "trail," however, is always downhill, so it's really not much of an effort to follow it. There is even a shuttle bus stop at the end of the near 15-mile trail. You can load your bike onto a school bus that will take you back across the road to the starting point.

Candice has to laugh, "I see quite a few couch potatoes trying to make their way here. I get to say that because I'm actually a couch potato, too."

"Okay, I'll go along with that," Erik replies. At least they resist the temptation to rent e-bikes immediately, offered here. That's not necessary unless they want to ride the route uphill.

THE TRAIL OF THE HIAWATHA

At the tunnel's east portal is the "trailhead," as the beginning of this section is called. They park there and heave the bikes out of the trunk. They pack, having been warned in "Lookout" to take enough to drink. The camera smartphones are with them, and they have also rented helmets. As if to confirm, the sign "Welcome to the Route of the Hiawatha" says that helmets and lamps are mandatory on this trail. The car is locked, the "tickets" are presented, and they crank towards the tunnel portal.

The ride is unusual because the tunnel is pitch black. It's good that the mountain bikes have lights. The cones of light shine on raw rock faces. Impressive, Erik thinks, how cold it is inside the mountain, an actual "temperature drop" compared to the warm sunny weather outside. They roll through the mountain. The ground is sandy but well compacted, so you pedal along with no problem making progress on the slightly sloping trail. You can actually hear the water rushing against the tunnel walls. He finds it strange that water is constantly running in a tunnel. I wonder if that's so good for stability. But the Forest Service will indeed have tested this tunnel. It's hard to believe that the 2.66-kilometer tunnel once took three years to build - and can now serve as a cyclist attraction.

On the other side, the walls are concreted and cycle through a small cut into the open air. The ride descends very slowly through the green fir forests. Only here can you imagine how nice it must have been to sit in a comfortable chair on the "Olympian Hiawatha" in the 1950s and enjoy the view of the mountains as the train rushes west toward Seattle. The hills here drop steeply into the valley beside the track.

At the next bend, there is a sign: "Turn on Lights" is written on it, and another small tunnel follows, through which they cycle. Then they reach "Johnson's Cut," an impressive wooden bridge that curves high above a mountain valley. Here, even the poles of the old overhead line, made of dark wood, still stand above the former rail bed. This is repeated a little further down the trail at the charming "Barnes Creek Trestle", and then especially at the high "Turkey Creek Trestle", a bridge with steel piers that rises much higher still. If you stop, descend, and lean over the railing, you'll look down into the gorge so deep it can make you dizzy. All the way down there, you can see the tops of the trees between the steel piers. It's a good thing the bridges on this trail have railings. The "Clear Creek Trestle" even crosses a valley at a height of 67 meters.

Erik discovers that more bridges follow - no wonder they chose this section of all to make an attraction out of the trail. It really is beautiful. Again and again, there are minor signs at the edge. At one pit, for example, he sees a sign explaining how a train carrying grain cars once derailed there. Some of the wagons tipped to the side and lay next to the railroad line; they were difficult to salvage. The grain was apparently fermented, and when bears later arrived, they are said to have eaten it - and staggered drunkenly through the woods.

After three hours and a good 14 miles, they finally arrive at the other end of the trail, the "Pearson Trailhead". Only here does he notice how mud-smeared they both are: From their legs to their torsos, mud from the tunnel is kicked up by their bikes. Candice doesn't like this at all; she grumbles and grumbles about the dirt. He doesn't think it's so bad, but his friend from Montana is taking quite a beating from the soil. He hands her a drinking water bottle, "Why don't you rinse off a little with this? You'll feel better." Scolding him, she starts cleaning. She is annoyed that her towel from her backpack is soon as mud-smeared as her clothes.

From the "Pearson Trailhead," the shuttle buses are supposed to go back. Because none is to be seen, they make a break at the edge of the trail, where they open the water and a bag with "Beef Jerky", the dried meat, which is so popular here, and strengthen themselves. Meanwhile, more and more cyclists arrive at this end. All are in good spirits, very talkative, and happy to have survived the outdoor adventure.

Later, after they've rolled back on the little school bus and dropped the bikes off at the ski area again, they can turn their attention to the question of where they actually want to spend the night. He would have favored the "Lookout Motel" at the ski area, but Candice wants to try out her father's camping equipment. Incredibly, she shows such a love of the outdoors when he thinks back to the earlier trouble he had with the mud. But so they drive to "Telichpah Campground," which is halfway between the trailhead and Avery. This small, wild campground is located in style on the former route of the Milwaukee Road. The "US Forest Service" runs the place where there is really nothing except a spot to pitch your tent, no sanitary facilities, and also no water.

It's good they've equipped themselves with more water bottles for another thorough wash. The cold stream that rushes by is too deep below the place for them to help themselves from it. But it is only good that the weather plays along. He wouldn't have felt like sticking the pegs into the muddy ground to set up the dome tent if it had rained. Damn, what is the ground hard, Erik thinks? Also, the thin sleeping pads from the spartan camping equipment hardly help make the tent's "bed" more comfortable. Some wool blankets, which are already a bit musty, benefit, and soon they have it reasonably comfortable. For dinner, they have sandwiches from the gas station on the interstate. "When the Hiawatha roared past here, the passengers in the dining car already got something else," Erik says.

"Well, maybe they were just eating sandwiches on their 'coach' seats, period style, with proper mayonnaise," Candice says. She opens two cans of beer and hands him one. "You can't have it in the wilderness without it. Cheers!"

Cell phone reception is fortunately available in the wilderness. So Candice calls her father. Of course, there is nothing new. But the sheriff is taking the matter seriously, he tells her, not just because he knows Candice's father well. He has already notified surrounding counties and issued a bulletin with a photo of Michelle. "Now it's back to wait and see," she notes.

In the middle of the night, Erik wakes up and wonders where he has ended up. They huddled under their blankets because it was getting cold outside. Candice is sleeping and breathing calmly and evenly. He hears an owl hooting. It sounds creepy. But there's something else breathing, and not so evenly. The sound seems to originate behind Candice. Yes, it's coming from outside. It must be pretty close to the tent. What is that? Something is pressing against the tent wall! An animal is clearly visible in the dark material. It seems to be sniffing. It's so close that it hardly dares to breathe itself, let alone make any noise. Can this be a bear? No, it's too small for that, fortunately, Erik reassures himself. Then maybe a wolf? A prairie wolf? A lynx? Whatever it is, only the thin canvas of the tent separates them from this monster. He considers a plan. As the critter sniffs, Erik decides it's time to drive it away. He can't possibly sleep with something like that creeping around the tent. So he very gently wakes Candice and tells her to be quiet. Then Erik gets up and picks up the flashlight. He points it at the tent wall, snaps it on, and yells as loud as possible, "Get out of here! Get out of here now!"

The beast pauses for a moment, then runs away. Saved! Whether that was the most brilliant tactic? Because it could have been something other than a shy and dog-sized animal nibbling on their tent wall. But the noise drove it away. "Let's put a light outside if we're not going to light a fire," says sleepy Candice. "The light should scare off animals like that, shouldn't it?"

Erik doesn't know what might drive the animals away. But he says, "Yeah, maybe it will," and quickly places the LED camping light in front of the tent entrance without venturing too far outside. Something is reassuring: a bright light outside the door, illuminating the darkness. They both fall back asleep, undisturbed until the next morning.

It is now slightly cloudy but still dry and bright in the mountains. Erik feels it is already an adventure to make coffee on the camping stove, which he serves to Candice, who has just woken up, and which she accepts gratefully. He had only made water hot and mixed it with instant coffee.

Later, after packing up and stowing their overnight camp back in the rental car's trunk, they drive to Avery for another "real" breakfast at the "Grocery Store." Candice loves small, family-run stores like this. You can buy everything there: groceries, housewares, pastries, and a café. This suits her, a small store in a small mountain town.

They also look at the railroad car left in the park next to the former station. It is a "lounge" car, and it even bears the name of the place, "Avery". That, in turn, came from Avery Rockefeller, the son of John D. Rockefeller, who was once one of the investors in the "Milwaukee Road." The lounge portion of the car is faithfully preserved. In contrast, the dining car portion is empty and contains only a few exhibits. "Oh, could we ride through the mountains in a car like this?" enthuses Candice, sitting on one of the bright green cushions. Triangular tables stand before it, with old railroad memorabilia stored under glass.

"Yes, that's right, I'd like that too," he replies. They discover that the former house for railroad employees in Avery is now a hostel. The town's residents are trying to make a little money as a tourist destination. Erik says, "I would have preferred that to chasing a beast away from near our tent at night."

Behind Avery, they roll down the "St. Joe River Road", which runs close to the former route of the Milwaukee Road. Because even though the tourist trail is behind them, the railroad track continues west, of course, although not as bike-friendly developed as east of the trailhead. That's why there are virtually no bicyclists on the road here anymore. Overall, the area is quite lonely. They ride through the long valley and, with stops at a former railroad bridge, reach the next larger town, "St. Maries" in Idaho, after an hour and a half. Here, in fact, there are tracks on the route. They connect a sawmill a few miles away to the following main line. It's nice to see a piece of railroad coming back after so much abandoned emptiness, Erik thinks. The eastern end of the "St. Maries River Railroad" runs from here to Spokane. The big, black EMD P9 locomotives in service here today are still from the old "Milwaukee Road".

Beyond the village of Plummer, to the west, the railroad branches off to the north. The "Trail" is back on the former railroad bed. Here, it is called "Palouse to Cascades State Park Trail"; they renamed it, although it used to be called "John Wayne Trail". From here on, it is 300 miles long and runs right through the Cascades. After all, the state still has the right of way for the route. Therefore, it could have the rail line back into operation at some point. But Erik and Candice first cruise with the rental car to Spokane, where they look for a motel to spend the night "properly". A long, hot, steamy shower is the most important thing on their evening excursion, followed by a visit to a diner across the street. Erik thinks there's something to be said for civilization after all, when you're the "passenger" and not the man from the mountains.

He gets along well with Candice again. She disliked the mountain bike tour so much because of the dirt. But she enjoyed the night in the tent, where he was threatened by animals. It's a joy to ride with her through Idaho and Washington State. And it combats the unease Erik feels about Amelia - and Candice, of course, about her sister. That's why, the next day, they both take the "big leap" to the second highlight of the "Milwaukee Road Pacific Extension": they drive from Spokane far to the west, into the Cascade Mountains. There, they set course for the "Snoqualmie Pass". Underneath, the railroad ran in a tunnel.

Erik already knows what Amelia would say, "Oh, a long tunnel. You love long tunnels in the mountains." In fact, it's actually the most extended section of a hiking trail that runs through a tunnel, and this time, it's 2.23 miles that they plan to hike under the mountain in the dark. "If that's not an experience," Erik enthuses. "I think it's a little scary. I also don't know how much fun it is. But what the heck: I'm in," says Candice.

They made the trip from Spokane in just over three hours. They park the car in front of the eastern tunnel portal. There is a vast parking lot here, complete with restrooms, but only a few vehicles are parked there. Again, a trail has been built on the former track bed of "Milwaukee Road", with the same "loose gravel", i.e., sand or debris, compressed together. By the way, not the whole route to Tacoma is paved as a hiking trail, but large parts of it are. So is this section in the "Cascade" mountains. They have their backpacks shouldered and flashlights with them.

The "trail" leads through a cutting; the two slopes on the right and left are lushly overgrown. Again, it is hard to believe they are standing on a former transcontinental railroad connection. In front of them is the opening of the tunnel portal in the mountain, a black hole into which the trains used to rush. A large gate can be used to close the tunnel, which is only open in summer.

Here, the "Milwaukee Road" management afforded itself a real extravagance in the 1930s, traces of which can still be discovered: In front of the tunnel, the company's own ski area was opened in 1937 to attract tourists. This included a two-story hut for day guests and even a ski lift, a novelty at the time. By train, people from Seattle could make day trips to ski. The area proved popular when the Seattle Times sponsored ski lessons for high school students. A round-trip train ticket cost a dollar in 1940 - about $22 today. However, the winter fun would end in 1949 when the lodge burned down on December 2, and the area was closed after the season.

On the right, you can still guess the "Company" ski area in the forest. The former train station is where the parking lot is today. The traffic on the wide Interstate 90 rushes by. Right next to them come cyclists again, some shouting, others waving. It looks funny, they both think, how the cyclists stop in front of the tunnel, turn on their lights, and then disappear into the darkness as fireflies.

Finally, they stand in front of the tunnel entrance them-selves. The portal is made of concrete and looks solid, as if it could stand there for hundreds of years. "Off to the night's adventure," Candice says, flicking on her LED lamp and leading the way.

"You're enthusiastic," Erik says.

"Wait and see when it's enough for me in this tunnel," she replies, walking with big steps. After a few hundred meters, they are swallowed up by darkness; the light from the portal doesn't reach long into the tunnel. But they are not alone. This is shown by the lights in the distance coming towards them: They are new cyclists, a whole group crossing the mountain from west to east.

Feet by feet, they march deeper into the mountain. This is how visitors to an old mine must feel, Erik says. Water is drip-ping down the walls again. It is also getting very cool inside the mountains; they put on summer jackets. The water has left traces on the walls - sometimes white, sometimes moss green, sometimes brown. Then the concrete ends, and the raw rock emerges. After a few hundred meters, the wall is concreted again; he thinks it must have something to do with the statics. When they have certainly walked one mile, they have the feeling of being very deep under the mountain. But there are no signs or explanations. The tunnel is a tourist attraction, but not a developed one. Again, wavering lights approach, and whooping cyclists - this time from behind, on their way from east to west. "I find this amazingly exciting," Candice says. "I didn't imagine it would be so adventurous."

"Is it like your science fiction worlds, maybe?"

"Oh yes, this could also be an alien planet here; perhaps Mars and the Martians once mined here." They take a walk in the dark. The tunnel was dug from 1912 to 1914. The line to Seattle had opened three years earlier, first running for a few years over an auxiliary route over "Snoqualmie Pass," high above them. This was a similar principle to the Moffat Tunnel and its past. Then, the tunnel served well for a fast connection to the Pacific. But no train has passed through here since 1980. It lay derelict for several years before Washington State took over and had it renovated in 2011: The concrete boarding on the walls was reinforced, and the bottom was filled with new, finely crushed stones. So, the trail is meant to last. It is a "nonmotorized trail". The fast cyclists are already enough for them as traffic in the tunnel; if cars drove along here or motorcycles, they could forget their walk.

They continue walking, and after twenty minutes, Erik has the impression that there is something like a glimmer of light at the end of the tunnel. Where better to experience the somewhat worn phrase "the light at the end of the tunnel" than in a disused railroad tunnel? "Well, a light could have been put here occasionally," Candice sighs. After her initial enthusiasm, she gets a little tired. "Look, there's a dry spot," says Erik, shining the flashlight against the tunnel wall.

Candice takes a seat right away and leans against the

concrete wall. She opens two cans of a "berry" drink he's never seen before. "Taste it," she says, holding the can out to him. He didn't know such a sweet yet tart taste. "There's enough sugar in there to chase us all over the mountain," Erik notes. "Then add a candy bar, and we'll make it to Seattle," Candice adds. It's incredible all the snacks she has in her little backpack. A few cyclists pass her, disappearing into the darkness with their lights on.

They are invigorated and tackle the last mile. There's this glow coming from somewhere, and they're walking toward it. "You know what would be really creepy?" asks Candice. "If you walked through here at night. Then you wouldn't be able to see a light at the end of the tunnel." They're getting cold by now. "Outside, we wouldn't have a summer afternoon to look forward to," Erik adds. With large steps, he advances. Indeed, the glow is the tunnel's exit, which is approaching. Other pedestrians haven't even seen it yet.

"It must have been great back then, on those luxury trains," Candice says. "That's when we would have had another cup of coffee in the lounge car while the train raced through the mountain."

"Yes, that would have been early in the morning, according to the schedule. That would have been a good time for coffee. And we would have been in Seattle by mid-morning."

"The schedule can wait," Candice says. Then she slips on the floor. Erik is able to catch her in a flash. She is in his arms. They look at each other for a second in the pale glow of the flashlights. Erik feels her closeness. The second seems to drag on for a long time. Then he helps her back up, and Candice leans against the rock wall. "Whew, thanks, I almost hit the ground," she says, a little embarrassed.

A few hundred meters more, then the light brightens the dark tube. "Let there be light, and there was light," Erik says.

Braces on the walls now support the tunnel. Finally, they stand outside holding their hands over their eyes; it's so bright. "Eww, I'm blind," Candice exclaims. "No, just wait, you'll be able to see again in a minute," Erik reassures her. There is even a restroom behind the portal. They seem to have arrived back in civilization. While Candice disappears into the cottage, Erik looks at the tunnel portal. God knows why, but it's a double portal. Only on the right is a tunnel excavated; on the left, there is nothing at all behind the portal except a rock wall. Maybe that was supposed to look good from the passing train? Or they planned to add another tunnel. Come to think of it, the whole "Pacific Extension" had been generously laid out by the company, so perhaps that was a possibility. When Candice returns, she says, "I don't like going back another 2.2 miles through that cold mountain. Let's see if we can get a cab up here to the wilderness."

In front of them, however, there is only the trail on the old railroad track. They walk down it for half an hour while deep below them in the valley, the Snoqualmie River flows, and the interstate runs along. Then they reach, as planned, the "Iron Horse & Anette Lake Trail Crossing". The latter is another trail that leads into the mountains to Anette Lake, which is also supposed to be stunning. This one, they just have to go downhill. They are no longer on the old railroad track, but they both like walking downhill through the woods in sunny weather, especially since they feel safe on the signed "trail". After only fifteen minutes, they reach the beginning of the trail. There is a parking lot here. It should come still better. A man in his mid-thirties, who is just dismantling the mountain bikes with his girlfriend to stow them in the car, asks if they need a "lift".

They are real bicyclists, as they say, but to get to the mountains and do tours like this, they still need a car. Interstate 90 runs pretty close to the tunnel exit, and because they want to go up "Snoqualmie Pass" again anyway, they might as well stop at the tunnel entrance to the east, where Erik and Candice parked the car. "We are completely on the tracks of the Milwaukee Road, which fascinates my friend here; he is a real railroad fan," says Candice.

It's not far, over the mountain by car, even though the interstate curves north. Soon, they are back at the starting point of their hike. After the hike, they say goodbye to the couple and throw their backpacks and summer jackets into the rental car, whose upholstery seems incredibly comfortable to them. Erik starts the engine and wants to take Candice to one last "railroad attraction" and to dinner. Because after their trek, they are hungry despite the snacks.

They drive back east on the interstate for half an hour and leave the highway in "Cle Elum". This was a tip from Otis in Kalispell: "You can take Candice out nicely in Cle Elum", he had advised Erik. They cross the shallow "Yakima River" to "South Cle Elum" and then to "Smokey's Bar-B-Que", a restaurant in a big wooden house. No doubt: The "Milwaukee Road" once came through here, right by the house the trail runs. He sits with Candice at one of the tables with the wooden chairs in the restaurant room. The doors, high windows, and the floor with its checkerboard pattern look like a train station. Outside is a yellow caboose, a trailer car of a train. Of course, the small village with its 600 inhabitants owes its existence to the railroad.

The Milwaukee Road had laid out supply stations, so-called "Division Points," about every 150 miles, as they learn in the small museum with a restaurant. Locomotives were serviced here. The station in Cle Elum lay between the terminus in Tacoma and the next station in Othello, Washington. Thus, the town was the last westbound transfer point before Snoqualmie Pass and the first eastbound stop into the Midwest. At the time, there was a switching yard with the depot, the roundhouse, of which only remnants remain today, the water tank, and a house for the train crew.

When the railroad discontinued its "Pacific Division" in 1980, the house became a boarding house for the staff. The restaurant was built in the station building. The remains of the marshaling yard were integrated into the park. The "Cascade Rail Foundation" runs the active museum. If you visit the restaurant, you can see it simultaneously. The old photos give you an impression of what must have been happening in this little village once: There was the marshaling yard, where freight cars stood in long rows. Locomotives pushed each other over the tracks; railroad workers ran back and forth between the roundhouse with its turntable and the substation. "What happened?" and "Pullin' the pin" are the captions on the panels. Many a guest must wonder what happened here in the Cascades mountains. The two know - and can devote themselves to dinner. Afterward, they stroll a bit through the "Palouse To Cascades State Park", as the large station area is called. Unfortunately, the "Iron Horse Inn" Bed & Breakfast seems to be closed.

In general, "South Cle Elum" is probably not the part of town where there is still much life, Erik thinks. So they take the car to the northern part of town, where the rival railroad company "Northern Pacific" laid its track. One place, divided in two, with two railroads, is "Cle Elum". With the "Traveler's Inn," they find a motel - one of those accommodations where you park your car right in front of your room. Erik still finds the concept, not so common in Europe, fascinating. Only that these are hidden under a pretty wooden veranda. But the thick white boxes with the air conditioners hang below the windows here, too, as in many motels in this country. The rooms seem to have been renovated.

THE RESCUE

At that moment, a "text message" arrives at Candice's smartphone with a piling.

"Help me. Michelle."

Candice's phone almost falls out of her hand in shock. She starts typing feverishly, "Michelle, where are you? Dad and I are worried. And so is Erik. Candice."

"Erik? That's good. Help me get out of here."

"Tell me: where are you?"

"I'm in the wash."

"Where's Wash?" types Candice. No answer. She adds, "Michelle, where are you?" Then another, "What's going on?"

But there is no further answer from her sister. The smartphone is silent. Candice calls her father. "Why don't you tell the sheriff quickly," he advises her. Candice does so and reports the text message. Then she explains to Erik: "The police are now trying to locate Michelle's cell phone with the data from the message to me. We have given our consent to this."

It doesn't take long for Candice's smartphone to ring, which she sets to loud.

"Candice? It's Dwayne Watson"

"What's up?"

"We tracked Michelle's cell phone. She's in a place in Washington, just off the interstate. There must be an illegal casino there; at least, that's my impression."

"Where is she?"

"Somewhere in eastern Washington. I'm calling the sheriff of Kittitas County now."

Without lingering, Dwayne hangs up, and Candice looks at Erik. "Where is that?" she asks.

"I don't know, but we'll take a look."

After a glance at his smartphone, Erik gets all queasy. "This is around here, Candice," he says, showing the map on the screen. "We're in Cle Elum. Behind that, there's Ellensburg. That's the biggest place in the area, with a population of 18,000. All of this is Kittitas County."

Candice reaches for her smartphone and calls the sheriff again.

"Dwayne, where's Michelle?"

"According to her cell phone, she's in Kittitas County," the sheriff said.

"Dwayne, is she in Ellensburg?"

"I shouldn't be telling you this, Candice, but she seems to be in Ellensburg. But wait a minute. Not that you're going there now, Candice. That's a long way. And you better leave that to the local police. They know how to do it."

"We're in Cle Elum, which is right next door. That's why we're going there."

"Candice, don't do that. There's a police operation going on right now. Stay where you are."

"I can't promise you anything, Dwayne," Candice says, hanging up. "Come on, Erik!"

He has already checked, and they run to his rental car from the motel room. Then Erik speeds off in the direction of Interstate 90. Ellensburg is just half an hour away. From the road, Candice calls her father. "Yes, I've heard. And, of course, if I were in the area, I'd go there, too. Hopefully, you'll find her. But just be careful and don't get in the way of the police operation under any circumstances," he cautions. Of course, Candice promises him to be careful. They exit the highway and find - nothing, just an empty road. "What do we do now?" asks Candice.

"We'll check out the area first. If Michelle ended up here involuntarily, it would have to have something to do with gambling."

"Sounds pretty likely."

"So if it's a gambling parlor, it's certainly not an official casino like the Indians run here. That just doesn't fit. It would have to be something illegal, a bar or something. And somewhere out of the way. I hardly think you'd run something like that in the middle of downtown. So we're going to search through the suburbs of this town."

They drive through Ellensburg: Via "Dollar Road," they enter the city, and via "Canyon Road," they leave on the other side. They don't even go downtown, following Erik's assumption. Then they take the road to the west, which runs parallel to the highway called "University Avenue". It is dark; only a few street lamps and occasional neon signs provide some light. Gas stations, small eateries, stores, and warehouses are on both sides of the road. As they come around a wide bend, Candice and Erik immediately see what's happening: "There's the police car," Candice calls out. Ahead of them, red and blue lights flash rapidly from the roofs of the patrol cars parked to the right of the road. There must be quite a few patrol cars, at least six. Erik slams on the brakes. But as the vehicle slows down, a man runs into the street. He comes from the lighted patrol cars and races into the lane. Erik hits the brakes again in a split second, but his car's radiator has already caught the man. With a dull bang, he hits the hood of the vehicle. Erik brings the car to a stop. He pulls the door handle and gets out.

"Don't make a mistake," the man, who has already sat up again, calls out to him. He is obviously only slightly bruised by the impact but still fully conscious. And he's holding a knife, Erik registers. "Don't make a mistake!" the man yells at him. Erik thinks he must be around 30 years old, tall, and quite muscular. His blond hair looks slightly oily, unkempt, and badly cut. He's wearing a denim jacket, and the knife he's holding is long and has an ornate handle. "Go on, get in the car. And then I drive off with you," the man hisses.

At that moment, two figures break away from the cascade of shining police lights and run in their direction. They have potent lamps in their hands. Erik stares, transfixed, in their direction. But as he is still thinking, the man with the knife runs around the front of the car and is on the other side of the vehicle in a flash. Quick-witted, Candice presses the door lock. Erik acts instinctively and throws his car door shut. The man with the knife faces him. "That was a mistake," the man hisses, glaring at Erik. "The doors stay shut," Erik yells. "He doesn't even realize how he just came up with that phrase. "There's nothing in here for you. Get away!"

"Oh no, my boy. Here's my ticket out," the man says, walking slowly to the car's rear. The blade of the knife flashes. What's Erik left to do? He has to keep up and move toward the front to keep the car between them. "Open the door now," the man yells. But Candice stays in the vehicle - thank God, Erik thinks as he moves around the hood while the man with the knife comes creeping after him. He now bangs on the window with the knife handle. But it holds. "I'll kill you!" he threatens Erik, raising the knife again.

Now, Erik has to deal with fear. But he can't think about it; he has to keep the distance between himself and the man with the knife. He has no doubt that this maniac, who has just survived a collision and is now waving the knife wildly, could really "finish him off." Then Erik stumbles and falls to the ground - he has overlooked a stone on the other side of the car. In a flash, the knife man jumps in.

"Freeze! Don't move!" a shout echoes through the night, and two spotlights bathe the scene in bright light. As the man with the knife stands over Erik, he raises the weapon upward. Like he's about to stab, Erik thinks. Then, a gunshot echoes through the night. "Bang." And another shot. Bang" again. The knife man is hit in the leg, Erik sees. He drops the knife. The two policemen were already with him, who had broken away from the crowd of vehicles and were running in his direction with their handheld searchlights. With their weapons drawn, they approach and keep the man and Erik in their sights. "We have two men and a woman in a car here," the one uniformed man says into the microphone in his breast pocket. "One man is injured by gunfire from an officer."

The other uniformed man pushes the knife away with his boot. While his colleague watches the man, the other puts nylon handcuffs on him. "Check on the woman in the car," Erik says. The adrenaline is still rushing through his body; he is wide awake and registers every detail. More lights approach from the throng of police cars. Now, a few squad cars arrive as well. "Can you stand up, sir?" the uniformed man asks Erik. "Yes, I'm getting up, I'm fine. I've got nothing." Rudely, the second uniformed man nudges the man with the oily hair, dragging him up. He waits until more officers have arrived, then leads him back to the lights. Only now does Candice open the car door. She gets out and hugs Erik. "How did you get here?" the policeman asks.

"I'm Candice. I'm the sister of Michelle, whose cell phone you tracked."

"Oh. Your sister is fine, you'll want to know that. She's over there!" he says, pointing to the police cars. "Now I understand why you came here."

"The man just ran in front of our car. I thought I had hurt him."

"You should have stayed in the car, sir. When there's an operation going on, and someone runs away, you shouldn't interfere. But who knows if he hadn't run away. It's good that we saw what was happening to you on the road. Now, why don't you move the car aside first, and then please join us up front."

Erik does as he is told. He gets in, starts the engine, and rolls the Ford toward the throng of glowing police cars. Then he stops the car, and Candice gets out with him. They both walk through the crowd of uniformed men standing outside a bar. The building is illuminated by the headlights of the patrol cars, and mobile spotlights have even been set up behind the building. A pretty big operation this is, Erik thinks. "Michelle!" yells Candice suddenly as she spots her sister standing beside an ambulance. She runs, Erik, following behind. "Michelle, there you are!" shouts Candice, and the two sisters fall into each other's arms. Both cry with happiness at having found each other again. Erik looks at Michelle. She looks pretty beat up. Her hair is tangled, her makeup is all smeared, and she has scratches on her face. But she seems unharmed. "How do you look?" exclaims Candice. "Well, I'm a little banged up." A nurse grabs Michelle's shoulder and says, "Your sister's been through quite a bit. But physically, she's fine. Did you get anything?"

"No," Candice replies, "I was in the car. What about you, Erik?"

"No, everything's fine. Fortunately, the knife man didn't get me."

Candice and Michelle sink onto a folding bench beside the ambulance. "So tell me, what happened here?" asks Candice.

"It all started out pretty funny. I had gotten a little bored in Kalispell, Candice. And then I met these guys at the bar."

While the police cars are still flashing, radio calls can be heard in the dark, and a second ambulance arrives for the knife man who was shot. They were on the road with a group of motorcyclists. At first, she thought they were pretty funny guys. They would have ridden west from Kalispell, stopping at a bar owned by the leader's friend. "And I found the leader quite attractive," Michelle confesses. "He was so fascinating to me. He was really charming. At the same time, he could do whatever he wanted. And the whole group listened to him." Only later, she says, did she realize that the group was not at all as peaceful as she thought. The conversations in the gang revolved around protection money they wanted to collect. "The police officer earlier enlightened me that organized crime likes to use gangs to work for them. In the case of the Seattle Mafia, for example, motorcycle gangs ride across the country, such as the Hells Angels. They do the 'manual labor' for the mobsters." Apparently, she had ended up in just such a group. Michelle knew she had to run when they reached the bar in this little town. "This seems to be something like their headquarters. But I didn't get another chance to get away."

The leader had noticed how uncomfortable she was and how much she had already witnessed. Michelle rolls a tear down her face. "That's when he hit me. I got locked in a room, right in that den there." At least no one in the gang had touched her. They left her alone and put food and drinks in her room. "I guess they didn't know what to do with me yet." Maybe that was for their bosses to decide, Michelle speculates. But then she got a hold of her cell phone while she was on her way to the bathroom, and one of her chaperones wasn't looking. "I was just able to text you in the restroom, and then they realized I had the phone and took it away from me right away."

A man comes up behind the three. It is the sheriff on duty. "That's how we were able to locate her sister," he says to Candice. "That took a little while. But when we got the data, I knew it could only be this bar. Because we've had our eye on that place for a while because there were rumors of illegal gambling. The search was already on our agenda, but now there was imminent danger."

"I didn't notice anything at first," Michelle says. "No sirens, no engines, nothing. I was in my room when a bang and loud voices were shouting for no one to move. A few seconds later, my door opened, and two officers came in at gunpoint."

"You were fortunate to get your hands on her cell phone. And you," he points at Erik and Candice, "you're lucky you caught the fugitive with the hood down. This is a very unscrupulous gangster whom we already know. He could have caught you with his knife if he hadn't been hit by a car. He somehow managed to escape the scene. He probably wasn't even in the building because there we shut everything down. I think he was outside, between the parked cars, and then tried to get away. This reminds me: when the police are on the scene, be sure to close the streets. We were a little quick on it tonight."

The fact that the sheriff admits this makes him sympathetic, Erik thinks, as he makes his statement and repeats what had happened on the street. Candice is also questioned in depth. "Now I just need to know where I can reach you if we have any more questions." Erik gives him his mobile number.

Candice says, "Why don't you call Dwayne Watson, the sheriff of Flathead County? That's where we're from."

"Yes, he informed us. That's what we're going to do. I think I can release you now. And you, miss," he turns to Michelle, "you be sure to report to your sheriff. And take it easy on yourself. It's best if you have another checkup." Michelle nods. Then, the three of them can get into the car. Very slowly, they pick up speed and drive away from the scene and the bar where Michelle had spent three angst-filled days and nights after Kalispell's gang arrived there. Erik doesn't get on the interstate, but they roll down the old highway that leads right back to "Cle Elum." Candice calls her worried father from the car and tells him everything.

Arriving at the small motel, Erik quickly takes a room at the reception. He puts the two sisters in the room that was actually intended for him and Candice. But he doesn't want to get in the way now. Besides, he could use the rest - after the exertions of the last few hours. Late at night, Erik falls asleep in the small motel in the Cascade Mountains, between Seattle and Chicago, not far from the Milwaukee Road substation.

Candice, Michelle, who already has a bit more color on her face, and Erik start the next morning towards the east. Shortly after "Cle Elum," the forested cascades end, and the hills follow, reminiscent of a desert and cut through by the interstate. A dam and an arch bridge lead over the wide Columbia River. Then, it goes straight through an area where intensive agriculture is practiced, with artificial irrigation because the fields are circular and have irrigation systems in the middle. A few hours after Spokane, they leave Washington State for Idaho. There, they enter the mountains again.

Near the town of Coeur d'Alene, they pass a large blue lake fed by the Spokane River. After the city with the atmospheric name "Wolf Lodge", the mountains await them again. But it still takes a while until they leave the interstate at "St. Regis" and go northeast along a state road.

Erik is happy that they have found their sister again and that he is now driving with them through the mountains. Candice is happily drumming along to the John Denver song on the radio on the dashboard. John Denver, of all musicians, Erik thinks. That's who they heard when they were out at Flathead Lake back in the day. Michelle stresses for the hundredth time how sorry she is about the whole thing and that she never wants to get involved with guys like that again in the future.

At Elmo, they again come to Flathead Lake, and from there, it is only a few miles before the car reaches Kalispell, passes through downtown, and then turns to the father's house.

"We were almost in Seattle," Candice notes as she looks at the route on her smartphone.

"That's right. Actually, we could have driven there," he counters.

"Oh no, it was such a successful rescue operation."

They take Michelle to her father's house, where she wants to lie down. "She will have to listen to reproaches from our father," Candice says. "He was so upset and so worried; I've rarely seen that. The best thing we can do is stay here and keep an eye on her."

Later, Candice and Erik head downtown to one of the restaurants. Afterward, they have an evening beer at "Moose's Saloon," which turns into several. "Was this where Michelle met the gang?" asks Erik.

"No, this is an excellent place here. There's a bar on the arterial road; that's where she went. That's where a whole different crowd comes together."

Candice looks at Erik with her brown eyes, and there is a trace of sadness mixed into her look, as he notes. Yes, she does look a little sad, as she now says, "Erik, sometimes I think we could have become something great."

He is surprised by this confession. But he feels similar. "Yes, Candice. If you knew how I thought about it while riding the train alone to Minneapolis."

"I guess that was our missed opportunity, huh?" she says, looking him in the eye.

"I'm afraid it was her. I sensed that she was."

"But everything is different now. And I understand that, Erik. You fell in love with your girlfriend from Canada. I fell by the wayside. I didn't take the step she did. Not only that, but I have only myself to blame. The distance between us was too great for me. What should I do with a friend from Germany who only comes to me every few months? Your Amelia was braver than I was."

"Candice, I look at it this way: I missed my cue, too. By the time I realized that, in Minneapolis, it was too late."

They look at each other for a while. Candice takes the floor. "It turned out that way. If our bond had been stronger, we would have gotten involved with each other."

"Yes, that's probably what happened."

"Then we would have pushed the beds together in Helena in the room."

"Definitely," says Erik, who has to laugh a little pained. After all, they had each spent the night on their side of the room.

"It is sad. But I feel that you have found someone for whom you need to be there. As I said, I want to help you because I like you."

The following day, she's up early and has made them one last breakfast - with pancakes she sizzles in the pan when he comes in. They drink coffee. Candice has to get ready to go to work, and he has to get prepared to go to the airport. He has a little more time since his flight doesn't leave until the afternoon. But he packs his things, and they leave her house together. Candice doesn't want to make a big scene out of the goodbye. "I wish you that everything turns out well. That you get back safely to your home. And, of course, that we meet again." Then she gets into her car and rolls down the street.

Erik starts the rental car and sets a course through downtown to the "Glacier Park Regional Airport". Much too early, he returns the rental car at the counter and checks in his luggage.

But he likes the small airport and sits down in the cafeteria. It's interesting how speeds change when you travel, he thinks. On foot, through the tunnel in the mountain, they were probably traveling at an estimated three miles per hour. But they had the greatest possible freedom because they could simply stop in the middle of the tunnel and have a picnic. With the bike on the trail, that was likely 12 miles per hour. However, they could still rest and take a break. While driving the rental car through the mountains of Idaho and Montana, they were doing 65 miles on the interstate. Again, they could have stopped at any time, but would have had to get off the interstate. Then, he was going up to 100 miles per hour by train. There would have been no way to just get off for that. And now? Soon, it will take off from the small airport in Kalispell. After that, he will fly east at 500 miles per hour - with the least possible freedom. It will be a tiny airplane seat in a regional jet that will take him to Minneapolis-Saint Paul, the twin city he had once visited by train.

After landing at the large airport, Erik changes from the small regional jet to a giant Airbus, taking him to Amsterdam Schiphol and taking off at 8 p.m. He sinks back into the airplane seat. These long, transcontinental trips are good at distracting him, he notes. You're so busy getting off and changing planes that you don't even consider the essential questions. But what about Amelia? How is she doing? Outside, he can hardly see anything; the plane flies into the darkness. It is not until many hours later that it becomes light as the Airbus descends to Schiphol Airport. Outside, he can make out the North Sea and a country that should be England. Later, Erik flies on to Hamburg in a small "KLM Cityhopper". Now he is back home. Everything is familiar and yet so far away. The airport in Hamburg, the way to the "S-Bahn" underground, the ride into the city. The trip has actually expanded his consciousness. The world hasn't really gotten smaller, but bigger. Actually, they say the continents are getting closer together, Erik reflects. But that's not true in reality. When you become more intensively involved with places and travel, for example, if you immerse yourself in a country as a passenger on a train, that is not the case. You get an entirely different view of the world. When you meet people on these trips, that are important to you, nothing stays the same. Especially when you meet someone like Amelia. The world has gotten bigger for him.

CHAPTER 6

The Canadian

EDMONTON

End of November this year

I think how hard it must be for Amelia. She left Erik in San Diego because she was facing the hospital. We sit together in her Edmonton apartment. "Amelia, you must come clean with him," I told her urgently. Amelia tells me again how bad she feels.

"I can't. I can't tell him what's going on. I don't think he'll like me then."

"That's nonsense. If Erik is like you described him to me, he will love you all the more."

"But you know how it was with Jack. When I had to go to the hospital, he left me."

"Amelia, your former fiancé was an evil guy. He simply abandoned you. I'm so sorry. But I told you that before you got engaged. You were blindly in love. But I don't think you will be blind this time."

"But what if he does? What if he doesn't like me anymore because he knows I'm sick?"

I've always found it difficult to argue with Amelia. She can be considerably stubborn. Since her unhappy engagement four years ago, my sister has become so cautious about making acquaintances. She is so afraid of being hurt again; I am very sorry for that.

"There's only this one way to find out how he really feels about you. You have to tell him: you had to come to Edmonton because you were waiting for a transplant and then straight to the hospital."

"But then I'm even more sorry that I just took off and left him in San Diego."

"Amelia, all I can tell is that if he loves you, he won't care. Because love overcomes such things. Because we love precisely to cope with such blows of fate."

"You really think so?"

"Amelia, write him what's going on. You'll see what happens. I have a feeling it's going to be fine. Please, write to him."

THE END AT THE ELBE

Hamburg, end of November

How has Erik been in Hamburg? First, it feels much cooler to him than it has in the past few weeks. That's because of his mood and the weather: it's much colder than Montana in the fall, not to mention Southern California. Erik is back in his familiar surroundings. Now, however, he feels pretty lonely after arriving. He could discuss his experiences with Candice in Montana, and new ones were added on their bike and hiking trip. But what awaits him at home? The loneliness of his apartment and a job that seems more and more like a misfortune to him. In addition, the uncertainty about what had actually become of Amelia gnaws at Erik more and more.

But a postcard was in the mailbox the day after his arrival in October. In front, it showed an artistically drawn maple leaf. He knew immediately, of course, who the card was from. On the back, Amelia just wrote, "I really love you. See you soon." So that was her signal from Canada. She still didn't explain what was going on. But she assured him that she loved him. This did little to reassure Erik. She must have sent the card a week ago, as he could see from the postmark. So he also got himself a postcard showing a pretty picture of the river Elbe. He took his old fountain pen and wrote back to her, "Amelia, I love you too. I am here for you. And I hope we can see each other again soon." Erik would have loved to write her a whole novel about his feelings. But it wouldn't fit on the little postcard. Her card was also brief. So, he sent the card to Canada with three sentences.

The first working weeks after the vacations weren't good. Autumn has arrived, and it's colder and rainier. The job becomes even more unpleasant because the publishing director, the "cookie monster," is acting increasingly nasty. But he can't get through to Erik. His most urgent problem is and remains Amelia. He thinks about writing to her, calling her, or sending another message.

The uncertainty ends as he stands outside his apartment building on a cold, rainy Thursday evening. He grabs two business letters and advertisements when he looks in the mailbox. But then he is literally struck by lightning. There is a letter from Canada. The address is written in Amelia's handwriting. She is the sender of the envelope. The letter almost falls out of his hand. Then he shakes as he takes the key out of his pocket and unlocks the front door. He puts the bag in the hallway and sits in the living room.

She writes in a curved cursive script. He misses her so much. The words on the page swirl before his eyes, and he feels sick. He has to force himself not to skim the letter but to read her text sentence by sentence and in its entirety.

"Dear darling," she begins, "I'm sorry I left in such a hurry. I didn't want to worry you and thought it would be easier to tell you in a letter.

Erik, I love you. Even though it may have looked different after I left San Diego. I first had to sort out my thoughts. Now I have the courage to tell you everything. You must first know how much I love you. Since we met, I have felt that we have a deep connection. In the weeks we have spent together, I have felt the relationship grow stronger and stronger. I love you for how you are and how interesting and creative you are. I love you for how thoughtful you are. Not only that, but I remember our laughter together, the humor that only the two of us under-stand. I am grateful to you for making me feel like the most important person. And because we two have big plans, no matter if we were together in Canada or in Germany or traveling around the world.

Erik, I believe we complement each other perfectly and are like the two missing pieces of a puzzle that found each other. Just the thought of leaving you tugs at my soul. I want to tell you that my love for you has become more precious every day since I went.

In San Diego, I was on the phone with the hospital in Edmonton, and they told me I needed surgery. Two transplants were necessary on short notice because I needed donor organs.

Today, I know it is time to tell you the truth. I should have told you long ago, but fear held me back. Erik, I have a severe disease. Type 1 diabetes has been with me for years, causing significant damage to my body unnoticed. I have had a pancreas and kidney transplant. Otherwise, I would soon have been dependent on blood washing.

But here's the thing, Erik, I didn't know how to tell you. I was afraid you wouldn't want me anymore. The fact that you cared for me so much scared me. I didn't want to lose you. You were the most important thing to me. My brother and the wonderful doctor made me realize that I had to tell you the truth. Otherwise, it would be dishonest, and I would have been unfair to you."

On the paper, a stain shimmers in the ink. She must have cried when she wrote this.

"Erik, I'm in Edmonton and I'm fighting. I have to take heavy medication and attend various therapies. I try to be brave. But I would be even stronger if you stood by me. I want to fight for us, for our love, for our future. Together, we can make it. Please forgive me for not telling you sooner. I'm so sorry if I made you suffer.

Unfortunately, the first surgery didn't go as well as planned. The pancreas failed, and my body didn't accept it. I had to go back on insulin and other medications. Another treatment will have to follow. The first one already cost a lot of energy. That's why I'm only writing to you now."

His heart feels heavy as he reads her words.

"Fortunately, the hospital here in Edmonton specializes in such transplants. What is scary for me must be the same for you. I know it must have been hard when I left so quickly. I don't like it at all when I think about it. But I couldn't tell you at that moment. I thought you were unable to take it. But I know that I couldn't bear to tell you. And what would you have done? You would have come with me to Edmonton, I know that. But I want you to know that I love you more than anything."

Erik realizes that tears are now streaming down his face. He just hopes they can be together again. The letter left him wondering what would happen next. "Yours forever," she signed it. With those three words, he knew that love could not end.

Erik is still sitting on the couch in his living room hours later. He takes heart and checks the time. Then he waits a bit before picking up his phone. He can't take it anymore. Despite the time difference, he calls Amelia's cell phone late that evening.

"I just read your letter. I missed you so much."

"I don't like what I did. But I couldn't help it," she says. "Erik, I'm so glad you called me now. I was so afraid you wouldn't."

"But you've told me now," Erik replies. "We're going to get through this together, Amelia. I'm not going anywhere."

He is delighted to hear her voice. She sounds brave, Erik thinks, not fragile at all. Unfortunately, as she confesses to him, her health situation has not improved.

The world seemed to disappear at that moment on the phone. The future is uncertain; he knows that. But love could be an unbreakable bond that would carry them through the storm. What he must do is immediately apparent to Erik. This is about Amelia from Canada, who has difficult hours ahead of her and whom he loves so much. He must travel to Edmonton as soon as possible.

The conversation at the publishing house couldn't have gone any worse. Erik could never have imagined the turn it took. "So, you want to go on vacation again? Do you want to relax instead of working? I've got a way for you to relax, and for quite a long time," says the "Cookie Monster" as he stands in his office. Erik feels he's about to eat him up like a giant cookie.

"No, I explained to you that my point was not to relax, but that there was an emergency and I have to travel to Canada as soon as possible."

"Oh, come on, that's just one of those stories I hear often enough when people absolutely have to have a vacation. Blah, blah, emergency in Canada. I think it's more like you want to lay on the beach with your American girlfriend."

He feels himself blushing and anger building up inside him. That was three turns too many that the "cookie monster" had tightened the literal screw: He had said, "Just a story like that". He had spoken in all seriousness of "blah, blah." He insinuated that he wanted to lie down on the beach - even more so with an American girlfriend, he couldn't know about. If not - indeed, if not, Andrea blabbed. She knew about Amelia because Erik had stupidly told her. She had been extraordinary in the past weeks, avoiding Erik wherever she could.

Erik is gobsmacked when the Cookie Monster goes on the counterattack. "Now watch this," he says condescendingly. That tone of voice had to be the fourth turn.

"The screw is about to be overtightened," Erik warns him, and the boss doesn't know how to classify that.

"Now, pay attention," he starts again. "We'll just dissolve your employment contract, and then you can take as long a vacation as you want. And if you don't," he adds, "I'm going to make you feel bad. Like, terrible."

This is it now, the fifth turn. Not only is the 'cookie monster' irritating him with his "patter," but he wants to take advantage of the situation to cut his job right along with it. He actually intends to use his situation as an opportunity to push through another of the many layoffs in the newsroom.

Erik can no longer stay cool. "My dear Mr. Publishing

Director," he says. "That's enough threats. This is really the last straw. I wanted nothing more than to request special leave for important reasons, and now you're trying to dispose of me. After all, I've done for this place, which you obviously can't save from going under. At least, you're not trying. Let others pay for you."

"What do you know?" the Cookie Monster yells at Erik. "If you in the editorial department want to make a lazy day of it, I won't allow it. I will single-handedly remove anyone here who opposes a reorganization course. And now it's your turn. You were due a long time ago. I know all about you, your adventures in North America, and the work you're leaving behind."

Erik is almost beside himself with rage. "What do you call that? When I'm here pushing 55-hour weeks and giving the shirt off my back to this store? Do you want me to take my turn? Oh no, Mr. Publishing Director, we won't let that stand."

"Yeah, you better find yourself a lawyer; you're going to need one," he calls after him as Erik leaves his office. He no longer knows what to say in response.

He tries to understand what just happened, but it is all very logical retrospectively. The "Cookie Monster" simply wanted to seize the opportunity. By taking advantage of a predicament, he could squeeze the costs that would undoubtedly be required to terminate the employment contract. But Erik couldn't fathom how he was able to do this. Hadn't he more than done his job the past few years? Hadn't he worked endless overtime and endured those eleven to twelve-hour shifts without grumbling? Only now, and this made Erik furious, to be "disposed of" in the cheapest possible way?

The fact that he immediately consulted a lawyer friend was the best thing he could have done after such a conversation. Hadn't the "Cookie Monster" also asked him to do this? Erik described to Peter everything that had happened. He nods in understanding as they sit in his office close behind Hamburg City Hall.

"I think we'll do it the hard way, dear Erik. You have to fight back now, and you have to fight back hard. Otherwise, they will overrun you. I'll help you with that, of course. But let me talk it over with a colleague." Peter picks up the phone and consults with a colleague. He looks out at the "Fleet" outside the office window, a canal that leads from the Elbe river to the Alster lake. He had worked near such a Fleet for years, and now it was all supposed to be over? It's a little bit your own fault, he thinks. They got you. You could have arranged it yourself by jumping out in time. Then they wouldn't have caught you cold.

After Peter has consulted, he looks up. Erik tells him how it pisses him off that he was "caught cold".

"No, I wouldn't see it that way after you told me your situation. On the contrary, now they want something from you. They have miserable cards when you add up everything that has happened. We'll use that to your advantage."

"But how?"

"Well, let me do that. The course is correct; the colleague also confirmed that to me. Watch out: You need to go to Canada. You will do that. The fewer who get their hands on you here, the better. I need a list of all incidents from the last few years. What your boss said, what the "Cookie Monster" said. How it was exactly with the working hours. Then we'll serve them a soup they won't be able to spoon out."

"I'll do that. And then you want me to fly to Canada?"

"Of course, that's what counts for you. Erik, there's no point in wanting anything else here. You no longer agree with this company. Which, given their economic situation, is also not to be recommended. You have already invested so much in this sinking store; now you must turn away. But check with your doctor first - you'll be able to figure out why you need a sick leave."

He adds, "I'll take over communication with the publishing house. You might as well get a new cell phone number because I don't want you talking to them again. I'll take care of it."

Erik has a load off his mind. That may sound harsh. But Peter had grasped what it was all about. How he could best get out of it, even if it was hard on the edge.

A short time later, Erik moves up in the queue at Hamburg airport. He thinks December is a lovely month, with Christmas just around the corner. It's clear to him that he can't stay here while Amelia needs support. Even more so when his job here is on the rocks. His flight takes him from Hamburg via Amsterdam and then directly to Edmonton.

But maybe it's time for a new chapter in life, and he doesn't want to experience it alone and not here. Erik thinks back to what he felt on the flight back from the USA: The world hasn't gotten smaller; it's gotten bigger.

There's a "ping" on the smartphone. A message has arrived. It's not from Amelia, even though he expected it to be. No, it's from Candice.

"What are you doing? What's next?" she asks.

"I'm standing at the airport and on my way to Edmonton. The job is gone," he writes back to her.

"Very true. Fly to Edmonton."

A NEW LIFE

The plane touches down on the runway after a long flight. Erik is flattened, but not only by the flight. But also from what he is doing. He's flying to Edmonton, to Amelia. "After all," Erik said to himself during the long flight, "the "Cookie Monster" has also brought the situation on himself and, in a way, solved a problem for me. I probably won't have a job in Germany soon. But I just wanted to have a special leave to come here in December. I most likely would have resumed my job. However, he wanted to take advantage of the situation. He can do that, but it won't be for nothing."

Then he thought about how fed up he was with "dependent employment". When a job consists only of being present in an office many, many hours a day. When one works for a publishing house, that is unlikely to have a future. When you try to stay afloat on a sinking ship. It gets gruesome in the process - especially with your colleague. Again and again, Erik shakes his head. But then he manages to put all that aside and adjust to what lies ahead.

He takes the bus the long way into town, then changes to a cab to West Edmonton. Amelia has gone to stay with her parents. She is standing in front of the house when he arrives in the cab. Erik's breath catches: There is Amelia, somewhat pale, in a thick winter sweater, her long brown hair blowing in the cold wind. She smiles.

He goes to her, takes her in his arms, and presses her tightly against him. They kiss for a long time, as long as they have ever kissed before. It is hard to believe for Erik. He is with his beloved Amelia again. He looks into her gray-blue eyes. "I love you," Erik says to her. "I love you even more. With every week that has passed, I have loved you more," she replies. She seems so glad that he has come, right to her, into her life in Edmonton.

Erik finally gets to meet her family. They seem like lovely people. The father, now retired, speaks enthusiastically but anxiously about his daughter. Her mother is charming and full of care for her guest from overseas. She works at the Edmonton Art Gallery. And there's me, Amelia's brother, with whom she has a close relationship. I'm friendly and squeeze Erik's hand. "You've really turned my sister's head. But you're here now to be with her. I think you're great," I say and hug Erik.

The parents live in a beautiful house: the foundation is stone, the facade is wood, painted dark gray. It is two stories and looks to Erik like it could be in Sweden. It is not overkill, but it is amicable and fits well here. They sit together in the living room in the afternoon. The sun shines through the wooden windows, and the logs are blazing in the fireplace. Over a drink, Erik talks about his trip from Amsterdam to Edmonton.

Amelia explains the situation in which she is. She bravely and without faltering tells about the first operation, which unfortunately did not bring the desired results. She received a new kidney and a pancreas, but her body did not accept the second organ.

"Amelia has suffered from type 1 diabetes since she was a child," her father explains. "It was always challenging for her, especially in school. She kept having life-threatening hypoglycemic episodes. And we were afraid of the secondary diseases caused by her severe diabetes."

"Well, I did take it in stride," she says.

"Yes, you really did. But Erik must know: When your kidney functions became weaker and weaker, it was clear that something had to be done. So the doctors wanted to transplant two organs at once." Turning to Erik, he adds, "If Amelia had already been on dialysis, you wouldn't have been able to travel to California together. Although we're glad, you did and could do it." His voice falters a bit. "If you knew what you meant to her and, by extension, to us."

Amelia talks about the new diagnosis and the second transplant that is to follow. In contrast to her father, she looks very calm.

"The fact is that only three-quarters of these transplants are successful. I just had bad luck; my body didn't want the organ. But I'm not giving up."

"Amelia, I noticed how you took your insulin. I just had no idea that you had such severe diabetes," says Erik.

Amelia looks at him and adds, "I know everything can go wrong. That would be a real pity. Now that you're here, it would be a real shame. And for you, too." At that, she looks at her parents and brother. Of course, in this situation, everyone tries to appease. But Amelia shakes her head. "It's going to turn out the way it's going. It's not like I can really change it. But I promise you: I'll do my best."

In the evening, Erik and Amelia drive to her apartment in Strathcona. So she lives in this part of town, of all places. He might have guessed that their paths would converge again here. They stop in front of her house. "That's pretty convenient for you," Amelia says. "I won't be far from you at all. Just a few blocks around the corner, at the hospital." Amelia's apartment on the second floor of one of the "brick stones," or old houses made of bricks, suits her well. The rooms have raw stone and wooden walls. She has hung colorful fabrics to add cheerfulness to the rooms. So this is where the girl he met in Jasper in the mountains and traveled with through Southern California lives, thinks Erik. This is her home, where he now makes his home as well. It's a little strange: Erik now grasps a great calm for the first time in weeks, he realizes.

"I think I've already reached the first goal," he says.

"Yes, I think so, too," Amelia replies. "But I hate myself for not telling you in San Diego."

"You can't hate yourself for it," he says. "Impossible. I'll admit that it wore me down. But unlike you, I didn't have to put up with nearly as much."

"Still, it's mean what I did."

"No, it isn't. I should have followed you right away. Now I'm with you."

"And you're not leaving?" she asks anxiously.

"Go away? Where to? You know what happened in Hamburg. You know that I love you. I have every reason to stay with you."

The next day, Amelia packs her bag. He helps her. She explains to him what works in her apartment: the light switches, the fuses, the hot water. This feels strange. Erik's neck tightens. Then she hands him the keys. He has tears in his eyes. "Now come on," Amelia says. "Where did your train journey begin again?"

"Our first train trip? That was in Chicago," he says, somewhat taken aback.

"Then you are the passenger from Chicago for me now. It's not like I'm not going to come back. I just want you to keep an eye on my place, that's all."

They put her bag in her little car, and she gives him the car keys; this is the second bunch he receives from her that day.

"Let's get going, then. Bye, apartment," Amelia says. They drive down the street, turn right, then left again, and arrive at the University of Edmonton Hospital, where Amelia checks in for the second time this year. Only this time, Erik can be with her.

Amelia puts aside the thick manuscript that she has read through to this point. On her bedside table is another coffee, not the one from yesterday. Again, there are cinnamon sprinkles on the milk foam. "That's quite a story you've written about the two of us," she tells Erik. Unfortunately, she seems a little paler than yesterday. "I like it a lot, even if I don't know the ending yet."

"Well, I'm glad, yes, that you like the story to some extent," Erik replies to her.

I have to think about what they are going through here. No wonder, Erik wrote down everything he experienced with my sister - and even more. I had already told him when we met in her apartment one evening. We were all a little skeptical about her boyfriend from Germany. Because it was so hard for her to tell him she had to go to the hospital urgently. But when Erik actually came to Edmonton, we were all amazed. When we saw what a loving person he is and how much he cares for Amelia, we knew he could only be the right one. He had also been through a lot in Germany.

"How are things in Hamburg for you?" I ask him.

"There's good news for a change."

"Is it about your publishing house? What's the situation there? Are they sorry about anything?" asks Amelia.

"Well, I really don't think so. But Peter argued with them, and they came to an agreement. He told them everything he could get his hands on - for example, the working hours with which they had violated the law. The fact that this was a criminal offense probably scared them. When the 'Cookie Monster' realized this, he is said to have become quite meek."

"So they have to make amends, huh?" I ask Erik.

"Yes, and not by a small margin. I wouldn't be surprised if that was the 'Cookie Monster's' last rogue act."

Now, however, he has a guilty conscience. Didn't he just want to put the events in Germany behind him? Now, at her bedside, he tells Amelia about the outcome of the legal battle at his old job. No, that was the past he wanted to put behind him.

Erik looks into Amelia's eyes, then at her brother, then back at Erik. "I wanted to tell you I now have a clear path," Erik says. "What matters now is that you get a clear run, too."

"I will try to fulfill this wish for you, I promise. After all, we want to experience so much together, if possible. We could settle down in Edmonton. Or in Southern California. You still would like to lure me to Argentina, as you told me."

The fact that she remembers is something Erik is pleased about. "I've already talked to my aunt on the phone. She already knows you. Her house is open to us."

"You're going to be quite the globetrotters," I say, remembering that Amelia was always the explorer of the two of us. While I stayed in Edmonton and found happiness here, my sister was drawn into the world.

Erik spends another night at Amelia's apartment in Strathcona. In the evening, he talks on the phone with Candice in Montana and tells her about recent events. He even phones Drake in Aspen, who is equally sympathetic. "We wish you both well. With all our hearts. Oh, and Erik, if you ever want a tip ..."

"Yes?"

"Why don't you make her a real coffee for once and bring it to the hospital with you? Don't go to that coffee shop from that chain in Seattle. You can make your own milk foam and cinnamon. Look, I'll send you some packs of decent beans."

Erik has another lonely coffee in Amelia's kitchen the following day. He then gets up in the morning and puts on his thick jacket. Outside, it has begun to snow. Thick flakes, he notices, are falling from the sky here in Canada. It's just before New Year's Eve, right after Christmas. A veritable "winter wonderland" has formed on the road he takes toward the hospital, as he does every day. He thinks there also seem to be more people on the road now than on other days. He imagines that they are a bit more cheerful than usual. Is that due to the snow?

Erik returns to the corner coffee shop - that's the habit. But as soon as the beans arrive from Colorado, he wants to make the coffee himself. The waitress wordlessly makes him two coffees - an Americano and a latte with cinnamon on the milk foam. She puts the coffee in two insulated mugs because it has to stay warm for a while.

Erik continues to the entrance of the hospital. He takes the elevator to the third floor, as he did many days before. The head doctor approaches him just before he can enter Amelia's room. By now, Erik has met him several times. He is a gray-haired man with thick glasses who carries much responsibility for his patients. "I want to talk to you for a moment," he says. Until now, Erik had always seen him with a severe expression as he described the diagnosis to him in a calm tone. Amelia had agreed to let him tell Erik everything. Bad minutes must follow when this man says he has something to say. Erik already suspects evil. They go around the corner into another corridor. But today, he is different than usual. The doctor's expression is now by no means as serious as he feared. He has something to tell Erik. And he smiles. Erik feels immensely relieved. They have a future together.

The End

312

About the Author

Nils Eriksen wrote this book after he traveled through the Northwest of the USA and Canada. The author rode the trains and visited the towns in the novel. He was particularly taken with the story of the "Milwaukee Road." The German-American thus knows the locations from Edmonton to San Francisco to Chicago well and did detailed research for the plot. He wanted to write a travel novel that is also a love story. This is the first novel by the author, who has written for numerous magazines as a journalist. Eriksen lives in northern Germany - and enjoys traveling by train through Scandinavia, Great Britain, and North America.

If you liked the book, we would appreciate a review. Otherwise, please write us your suggestions and comments to info@nils-eriksen.de.

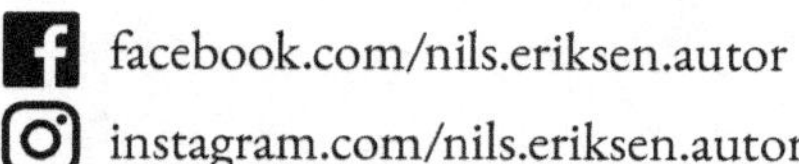

facebook.com/nils.eriksen.autor

instagram.com/nils.eriksen.autor